Against the Grain

Against the Grain

Developing your own management ideas

Sheila Cameron and Sue Pearce

BUTTERWORTH
HEINEMANN

Butterworth-Heinemann
Linacre House, Jordan Hill, Oxford OX2 8DP
A division of Reed Educational and Professional Publishing Ltd

ℛ A member of the Reed Elsevier plc group

OXFORD   BOSTON   JOHANNESBURG
MELBOURNE   NEW DELHI   SINGAPORE

HD
38.2
.C36
1997

First published 1997

British Library Cataloguing in Publication Data
Cameron, Sheila
  Against the grain: developing your own management ideas
  1. Executive ability   2. Industrial management
  I. Title   II. Pearce, Sue
  658.4

ISBN 0 7506 2779 4

Composition by Genesis Typesetting, Rochester, UK
Printed in Great Britain by Biddles Ltd, Guildford and King's Lynn

Contents

Preface

If you have picked up this book you are probably not the sort of manager who is prepared to 'go with the flow', preferring instead to feel more in control of your working life. Like most managers you may well be under a lot of pressure at work, much of it caused by the rate at which changes are happening within your organization. You have to respond to new situations quickly. And as a manager you are expected to take decisions and to get them right. In a climate of constant change it is no longer enough to rely upon old ways of thinking or to hope that applied common sense is all that you need to get by.

This book is intended to help you to develop a new kind of 'common sense' which you will need to meet the many and varied challenges which face managers today. It was written because now new ways of thinking are essential and because management theory and teaching seem to offer little help in developing these skills. We have drawn upon conventional management theory in the book, but we suggest that you use theory to develop and expand your own thinking in a way that is far from conventional. A number of creative techniques have been included to help you to do this.

Many managers are beginning to recognize that it is time to question 'the way we do things around here', but organizations do not always make it easy to do this. The kind of questioning, thinking approach to managing, which we believe is so important, may not be welcomed because often it produces responses which do not fit comfortably with the prevailing organizational culture. This is why we have called the book *Against the Grain*. It is an image taken from working with wood and is entirely different from the idea of 'going with the flow'. It requires more effort, but it can produce very effective results.

The effort which you need to make in order to change your long-established thought habits starts here. You will need to do more than simply read. Follow the prompts to stop and reflect and also do the Workouts. If you are busy, you may not have the time to work from cover to cover. Although the book does develop an argument as it progresses, it has been written to allow for the likely demands upon your time. Each chapter is fairly self-contained and so it is quite possible to read them out of sequence if you feel that you do not need to be convinced by argument and just want to concentrate upon particular ideas or skills.

In writing this book we have also drawn upon our own experience as managers, and on that of the many hundreds of practising managers we have taught through the Open University Business School. The process is always interactive and one through which we also continue to learn. If you would like to let us know your own reactions to the ideas presented here, please do contact us. Although we planned the book jointly, Sue Pearce was primarily responsible for Chapter 3 and Chapters 8–12, Sheila Cameron for the remainder, save Chapter 13, which we shared.

We hope that you will find the process of challenging your own thought processes, and those of your colleagues, interesting and productive, even if it is hard work at first. We hope too that before you have finished with this book the way in which you respond to the challenges you face will have changed significantly, because of the very different way in which you will be thinking about them.

Finally, we should like to thank our families for their support, and the Open University Business School and its students for allowing us to develop these ideas.

Sheila Cameron
Sue Pearce

Chapter 1
Do managers need uncommon sense?

Organizations today are changing at an unprecedented rate. Competitive forces, political pressures, technological developments, and sometimes the mere following of the latest management fashions are leading to rapid and dramatic change. Strategy, structure and staffing are being drastically altered as organizations try to survive the turbulent environment in which they find themselves. This constant flux presents huge challenges for managers. To survive, better still to thrive on such rates of change, managers need new ways of thinking. They need to be able to react as quickly as when a response seems to be 'common sense', but in a way that is probably radically different from the common sense of the past.

Changing habits of thought ingrained over a lifetime is extremely difficult at the best of times. If these habits are shared by those with whom you work, and form part of the culture of your organization, change will come about only if you make conscious and determined efforts. However, it is the task of making this difficult change that this book addresses. If you work at it, and it *will* be hard work, you should be on the way to using more flexible and creative thought processes than at present. Even more importantly, you will develop the habit of being aware of how you are thinking, and of continually modifying your thought processes to increase their effectiveness. This habit is essential if you are to be able to react quickly and appropriately to the rapidly changing context in which you are likely to work for the foreseeable future.

This chapter outlines the argument central to the book as a whole, that there is a need for a different way of thinking to cope with the demands which managers face today. It establishes some of the characteristics which such thinking needs to exhibit. This will form a basis for your reading of the rest of the book, allowing you to see how the ideas or techniques introduced in subsequent chapters fit in with the wider approach, as well as to appreciate the force of the central argument itself.

By the end of this chapter you should therefore:

- Be more aware of the role, and the limitations, of managerial common sense
- See how 'common sense' may need to be expanded to meet current demands
- Appreciate the place of rationality in managerial decisions
- Accept the effort that will be required to change your own ways of thinking
- Be wondering what assumptions are built into your present thought habits.

Decisions and common sense

It is generally assumed that managers spend much of their time on decision making. This is the implicit assumption underlying the cartoon which shows a picture of a suited executive, Mercedes smashed into the 'Pass either side' sign, captioned 'But, officer, there are only so many major decisions you can take in a day'. The cartoon would not be funny if the assumption were not generally held. Indeed, the assumption is still built into many management courses, particularly those aimed at senior management.

But is this assumption correct? Do managers themselves feel that they spend their time carefully weighing evidence and taking decisions of great importance to the organization? A research project looking at how decisions were taken in an organization (Mangham 1995) found it extremely difficult to find out from managers just what happened. When asked to 'walk the researcher through' a recent decision, many seemed genuinely puzzled by the request. A typical reaction was 'It's common sense, isn't it? You look at the issues and decide . . .'

This may be your experience too. Studies of managers and how they spend their time show that they typically deal with dozens of issues in a day, flitting from one thing to another every few minutes. They seldom have the luxury of setting up major projects to evaluate issues rationally, of gathering evidence, weighing probabilities, and finally deciding which option maximizes the chance of a favourable outcome. Far more often decisions are taken almost instantly, on the basis of 'common sense', or 'the obvious' thing to do.

But as George Bernard Shaw pointed out some time ago, 'No question is so difficult to answer as that to which the answer is obvious'. What is obvious to you may be less so to others. What is obvious to all of you may be wrong. Yet because your view *is* so obvious, it can be extremely difficult to escape from it, and look at the situation in a different way.

With the pressures on managers increasing all the time, there is more demand than ever for the complex but rapid mental processing described as common sense. And although the issues decided in this way may individually seem trivial, taken together they are a major determinant of the success of an organization. Indeed, in many organizations the strategy that 'emerges' from the multitude of small decisions taken by individual managers *is* the organization's strategy. Unless common sense is common, and driving in a fairly uniform and appropriate direction, this may not be an ideal way to operate. And because of the trap of the obvious, it may be hard to see how things could be changed.

The constituents of common sense

If you look at the likely ingredients of common sense, variation is not altogether surprising. The 'obvious' answer to you is likely to be based on things you have been told by people you trust, what you have learned for yourself from past experience, and similarities that you perceive between the present situation and situations encountered in the past. You will probably concentrate on a very limited number of factors in the situation, and a few clear 'lessons' you have learned. These factors will be somewhat tempered by the values that you hold in general, and your overall view of the nature of the world. Together they make up your existing 'models' of reality. Figure 1.1 shows the basic constituents of 'common sense'.

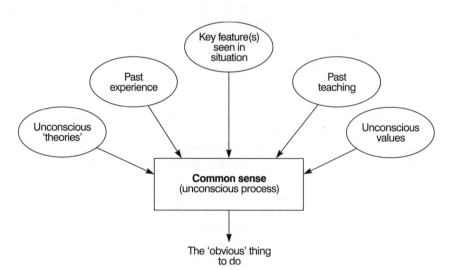

Figure 1.1 The basics of common sense in management

This figure points up one of the problems with reliance on common sense. Variation is to be expected, as what you have been told about various aspects of work will not be the same as what others have been told. Their work experience has probably been very different from yours. It is possible that neither you nor they have thought very deeply about that experience, and may have interpreted it in ways that are different from each other. Such variation may lead to conflict that is difficult to resolve.

But shared common sense may be even more of a problem, if it misinterprets or misses out key aspects relevant to the present situation. If your basic view differs from those with whom you work, and if you are good at handling conflict, you may just start to explore the different views of the situation which you hold, and come up with a much richer view in consequence. If you share the assumptions, and in many organizations there is a strong culture based on such shared beliefs and meanings, then it is highly unlikely that you will ever question your underlying models. Without such questioning you may be permanently trapped in an inappropriate interpretation of a situation.

Experience as limitation

This leads to a subtle but dangerous problem, where experience, normally seen as a source of learning, may act to *prevent* learning. Successful organizations with firmly established ways of doing things may find their very success a millstone if circumstances change. The weight of tradition, based on this success, may make change or even the questioning of established practice very difficult. If the present is *different*, unquestioning reliance on past experience and the models which worked then may be unhelpful. The same limitation may apply to individuals.

This can happen if the 'lessons' learned from experience are a limited set of 'models' of the world. An example of such a model might be the belief that people will only work hard if threatened with serious punishment if they do not. Use of such models will restrict the information that you extract from any situation, as you will tend to observe only those things which are significant within your model. In this example you might concentrate only on the penalties for poor performance. Mitroff and Linstone (1993) call this 'model myopia'. If your basic models are limiting, then your ability to learn from experience is seriously diminished. You may become locked into an increasingly narrow and restricted view of the things around you. One of the important aims of this book is to help you develop different ways of reflecting on and benefiting from your experience, so that it becomes a rich resource rather than a potential constraint.

Prescriptions or theories which you have been taught by others may offer few advantages over models based on experience if such theories are used uncritically or inappropriately. What you were taught may no longer be all that useful, or if it is, you may not have been taught how best to use it. One of the observations which led to the writing of this book was that the bulk of what is taught on management courses seems to be surprisingly common, and does not seem to have changed all that much in ten or fifteen years. There is clearly a 'gospel' of management. But the parts of this which are most frequently examined, and which students remember, are often not used in any way in their jobs. The superficial way in which they are taught and regurgitated may be part of the reason. Also these 'theories' may not be appropriate to today's situation. The book aims to show some of the limitations of some of these 'authorities'. It also shows that if used as prompt rather than prescription, some of them at least *can* broaden your perspective and help you to cope with the complexities around you.

Simple or simplistic?   Models as tools

Both common sense and many management theories tend to cope with complexity by simplifying, usually describing a situation in terms of only a very few factors. You must have heard people say confidently, 'The problem is . . .' and offer solutions based on the identification of a single cause. Yet despite their confidence you may have thought that the problem was something quite different, not only because of your different experiences but because you identified different factors in the situation as being relevant and therefore drew on different aspects of your experience, or different sorts of authorities in assessing the situation.

Simplification is clearly necessary. Brains are not all that good at coping with a mass of different things at once. What is needed is a way of simplifying which can be built up into a better understanding of the underlying complexity, rather than a denial of that complexity. Again this is something which this book is intended to help you achieve.

This book suggests a variety of ways in which you can develop your mental processing ability to an *uncommon* degree. It addresses the practice of management thinking, and some implications of this thinking for management practice. It should enable you to become more aware of the complexity of situations facing you as a manager, to identify a wider range of important aspects than perhaps you do at present, and to cope with this complexity once identified. To do this you need to increase your repertoire of models and frameworks for making sense of the diverse factors identified.

Using these frameworks you will be better able to go *beyond* your past experience, modelling *new* situations in a truly creative way. You will become more aware of just what decisions you *are* taking in exercising your common (or uncommon) sense, of the process by which these decisions are being taken and of the factors that are important in both deciding and evaluating the success or otherwise of the decision. Through this reflection and evaluation you will also develop the habit of *learning* from your experience, so that it becomes a rich resource, rather than a limitation. Your response to organizational challenges will show continuous improvement.

Going beyond the rational

For those decisions which you were already taking consciously the approach suggested in this book is still highly relevant. Much management training has been devoted over the years to developing 'rational' decision taking. And yet such rational approaches may be as limiting and misleading as the quick exercise of common sense. If the emphasis is only on what can be measured, as is commonly the case when the emphasis is on rational decision taking, many relevant factors will be left out. If past experience acts as a constraint, creative options may never surface, and the decision will consist of a choice between an uninspired set of alternatives, none of which addresses the 'real' problem. If the range of options considered is seriously restricted, the resulting decision is unlikely to help the organization no matter how rational was the process for deciding between the options.

The first stage of the standard rational decision-making process is problem definition. But the approach frequently fails to emphasize the importance, or the difficulty, of making sure that you fully understand the key features of the situation to which the decision relates. Even if this means facing up to more complexity than is comfortable. This will require the exercise of thought processes which are far from common. It may also be necessary to work hard at generating a wider range of options than are immediately obvious, using the sort of creativity techniques described in the later part of the book.

So although 'irrationality' is not normally suggested (except in deliberate pursuit of creativity), it is important to go *beyond* what is normally seen as the rational decision-making process. Only thus can you incorporate the less obvious, invisible features of a rapidly changing situation, and the differing perceptions and assumptions which may be key aspects of the problem or challenge. Faced with today's complexities you will not be able to make an appropriate and sufficiently creative response otherwise.

Developing 'uncommon sense'

The discussion above has started to map out a different way of thinking, one that is more conscious, more complex, more tentative, and more experimental than the unthinking exercise of common sense. Figure 1.2 shows some of the constituents of this different way of thinking. Major differences are a much more conscious thought process, a constant testing and refining of ways of thinking against experience, and the realization that models are no more than models, tools to be built, tested and used as best suits a situation, rather than unconscious and immutable constraints upon your thinking.

The process of moving from 'common' to 'uncommon sense', with its more complicated and more conscious thought processes, represents a kind of circularity that may sound impossible. How *can* you change the way in which you think? Thinking about your own presently unconscious thought processes is certainly not easy. But it can be achieved through a combination of reflection on your reaction to questions, deliberate use of particular models to describe your own work situation in different and varied ways and help reflection on your own experience, and practice of certain techniques for working with yourself or with a group of colleagues.

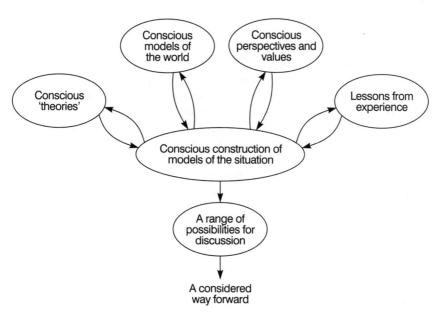

Figure 1.2   Uncommon thinking

Be warned. This will be difficult at first. You will be going against thought habits ingrained in you by years of education, and against the ways of thinking prevailing in your organization. But the effort *is* worth while, and the following chapters will include exercises to help you make the change. The remainder of this chapter goes into a little more detail about why thinking about thinking is so important, why it is so difficult, and how you can use this book to develop a way of responding to new challenges that will single you out as a manager of *uncommon* ability.

Thinking about thinking

It has been argued that thinking is *so* important for managers today because of the constant change which characterizes organizational life at present. For the few who query this, the next chapter outlines the sorts of experiences managers are currently having to cope with, but broadly these comprise:

● High, and increasing workloads for themselves and those they manage
● Increased levels of responsibility as authority is devolved
● Repeated redundancies, with worries about job security being prevalent
● Repeated major changes to organizational structures and practices.
● Increased influence of national and European policy initiatives on many organizations

The sheer increase in workload presents problems enough. Long hours at work can leave you feeling incapable of coherent thought! A common symptom of prolonged stress is the inability to concentrate. Yet the demands on you to think are almost certainly increasing. Devolution of authority may have given you responsibilities previously exercised by your now-redundant boss. The quest for flexibility and increased responsiveness to customer needs which drives much of this devolution may well have increased the number of decisions to be taken. And redundancies of colleagues at your own level may be further increasing the range of your responsibilities.

All this means that the job is offering challenges and opportunities that are totally new. Yet at the same time, old prescriptions and rules of thumb may no longer work, and there may not *be* any 'obvious' answers in a situation radically different from any you have previously experienced.

One result of this has been an almost desperate search for some kind of 'magic' answer. It is perhaps no coincidence that the management 'experts' whose books now frequently reach the bestseller lists are referred to as 'gurus', nor that academic writers on management are seriously comparing management consultants with shamans and witch doctors. Organizations may embrace the latest 'fashion' wholesale. Total Quality Management, Business Process Re-engineering and Empowerment are among such fads to have passed across the management stage in recent years. (By the end of this book you should be somewhat sceptical of such fashions, and questioning the validity of the assumptions upon which they are based and the way in which they are implemented.)

In opposition to these movements, the central argument presented here is that there *are* no ready-made solutions. Instead you need to step back from the 'buzzing blooming confusion' of the organizational world in which you are operating, and make your *own* sense of it, sharing this sense with others involved. You need to act in the light of this understanding in ways appropriate to a particular situation, which will make things better, not worse. This process of making sense may involve challenges both to received wisdom and to your own preconceptions. It may well require the conscious use of a variety of mental models, frameworks and metaphors to increase your understanding of the relevant complexity in the situation. It may indeed need a highly rational approach at times. It will probably also involve consideration of factors which cannot easily be measured, and will need to draw on techniques for doing this.

Thinking is hard work

This was the caption of a poster showing a man reclining in a hammock which graced a colleague's wall for many years. And it is clear from the discussion so far that 'thinking' as a manager means more than quiet contemplation, and more than taking a set of assumptions and following them logically through to the end point which they imply. Reflection has its place, and an important one. And logical thought processes are extremely valuable. But there is another form of thinking which is equally important, and all too rarely a habit. This is the more 'dynamic thinking' involved in carrying out 'thought experiments'. It is far more creative than either conventional common sense or highly rational approaches. It identifies a range of possible starting points, and asks questions such as 'what if . . ?' rather than 'what . . .?' It deliberately operates with a number of models at any one time rather than assuming that any one model is *the* model of reality.

This allows a far richer if more tentative understanding to be developed than is possible by using any single model. (*Any* model is, by definition, a

simplification, so to use only one risks omitting too much of importance.)
It also keeps the idea of model as *model* to the fore – if using only one, it is
all too easy to equate the model with reality, risking the model myopia
referred to earlier.

This sort of thinking does not come naturally to most of us, for a
number of reasons. We have been trained from our first experience of
school to value facts and certainties, and to think in terms of an
undisputed 'reality'. Our training, particularly in the physical sciences,
has led us to look for simple explanations such as 'B happened because
of A'. We feel uncomfortable with the idea that the way we view the
world is not the 'right' one, and even if eventually faced with over-
whelming evidence that this is the case, will look for the 'real' right
view.

In sheer practical terms there are pressures against this more complicated approach to situations. The time pressures on managers have already
been mentioned. How often have you felt that you 'haven't time to think'?
In many organizations decisiveness is seen as a major virtue, essential in
those destined for promotion. For both these reasons a speedy diagnosis
that 'the problem is . . .' may be more attractive than the response that '. . .
it is all rather complicated, and it isn't really clear what is the best way
forward'!

However, if the nature of the world is now such that the simple or
'obvious' solution will all too often make things *worse*, then it is important
to resist its allure. If simple causal models do not work, a battery of models
may be needed. Bending the present to fit past experience is no longer
enough. Until *uncommon* sense becomes second nature, these less familiar
models will need to be 'played with' consciously.

This book offers a selection of models, metaphors and frameworks that
should help you to do this. Many of these will be part of the 'gospel' of
management that forms the stock in trade of most management trainers
and developers. The emphasis differs, however, from that of most
'introduction to management' books. First, there is no attempt at
comprehensiveness. This is not a crib to the basics of management theory.
Such cribs may help you pass exams, but ideas are treated so briefly that
their significance (or otherwise!) is seldom clear. Most management ideas
are pretty simple. Some are fairly clearly wrong, or if used as prescriptions
will be useful in only a very restricted set of circumstances.

Yet used as a basis for 'experimental thinking', some of these simple
ideas can prove a powerful lever to increasing understanding. By taking a
few such ideas, and putting in the mental effort needed to use them to get
to a greater understanding of a real situation, you will gain far more than
by learning a wide range of such ideas by rote, but never really
incorporating any into your personal approach to the management
challenges you face.

Developing 'uncommon sense'

To help you make this effort, the following chapters will include the rather peremptory prompt 'Workout!' at points in the text. This is not intended to be dictatorial, merely brief. The prompts are, however, important. You will not change your way of thinking merely by reading this book. As with all skills, you need to practise, although it is mental dexterity rather than physical that these 'workouts' are intended to develop. Initially this practice is difficult, and you will need to discipline yourself to achieve it. The exercises which follow the prompts will point to reflections on your own ways of thinking, or discussions with others to find out about how they see the world. They are intended to make the process of changing your ways of thinking as focused and straightforward as possible. Unfortunately they cannot make it easy.

If you succeed in forcing yourself to follow the prompts, a number of things should happen. First, you should become more aware of your existing habits of thought, and of the roots of your own 'common' sense. You will then become more aware of the assumptions and other influences which make others see things differently from you. You will see that these differences, far from indicating ignorance or stupidity, are a valuable resource. They may indicate aspects of a situation which have so far escaped you, and which may indeed hold the key to a valid way forward. But, of course, because of the difficulty already referred to in changing your way of thinking, you will gain these benefits only if you do make the considerable effort required to reflect on ideas presented, to try to *use* them in real situations, and to *discuss* their use with colleagues.

Success in expanding your mental repertoire, and greater awareness of the processes underlying your response to situations, can have profound effects. If you can make time for 'thought experiments' on real situations, then you may be truly surprised at the extent to which your approach to management changes. You may become more cautious, and indeed critical of 'solutions', whether produced by colleagues or by the latest guru. You may initially respond to situations more cautiously yourself, though as the 'experimental' approach to thinking becomes second nature this will become less apparent. Above all, you should be responding more *appropriately*, even to totally new and difficult situations.

All the time you will be developing your capacity for appropriate and creative response still further. You will be learning from all aspects of your experience. 'Going against the grain' of your own thought habits, and the ways of thinking common in your organization will become less painful. And before long this will mark you out as a manager possessed of uncommon ability, reflecting the 'uncommon sense' which your efforts will have enabled you to develop.

Summary

This chapter has aimed to make you more aware of the contribution of both common sense and a rational approach to managerial decisions, and the likely need to go beyond both to respond effectively to today's challenges. It has discussed the reasons for 'common' sense being far from common on occasion, because different managers will respond to situations in ways influenced by *different* experiences, *different* beliefs and values, and *different* models of the world. Even where such experiences, beliefs and models are shared, as may be the case in organizations with a strong culture, they may be based on the past, and not totally appropriate to a present which is dramatically different.

Unless common sense is challenged, experience may become a limiting factor rather than a strength. Similarly, while being irrational is not recommended, strict reliance on the rational and the measurable may restrict the range of response. Greater creativity, and the ability to deal with differences in perspective and include things not easily measurable, will be needed if responses to future situations are to go beyond what has worked in the past.

This will be achieved only if considerable effort is put into becoming aware of one's own unconscious thought habits, and breaking out of these into a more conscious and experimental way of thinking that continually tests a range of models against experience. By using multiple models, and developing such models continually, a responsive and 'uncommon' sense can be developed as an approach to managerial complexity.

Chapter 2
The complexities of management today

A complex and changing management environment requires managers with the ability to grasp the key features in complex situations, and to think constructively and creatively about appropriate responses to these. Part of this ability to make sense of situations lies in accepting that they really *are* complicated, and the challenges they present are formidable. If you realize this, you will mistrust any facile and obvious solutions that you may be offered. This chapter explores some aspects of the complexity faced by mangers in the 1990s.

Later chapters will look at ways of building up a better understanding of complexity, and of your own role as observer of, and participant in, complex situations. Here we look primarily at the assumption underlying the whole argument for the need for thinking, the claim that the environment in which organizations are operating is changing at an unprecedented rate, and that this is impacting heavily upon the demands made upon the managers within those organizations.

This should help to reassure you that you are not alone in encountering these demands, that you are not going mad, that your part of the world is not unusually crazy, and, most importantly, that the difficulties that you face do not result from inadequacy on your part. To give you a feeling of how common such experiences are, this chapter draws on a survey of some 200 managers from a wide range of organizations, and their descriptions of some of the issues they faced. All were studying part-time for a Master's degree in Business Administration (MBA). During late 1994 they were asked to identify issues of current concern to them. Where quotations appear below, they are from managers taking part in this survey. Overall, their experiences support the assertion that these are times of unprecedented change for managers.

The other claim in the previous chapter was that in order to think clearly about complex situations you need the help of some models or frameworks. To impose some structure on what the managers said in response to a totally open question, a very simple framework has been used here. This is a description of the managerial role, provided as long ago as 1916 by the first management guru, Henri Fayol. By considering the issues which managers raised under the headings Fayol used, and by looking at your own experience against the same headings, you should become more aware of some of the strengths and the weaknesses of this framework as a way of organizing your own thinking. You should also see how it might need to be modified to suit the particular purpose for which you might be using it.

The chapter thus has a triple aim. By the end of it you should:

- Appreciate some of the major and varied challenges facing managers today
- Have started the process of reflecting on your own role as a manager
- See some of the advantages and disadvantages of using a simple framework to structure your thinking.

What *is* a manager?

You may well have managerial responsibility without your job title including the word 'manager'. It is important therefore to start with a definition of management, before saying much more about the pressures on managers, or about why thinking is one of the skills needed to cope with these pressures. (You may be surprised that academics *still* devote considerable effort to debating the nature of management.) The definition which is still the starting point for much teaching is the first formal definition of the role, that provided by Fayol. Indeed Fayol still appears among the top-ranking management 'gurus', whether measured by academic ratings of importance or by the number of times he is referred to in management texts.

Drawing on fifteen years of experience as managing director of a French mining and metallurgical concern, and his earlier experience as an engineer and manager within the organization, Fayol suggested that the manager's role was composed of five elements:

- *Forecasting and planning* for the anticipated future
- *Organizing*, or building up the physical and human structure of the organization
- *Commanding*, or setting in motion and maintaining the activities needed to implement plans
- *Coordinating* the various activities so that overall goals are achieved
- *Controlling*, or ensuring that 'everything occurs in conformity with established rule and expressed command'.

Other nice definitions of managers include 'people who are responsible for more work than they can do themselves' and 'people who can keep a lot of balls in the air at once'. While busy managers will feel both represent good descriptions, neither offers much help in organizing the survey responses. The more specific framework offered by Fayol suggests one way of breaking down the role into a manageable number of different aspects. Each of these can be explored to see whether there are reasons why it should present more challenges today than may have been the case twenty years ago. If so, this would support the assertion of increased pressures on managers today.

Curiously, Fayol's list is now more commonly quoted as 'plan, organize, coordinate and control'. This may be because 'command' sounds altogether too authoritarian for the current context, or simply because four things are easier to remember than five. But initiating and maintaining activity would seem to be an important element of a manager's role. Perhaps means other than 'commands' are needed for this – indeed the area of motivation is a high priority today, and is dealt with in considerable detail later in this book. The full list is therefore used here, though with a broader interpretation of 'command' than Fayol may have intended.

Fayol was writing from the perspective of someone whose responsibility was to determine strategy for the organization as a whole. In this he was the first of a long line of senior managers including Sir John Harvey-Jones, Lee Iaccoca and Akio Morita, who have attempted to make sense in retrospect of their management experience, and pass on their insights to others. In the case of some of these authors you might want to question the relevance of the senior management perspective for managers operating at more modest levels.

Fayol's definition of roles can, however, be applied at all levels of management. Almost all managers will have elements of each of the five roles in their job, albeit to varying degrees. The more junior the manager, the shorter is likely to be the planning time scale. At lower levels human and other resources may be more limited. But the functions will still exist. Although middle managers may have to energize staff by ways other than giving orders, the function of motivating and of coordinating and controlling will be crucial at all levels.

Sources of pressure

So why do so many managers claim to be experiencing more pressure today than ever before? What are the organizational and wider factors contributing to these feelings? Is change really taking place on a wider scale, and more rapidly, than ever before? If we look at each of Fayol's elements in turn, a fairly clear picture starts to emerge.

Forecasting and planning

Planning relates to preparing for some future state, and this involves forecasting future requirements. Many organizations are finding it very difficult to anticipate, and therefore plan for, the future. This difficulty cascades down to middle managers and lower. The combination of recession and increased competition has created considerable pressures. The growth of manufacturing in the low-wage economies has had a major effect. Technological advances have had huge impacts on most organizations, in the service sector as much as in manufacturing. A manager working for a computer services company said, for example, that '. . . the introduction of PCs radically changed our market. Our competitors are more aggressive. Our customers demand tailoring to meet their needs, and faster, more flexible, more cost-effective solutions. We failed to respond in time to these rapid changes in our market.'

Government action is another major factor which is not always easy to forecast. Pharmaceutical companies, for example, have been seriously affected by UK government restrictions on prescribable products and pricing, and controls on promotion. As a manager in such a company said, when discussing the organization's response to these restrictions, 'The new CEO is determined that the organization become more flexible, goal-seeking and market oriented'. Few (if any) UK beef farmers will have forecast the impact of European action on BSE.

The impact of government action on the public and quasi-public sector has been even more dramatic. Policies aimed at reducing public expenditure and allowing market forces to play a major controlling role led to considerable uncertainty about the future among those surveyed, as the following typical quotes demonstrate.

> It is likely that within two years the [local] authority will be split into two . . .
> Within three years we shall face either privatization or at least CCT [compulsory competitive tendering].
> Engineering and Planning departments were merged, and a purchaser provider split introduced in anticipation of new legislation. Now the legislation is clearer, we need further restructuring!

Upheavals like this, driven by forces outside the organization, have had a major impact on middle managers' own planning. When senior management forecasts are wrong, or there is a planning vacuum at high levels because it is *impossible* to forecast, organizations may make major strategic changes at very short notice. Middle managers may have great difficulty in implementing these changes in a planned or controlled fashion. One manager referred with feeling to the difficulties she was encountering in September, when faced with the *third* complete change of business plan since April!

Uncertainty for the organization as a whole means that middle managers may be unable to forecast the internal factors which need to be taken into consideration in their own planning, meaning that they too are often having to respond very rapidly without the luxury of detailed exploration of available options. The widespread pursuit of greater flexibility to customer needs demands similar rapid response. Under such circumstances, it is essential to be able to extract key aspects in a situation, and consider ways forward, very quickly. 'Uncommon sense' is at a premium.

Consider those aspects of your own role that involve planning and forecasting and jot them down. How often recently have you been forced to respond in a unplanned way because of rapid changes of direction at higher organizational levels?

Organizing physical and human structure

One of the responses organizations have made to the increasingly competitive environment and to the difficulty of forecasting key factors in the future has been to *restructure*. The goals of restructuring are almost always said to be greater flexibility and proactivity, greater customer and/or commercial focus, and greater efficiency. The structural changes which seem to have been favoured by both public and private sectors are:

● Delayering or flattening
● Devolved autonomy
● Decentralization.

Associated with almost all of these changes has been a fourth, though less advertised, change:

● Downsizing

Delayering

In *delayering* whole levels of management are removed. This in itself increases the number of staff reporting to the manager in the level above that removed. Even within the levels which are retained the number of managers is often severely reduced, so that spans of control are increased still further. Thus one manager whose organization, an educational institution, had flattened itself in a fairly modest way described how one whole layer of management had been removed, while the span of control of the remaining two levels had been doubled through selective redundancy. Another's Japanese-owned company had taken a rather more radical approach, removing *all* middle managers! The CEO met all staff twice a year in small groups. Between these meetings staff relied heavily on electronic communications.

These managers are not in any way unusual in their experience. Three quarters of 150 companies who took part in a survey in 1992 reported that they had made changes resulting in increased spans of control for middle managers, while a survey of middle managers who had experienced restructuring found that three quarters of these managers had experienced a significant increase in workload in consequence.

Some of this restructuring has been made possible by increasing use of information technology. Before the use of computers became widespread, many managers spent considerable time and energy in recording data, processing it, and communicating the information so derived to others in the organization. IT developments have removed the need for the manager to do much more than respond to the information that relates to his or her particular area of responsibility.

Devolved autonomy and decentralization

Developments in IT have also aided the move to *devolved autonomy*. This involves giving increased responsibility to lower levels in the organization. The argument is that greater flexibility and responsiveness will be achieved if decisions are taken at the lowest possible level. It is here, after all, that much of the relevant information resides, particularly if IT's information *processing* capabilities are exploited. Devolved autonomy is often achieved by the creation of multi-skilled teams with accountability for the quality and quantity of their output. Clearly, devolution will increase the need for decision taking by middle and junior managers.

Devolved autonomy is often linked to *decentralization*, where organizations try to move operations closer to the customer in order to increase customer focus and, again, flexibility. They will therefore move away from a structure based on *functions*, such as marketing, production, personnel, and finance, and towards divisions based on the product and incorporating within them all the necessary functions. These will often be referred to as *strategic business units*. In consequence, line managers may find themselves taking on personnel and financial responsibilities which were previously the role of centralized specialists. This trend is by no means confined to manufacturing. The 'product' referred to may just as well be a service. Police forces have created strategic business units, and local authorities have done so for several years.

Downsizing

All the forms of restructuring described have in recent years been frequently accompanied by redundancies. Sometimes these are implicit in the form of restructuring adopted: in delayering, almost by definition, several layers of management are likely to go, while in de-centralization it is specialists who are particularly at risk. But even where redundancy is not an inevitable consequence, restructuring exercises are often accompanied by 'downsizing' or one of the other euphemisms for redundancy. Thus a manager with a motor manufacturer described a reduction from a workforce of 6000 to one of 1500 in conjunction with restructuring, and another in a quasi-governmental agency talked of a 50 per cent reduction in the workforce over five years together with a move to a product-based structure. Another, this time in a local authority, spoke of a reduction from 34 000 in 1987 to 25 000 in 1994, with further redundancies anticipated.

In such situations managers frequently complain that it is virtually impossible to 'organize' the human resources necessary to meet their objectives. A frequent immediate response to current or anticipated restructuring is a ban on external recruitment. At the same time, employees with skills which are in demand may be leaving for more secure employment. Teams are therefore left seriously under strength and lacking key skills, yet managers are not allowed to take action to secure the resource they need. Thus a librarian bemoaned the impossibility of attracting suitably skilled and qualified recruits when there was an embargo on external recruitment. Those in other departments in the authority were not, on the whole, trained in librarianship! Nor are those selected for redundancy always chosen with a view to future skills requirements. A manager in manufacturing complained that '. . . these massive redundancies have been declared with no explicit medium or long-term strategy, and with no analysis of the skills required for the future'. Another claimed that not only was it now impossible to obtain resources for new ventures, but that current workloads were straining the severely reduced workforce. There were already signs that staff were breaking down under the load, particularly those who were most committed to the job. Yet 50 000 further redundancies were planned for the next five years. 'How', he asked, 'can we prevent corporate anorexia?'

Commanding

To speak of managers 'commanding' is not very fashionable. Talk today is all of 'participative management', 'employee involvement', and 'enabling'. This may be the rhetoric. But the overpowering impression gained from the survey responses was that as far as senior management is concerned, commanding in the authoritarian sense is still very much alive and well.

Managers made frequent reference to the announcement of major changes from on high, without consultation or any other form of employee participation in the decision process. As one manager said, 'Higher management announce to all, and middle managers are left to explain, without understanding the reasons themselves'.

Unpopular decisions taken in response to an imminent threat to the organization's survival may well be felt to be best handled in this way. But it leaves middle managers like the one quoted above in a very difficult position. They are faced with the problems of implementing the change without warning or preparation time, and often without the goodwill of those whom they need to manage through the process.

This is particularly difficult, as 'commanding' in the sense of issuing orders is not an option for many managers lower in the organization. Authority relationships in organizations have changed considerably since Fayol's day. Employee legislation, terms and conditions of employment, equal opportunity policies and union agreements may seriously constrain what a manager can actually *require* of subordinates. Authority may be poorly defined. Even when managers feel sufficiently confident in their right to take a decision, this may be overturned by a (possibly less confident) superior. Many managers have received little (if any) training in their role, and restructuring and devolved autonomy may have made them even more confused about their responsibilities than they were before.

One factor which may be increasingly available to middle managers to supplement their perhaps diminishing authority is involvement in deciding rewards. Large numbers of managers surveyed referred to the introduction of performance management schemes, in which pay is to some extent dependent on level of performance. This level is frequently determined through the annual appraisal process, this appraisal normally being carried out by the line manager.

Despite the increasing importance of appraisal, there are still many managers who feel that even though they have very limited authority they are being required to 'initiate and maintain the activities necessary' to further the organization's (often rapidly changing) plans. This means that they are having to motivate staff, often under very difficult conditions. A large number of the managers in the survey described problems of motivating teams on whom *yet another* change had been imposed, who still did not feel safe from redundancy, and who were often already working harder than was felt to be sustainable because of the redundancy of others.

Thinking about motivational effects of decisions, and the way they are handled, is something which many managers find difficult. If they do have assumptions, or models, which underpin their thinking, these are often very simple, and may be misleading. Yet the difference between a motivated team and an apathetic one is enormous, and the ability to generate commitment to the job is vital to a manager's success. The topic will therefore be re-visited, and dealt with at greater length in Chapter 6.

Reflect on those parts of your job which involve maintaining the activity of your staff at an appropriate level, and list them. How do you achieve this? To what extent is it by authority, and what other means do you have at your disposal?

Coordinating

Surprisingly, no manager specifically raised coordination as an issue, although some mentioned it in passing, for example in the context of a move to a 'just-in-time' way of operating. Here, the removal of buffer stocks and reduction in work in progress means that a high level of coordination is needed. It is possible that new technologies have made coordination easier. It is more likely that new structures, with a shift to a product focus for organizations, and the widespread adoption of devolved authority have to some extent reduced the difficulties of coordination. Certainly the more fragmented a task and the narrower the area of an employee's responsibility, the greater is the need for coordination by supervisor or manager. Similarly, where firms have been organized according to functions, communications may have needed to go a long way up the organization before reaching a crossover point (Figure 2.1).

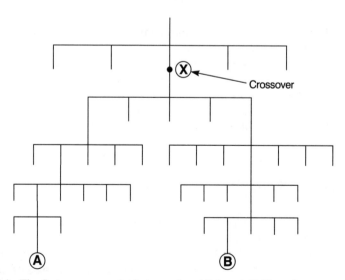

Figure 2.1   The first crossover point between A and B in a rigid hierarchy

Again list those parts of your job which relate to the aspect of the role discussed, here coordination of the activities of those you manage.

Controlling

This is a major issue for managers, responsible as they are for meeting performance and quality standards. Changes in structure are increasing the level and breadth of junior and middle managers' jobs. Managers are finding they have responsibility for budgetary control, and have personnel responsibilities which previously belonged to specialist functions. There is now a strong focus on quality in public and private sectors alike, with many organizations seeking or having gained BS 5750/ISO 9000. This has considerably raised awareness of the need for quality control in the broadest sense of conformity to specified standards at all stages. In the public sector there has been a marked move towards the adoption of performance measurement, driven by legislation and government pressure of other kinds. Cutbacks in public spending or, in the private sector, increasingly competitive markets have led to pressure on resources, and a need to control their use closely.

IT developments have the potential to provide much of the information essential to any effective control, but managers still complain of 'too much' or 'the wrong kind' of information. Or they may feel 'out of control' because of the level of pressure on them generally, and because of the difficulty of *exercising* control given the changed authority relationships described earlier. Sometimes they may simply not know 'what levers to pull' if things seem to be going wrong.

Control may have negative overtones for some, particularly when linked in 'command and control'. Exercised with a heavy hand it can lead to inflexibility and demotivation. Nevertheless it is an essential part of any manager's role, and may be seen in a much more positive light. It is discussed in more detail in Chapter 5.

As before, list those aspects of your job which involve some form of control. Now you can start to think more seriously, in order to see how useful Fayol's framework is for *you*. Spend a little time thinking about the proportion of your time devoted to each of the five elements of management which Fayol identified. In particular, note any parts of your job which do not appear on any of your lists, and therefore do not seem to fit into the given categories.(If you are not currently a manager, but are sufficiently close to someone who is, ask them to cooperate with you. Ask them about their jobs and find out how they distribute their time, and what problems they encounter in mapping their job onto these five areas.)

How useful *is* Fayol's framework?

You probably found that you could not account for 100 per cent of your job under Fayol's headings. This does not necessarily mean that you have not classified your work properly - for example, by not being aware that you are coordinating, when this is actually what you are doing. There are two possible reasons for a shortfall. You may have identified tasks which you do yourself, *in addition* to managing. This is a common situation. The other possibility is that Fayol's categories may not fully represent the role of many of today's managers.

This second possibility raises interesting questions. You may have identified areas of your work that are clearly managerial in nature, but which cannot be fitted reasonably easily into one of the five categories listed. It is possible that, given Fayol's 'top management' perspective, his categories omit aspects of middle management life. One obvious omission involves managing boundaries between the area under the manager's control and other areas within the organization which are not so controlled but with whom cooperation is needed. It may also be that in a highly competitive environment there are important aspects of at least some managers' roles which have to do with managing relations with external parties, another form of boundary-spanning activity.

Look at the areas of your job which were difficult to categorize, and decide whether they are non-managerial in nature, or need additional categories. If more are needed, try to invent appropriate ones.

If you needed additional categories, you may like to compare your final list of roles with two more recent lists. The more widely quoted of these was derived sixty years after Fayol's (though still several decades ago) by Henry Mintzberg. Again it is based on chief executives. Mintzberg's list has ten key management roles, some of which map quite neatly onto Fayol's categories, some apparently quite distinct. The roles are: leader; figurehead; spokesman; liaison; negotiator; disturbance handler; monitor; disseminator;

entrepreneur; and resource allocator. The second list was derived from observations of middle managers made by Luthans in 1988. These managers worked in a range of different organizations in the USA. Luthans suggested that 'real' managers' activities can be broken into four major categories:

- *Communication*: exchanging information, and paperwork
- *Traditional management*: planning, decision making, and controlling
- *Networking*: interacting with outsiders, socializing/politicking
- *Human resource management*: motivating/reinforcing, disciplining/punishing, managing conflict, staffing, and training/developing

Here, then, are three possible frameworks for thinking about the manager's job in terms of the roles performed. Each allows you to look at what you or other managers do in a structured way. One may suit some purposes, another may be appropriate for others. Nor are they the only possible frameworks. The literature contains a number of different such lists. You could draw up one particularly suited to your specific job, with more or fewer categories. Some organizations do this with a view to providing a structure for performance appraisal and/or training. There is also a framework of competences devised by the Management Charter Initiative (MCI) and the basis of National Vocational Qualifications for managers. This is built around four key roles, relating to the management of operations, of finance, of people and of information. Additionally, there are a set of personal competences, implying a fifth role of managing yourself and your relationship with others.

The provision of these different frameworks, all of which have some merit, makes the point that there is no simple 'truth' about the management role. Not only is there the obvious point that there must be hundreds of thousands of very different jobs all labelled 'manager', but there are also many different ways of organizing your thinking about these jobs. As a broad framework for looking at management challenges today, Fayol was simple and provides a starting point for thinking about your role. Without some such structure you might flounder in the complexities of your job, not knowing where to start. Luthans or Mintzberg would have served the same purpose, whether as well or even better would depend upon your job and your preferences!

As a basis for designing a comprehensive management development programme suitable for managers from a wide variety of organizations, however, something more detailed would be needed, perhaps along the lines of the MCI standards. For selecting a manager for a particular job, something much more specific to the role in question would be required as the basis of the job description. When deciding on an appropriate model to use it is essential to be clear as to your purpose, and to select one (or more) that fits it.

The basic and crucial point to take from this exercise, however, is that while each of these frameworks may have some uses as an aid to thinking about what managers do, it would be very dangerous to regard any one of them as the *only* way of viewing management as an activity. To use only Fayol, for example, tried and tested and quoted many thousands of times though his set of roles may be, could mean that you ignored important aspects of what managers do today, and might be blind to important areas where you should be devoting your energies and developing your capabilities.

The management challenge

From the previous section it will be clear that the managerial life is no bed of roses, whatever the framework you use to organize your examination of it! Organizations *are* changing, drastically altering their corporate strategy, their very structures, and their ways of doing things. These changes may be frequent as well as radical. In consequence, managers may find their responsibilities increased, while at the same time they may feel that their authority is diminished. The rate of change may be such that they are trying to manage totally new situations while not sure of what they should be trying to achieve, nor of how best to achieve whatever it may be.

All this may be taking place in a context of work overload for both manager and those managed, as major reductions are made in the workforce. The stress of overload is added to by worries that the manager may be one of the next to go if further cutbacks are made. While a stress factor in itself, this fear may additionally increase the pressure on managers to 'perform': a high level of achievement *may* make their jobs more secure.

If this sounds unnecessarily gloomy, it is worth noting that the changes described above were undertaken in pursuit of greater competitiveness and effectiveness, and many of the managers surveyed indicated that the organizational changes they had experienced did seem to have achieved at least some of their aims.

Indeed, there were one or two managers who even in 1994 mentioned difficulties caused by rapid growth. Interestingly, many of the problems of growth can be similar to those of contraction. There may be a need for restructuring as an organization grows. Also resources may not grow as fast as demands upon them, again placing managers and their teams under pressure from work levels greater than can be comfortably sustained for long. If the industry as a whole is growing then it may be difficult to keep good staff, exacerbating the problem.

This, then, is the context for management today. To respond creatively and effectively to the challenges of rapid change, whether posed by growth or decline, you need skills and knowledge. You need to *know* a lot about your own organization, and about the processes for which you are responsible. You need to know what resources, such as specialist advice, are available when required, and how to obtain these. You need to know what *could* be available, provided you can make a good case, and how to make that case. And you need to be fully aware of the constraints imposed upon them, for example, by organizational policy and legislation. You need to be able to tell which of these constraints are absolutely firm, and which can be flexed slightly. You also need to appreciate the constraints placed upon you by factors outside the organization, such as employment legislation.

Managerial skills to meet the challenge

If you are managing in the present context you will need *technical* skills, both to exploit the information processing facilities available and to cope with the accounting and other systems which you have to operate, in addition to any skills associated with the operations for which you are responsible. Devolved autonomy and decentralization are likely to have increased the level of demand for such skills.

Managers today can seldom rely simply on giving orders to those they manage. To run an effective team you need a huge range of *interpersonal* skills to enable you to motivate, support and control (in the best sense of the word) your staff, and to negotiate with them, or on behalf of them with others in the organization. You need skills in communication, whether with those inside the organization, or with customers and others outside. The need for interpersonal skills has been further increased by structural changes, making horizontal communication and negotiation as important as communication up and down a hierarchy.

But above all, as was argued in the first chapter, you need *conceptual* skills. The mental agility to respond to rapid and major change, and to plan quickly and appropriately how best to move forward has been made far more important both by structural changes within organizations and by the continuing pressures on organizations and the rapidity of response needed to meet these. Your role in implementing change in the midst of complexity means that you need to be able to take into account a wide variety of different factors and a high level of uncertainty. It requires conceptual abilities that conventional education frequently does little to develop.

Throughout the remaining chapters the emphasis will be on developing these conceptual skills. If you are to flourish in an organization which is changing as rapidly as many of those described earlier, you need to be able to approach each situation as it arises, and tease out the relevant factors from the complexity. To make sense of these factors you need to use whatever past experience is of relevance, and whatever theory may be helpful. Above all you need to develop the ability to explore *different* ways of looking at the situation, and different ways of making sense of it, in order to increase your chances of including all the factors which are important and of interpreting these factors in an appropriate and creative way. To help you derive new ways forward based on this sounder understanding you also need techniques which will develop your *creativity*.

The starting point for this change to your way of thinking is to become aware of the thought habits which you already have, and the assumptions which are at present limiting your view of any situation. You need to go *beyond* these, forcing yourself to play mental games which compare different versions of 'reality'. This mental modelling, or experimental thinking, which is an essential component of the elusive *uncommon* sense which you need to develop, is the most important conceptual skill you need. The next chapter should start this process of making you aware of your own starting points, so that you can see how to go beyond these. It will begin the proces of 'thinking about thinking' needed if you are to develop your own conceptual skills, and the ability to continually learn from experience and adapt to a rapidly changing and increasingly demanding managerial world.

Summary

This chapter has drawn on the experience of a range of managers to support the assertion that the context of management is rapidly changing, and that great demands are being placed upon managers as a result of this. The impact of increased competitive pressures and government initiatives in particular, and the consequent major restructuring undertaken by many organizations were major themes.

These impacts were explored in the context of an early definition of the manager's role, which was then used as a framework for studying your own experience as a manager. From this you should have been able to see both that a simple framework can be a useful starting point, and that it is unlikely to totally reflect your own experience as a manager. There is a need therefore to think critically about the framework, and its suitability as a model in a particular context.

This suggests the need to use more than one model, and to be aware of models which you are already using, in order to be able to consider their usefulness, and modify or supplement them.

---------- *Chapter 3* ----------
Your own management philosophy

No one can become a carpenter, a doctor, a social worker or a secretary without some form of training. But people can and do find themselves in management positions without having been trained. They become managers by stealth. Many of them muddle through, relying upon an approach to management which is an amalgam of knowledge acquired randomly, their own experience of being managed or of seeing other managers at work, their personal beliefs, assumptions and values. Few people, once they have established their own management philosophy, will challenge or change it without some significant external stimulus. This is particularly so as they move up the management ladder.

Yet while some muddle through, other people become very capable and effective managers. This might be because, in the course of management training or development, they have been persuaded to reconsider their own management philosophy. But it may be that they are *thinking managers* who constantly evaluate the outcomes of what they do and, as a result, look for ways to become even more effective.

However, management education and training in the formal sense are not the only means to this end. In fact we would argue that managers need to approach the management education and training that they are offered with a critical eye, questioning the value of the theories and concepts they study and testing whether they are applicable and relevant to their own circumstances and experience. This is not to say that as a manager you should not be looking for development through education and training, but your aim all the while should be to build up your own *personal* set of tools. These can then be used creatively to tackle the situations that confront you day to day in your job. In other words, the *way* in which you think can be equally as important as *what* you think, and later in the book you will find some techniques to help you to develop new ways of thinking at work.

As you saw in Chapter 1, the most effective managers constantly re-examine their understanding of management, reflecting upon their experience of working in organizations, challenging their previous assumptions and reconsidering any theoretical frameworks that they have studied. In this way they remodel their old 'common sense' approach to managing. They may not do this consciously, but the habit of reflection and re-evaluation is part of the thinking process of successful managers. We have called this process uncommon thinking. As well as rejecting the common sense approach as the only way forward, effective managers also recognize that the beliefs and values which constitute their own common sense are part of a purely personal philosophy, which may not be shared or understood by others.

But before you can begin to reflect upon your own effectiveness as a manager you need to establish 'where you are coming from'. This chapter, then, is about helping you to understand what goes to make up your own management philosophy and what parts of it might be due for an overhaul. By the end of it you should:

- Understand some of the assumptions that you bring to management situations
- Recognize that theory can be used to challenge your experience, and that you can also use experience to assess the practical value of management theory
- Want to explore other concepts and frameworks
- Wish to extend your thinking

Knowing where you are coming from

I have used the terms 'approach' and 'philosophy' so far in this chapter to describe the ways in which people apply themselves to the tasks of management. However, just having a philosophy is clearly not going to help a practising manager, who has not simply to philosophize but also to act!

The aim of management development and education should be to provide a range of tools which can help a manager to act more effectively at work. If you have studied management, you probably found that the models or theories were interesting and could be helpful in analysing situations, but they failed to show you how to deal with them effectively. This does not mean that they are never going to be of use to the practising manager. However, their value lies in the extent to which they can stimulate further thought about the situations that confront you, and this includes being aware of the range of perspectives that there might be on that same situation.

The idea of perspective is an important one and is a theme which will run throughout this book. My view of the world is shaped by my own experience, which is personal to me. I will interpret the events and situations that affect me in the light of this experience. Events that fit with my vision of the environment in which I find myself will reassure me. Those which don't can make me react in a number of different ways. I may feel uneasy or angry. I may try, consciously or otherwise, to distort the nature of the event so that it *does* conform with my view of things. I may become defensive about my own view of reality. I will certainly want to discover allies whose perspective on an issue is similar to my own.

Imagine that you are asked to be a member of a working group. The other members are known to you by sight only. One of the things you will want to gauge at the first meeting is where the other individuals are 'coming from'. You need to form a view of their perspective on your shared work environment as well as on the issue you are addressing, so that you can assess which of your views is likely to gain support and with whom.

Recognizing the importance of other perspectives does not mean, for example, that successful managers only make a decision once they have taken all views into account. It may simply be that such managers are more aware of the strength of the opposition to a particular plan and where it might be expected to come from. Or that they recognize, when putting together a team to work on a particular project, both the strengths as well as the difficulties inherent in accommodating a range of perspectives.

Selecting the tools for the job

A large part of a manager's role is taking decisions, not about the big strategic issues of importance but about the myriad simple issues that crop up each day. However, as we shall see later, even simple decisions can have far-reaching and unforeseen consequences. Any management tools which help you to decide wisely are an essential part of the manager's 'toolkit'. However, these models and ideas do not have to be imported wholesale from a management theorist or current guru. The important thing is that you select those which will help you to manage better and to adapt others to suit your own particular needs and working environment. As you read this book, you will recognize that you have some of these 'tools' already, though they may be a little blunt or rusty. You may reach the conclusion that you should have stopped relying upon some of them ages ago. Depending upon the nature of your management role, you may consider that you need to acquire some specialist tools, but that others you could create yourself or adapt from what you can find, bearing in mind all the time the nature of the task for which they are designed.

The point is that you cannot go on relying on this set of tools indefinitely; you will need to select others and perhaps adapt more as each occasion requires. The demands upon managers are constantly changing as the management environment itself changes, and also the tools that you use need to remain fit for today's purpose. Nor can you hope to discover a set of theories and models sufficient to cover the range and complexity of the management situations that you are likely to encounter. Scouring management texts will not provide you with answers. In the end it is the quality of *your* thinking, plus *your* understanding (based upon theory and experience) of how people and organizations behave in their environments which will make you effective as a manager.

Before you examine the value of theories and management models to you in your own management situation, you need to recognize what constitutes your current management philosophy, made up, as we said, of a complex array of knowledge, experience, assumptions, beliefs and values.

Looking at your own approach to management

If you have been a manager for some years you may seldom ever think about how you go about doing your job. Your responses are likely to be instinctive, just 'common sense'. Indeed, colleagues can probably predict how you will react in a given situation. On the other hand, if you are a recent manager you may still be hoping for that time to come when you can feel this comfortable with your role. However, comfortable and predictable does not necessarily mean effective, and it is possible that newer, more junior managers who are thinking hard about what they are doing are actually more effective, though, because their sphere of influence is smaller, this may not be generally noticed.

The quiz below is designed to set you thinking about where your own approach to management has its roots. Do they lie principally in past experience or in theories and concepts you have learnt?

Management philosophy quiz

There are no right or wrong answers to the questions below.
Scoring is as follows. If you *strongly agree* with a statement, award it 5 points, 4 if you simply agree. If you *strongly disagree* with a statement award it 1 point, 2 if you just disagree. If you really can't say either way, score 3.

1 People are generally lazy and need close supervision in order to make them work

2 The most important thing for an organization is to have a charismatic leader

3 An organization chart tells you virtually everything you need to know about an organization

4 Every organization needs to have proper procedures in place to guarantee quality

5 It is dangerous to keep on modifying objectives ☐

6 Most people work harder if they are paid by results ☐

7 A manager's job is to control ☐

8 Women tend to be more creative and innovative than men ☐

9 Whenever things go wrong in an organization there is usually a simple solution ☐

10 Good managers are born, not made ☐

11 It is not a manager's job to predict the future ☐

12 Gathering feedback is much less important than keeping your eye on the ball ☐

13 Dynamic organizations need to appoint young dynamic managers ☐

14 Communications are only effective when they go upwards and sideways as well as down ☐

15 In order to get things done you need to build effective teams ☐

16 Every organization needs to have a mission statement so that every employee knows where they stand ☐

17 All change is a threat ☐

18 A manager's main responsibility is to the shareholders ☐

19 It's the job of those in sales and marketing to look after our customers ☐

20 It is essential to focus on strengths and look out for opportunities ☐

None of the items in the quiz is unambiguously true or false; they are all statements of opinion about organizations, the people who work in them and the way in which managers work most effectively. Your answers to them express in part your own management philosophy. If you refer to the notes at the end of this chapter, you will find some comments on each of the questions, cross-referenced where appropriate to other chapters in the book.

What other managers thought

We asked a group of managers to complete the same quiz. All the managers were studying for a professional certificate in management. There were 58 responses, 36 from managers who were nearing the end of their studies and 24 from managers who had just started to study for their certificate. Perhaps you won't be surprised to learn that there was no consensus about the answer to any of the questions. The answers from the students who had just begun their course showed that in only two cases was there a tendency for them to agree (on questions 3 and 4). The rest of the time there was a complete spread of opinion, even if it was only one or two of the respondents who held an extreme contrary view.

If you would like to compare your own responses with those of the students, their responses have been analysed in Tables 3.1 and 3.2.

Table 3.1   Results of management questionnaire: replies from new students
Range: 5 (very strong agreement) to 1 (very strong disagreement)

Question	5	4	3	2	1
1	0	3	2	**13**	6
2	1	6	6	**9**	2
3	0	0	5	9	**10**
4	11	**12**	1	0	0
5	0	5	6	**8**	5
6	4	3	**8**	7	2
7	2	5	**11**	4	2
8	0	5	**10**	5	4
9	0	5	7	**8**	4
10	1	1	5	6	**11**
11	3	4	2	**10**	5
12	2	0	4	**10**	7
13	1	6	5	**7**	5
14	**16**	6	0	1	1
15	**15**	7	1	1	0
16	6	**14**	3	1	0
17	2	1	3	3	**15**
18	1	1	3	6	**13**
19	3	4	1	7	**9**
20	**17**	5	2	0	9

Note: The figure for the largest number of replies to each question is in bold type.
Total number of replies = 24

Table 3.2   Results of management questionnaire: replies from completing students
Range: 5 (very strong agreement) to 1 (very strong disagreement)

Question	5	4	3	2	1
1	0	2	3	14	**17**
2	2	9	6	**16**	3
3	0	3	4	**16**	13
4	12	**18**	5	1	0
5	1	8	11	**13**	3
6	3	6	10	**13**	4
7	5	7	9	**10**	5
8	2	5	**13**	11	5
9	2	7	5	**11**	11
10	1	7	4	7	**17**
11	2	3	4	**15**	12
12	0	5	4	**18**	9
13	0	9	6	**12**	9
14	**20**	11	2	2	1
15	**19**	14	2	0	1
16	**13**	10	8	3	1
17	3	4	3	6	**20**
18	0	2	8	9	**17**
19	2	5	2	13	**14**
20	**20**	10	2	3	1

Note: The figure for the largest number of replies to each question is in bold type.
Total number of replies = 36

Understanding your answers

Among this group of managers working in different organizations there is no single view about management and the way in which organizations and people behave. Every individual response will be a reflection of that person's experience. And, there are some useful things that you can learn by looking at your own responses to the statements.

Strong agreement or disagreement

First, look at the strength of your agreement with the items in general. If you tended to agree or disagree strongly with the majority of the statements, this suggests that as a manager you have a very clear set of perceptions and values. This can be, and can be seen by others to be, a great strength. It means that you are likely to be able to assess situations very rapidly and reach a firm decision about what needs to be done. Even if others do not agree with you, your conviction may be so strong that you will not be influenced by their contrary views. (When I asked a senior manager working in a demanding role in the telecommunications industry to complete the quiz, his responses were nearly all at the extremes of the range. This may be a function of his personality or perhaps the nature of the environment in which he finds himself working.)

Of course, this same strength can also be a weakness when it comes to situations where decisions have to be negotiated or where the cooperation of others is needed. In these situations it is important to be able to set aside your own firm views in order to take into account the contributions and perspectives of other people who are involved in the particular issue. It can also be seen as a weakness if despite having firm views you turn out to be wrong from time to time. Management is not like a scientific experiment where, in a particular set of circumstances in which all the components and their values are known, you can expect a previous result to be repeated. In management the circumstances, the components and their values are never the same. You can never be sure that repeating a set of procedures will produce the results you expect. Check out particularly your answers to questions 7 and 12. If you *strongly agreed* with these statements, is there a possibility that you may not be open to inputs from others? Notice too your responses to items 14 and 15. If you *strongly disagreed* with these as well then perhaps you should reflect upon whether you are allowing your staff sufficient autonomy as they would wish in your determination to 'lead from the front'.

You may be very effective in dealing with situations which are more time-critical than complex, since you do not waste time collecting information which only serves to obscure the issues. You tend to go right to the heart of the matter and then act. However, this approach could be a disaster when the situation is complex. In such cases it might be advisable to consider different angles and perspectives and to gather as much data as you can from others before reaching a decision.

No strong views

If, on the other hand, you found it difficult to either agree or disagree with the statements because you felt that they oversimplified reality you are probably someone who has the ability to see a number of sides to every question. This can be a positive asset in dealing with complex situations. You tend not to go for the immediate answer, nor to address simply the situation as it is presented, but to consider the various issues in some depth before reaching a decision. You need time to explore the situation and to gather information. You may want to consult with colleagues before making up your mind about how to proceed. However, unless you are sure that you can assimilate detail and a mass of information, there is the chance that you could start going round in circles, producing at the end of the day no more effective decision than the manager who had the clear perspective, but having done so more slowly and having used up valuable human resource in the process. As you will see later, creativity is about adopting a questioning approach. However, it is also about asking *appropriate* questions which challenge given assumptions, not about questioning everything so that you end up in a state of paralysis!

For example, you may feel that the statement 'Every organization needs to have procedures in place to guarantee quality' is not a simple one. If you examine it more closely, you might wonder whether the procedures *themselves* can actually guarantee quality, or does this have more to do with the people who operate them? You may feel that the statement is more true for certain organizations than for others. Would it necessarily be the case in an advertising agency, or the customer complaints operation of an airline company?

Again, is it *really* the manager's job to control? Or is this just one of the many tasks of a manager? Certainly you will have a responsibility for the resources which you manage, but do you control the human resources in the same way that you control the financial ones, or is your approach different?

If you found that you were asking these kinds of questions as you worked through the quiz, you are already someone who tends to use their experience to evaluate management concepts and who thinks about the complexity of organizational life.

The many roles of a manager

Thinking more deeply about the statements in the quiz will remind you about the complexities as well as the subtleties of management. For, like an actor, a manager is called on to play a number of different management roles. For example, these might include being a team player, a coach, an examiner, a negotiator, a counsellor, an arbitrator, an innovator, a regulator, a sage, an instructor or a choreographer. You can probably think of other 'roles' that you play regularly in the course of a day at work. They may be different from the list of ten which Mintzberg drew up, which were referred to in Chapter 2, but he, you will remember, was just concerned with the roles played by chief executives.

Effective managers cannot afford to be one-dimensional. If you rely too heavily upon a single management persona, it is likely that you will find it difficult to respond adequately to the kind of complex situations which require a different kind of approach. To take the theatre analogy a step further, at times managers have to be quick-change artists, ready to take an *appropriate* part in a new scene or a different management drama.

Questioning your own assumptions

While responding to the quiz, and thinking about the responses which our other managers gave, you may have begun to question some of your own assumptions. For example, many people do regard change as a threat, whether it affects them directly or not. Some, on the other hand, welcome the idea of change, but only if it does not interfere with their own preferred way of doing things. You may have agreed with the statement that all change is a threat, basing your response perhaps upon a major change that is occurring in your own organization and how it is being handled. However, if this view is never challenged, if it becomes embedded in your personal management philosophy, you may be in danger of forgetting that change can also bring opportunities for improvement if handled effectively.

As the quiz suggests, for every view that you have about the management environment there are likely to be other managers who hold the opposite view with equal conviction. Try discussing some of the statements with colleagues or friends to get some idea of the range of views. Alternatively, try to set out for yourself the arguments that someone who took the opposite view might put forward, perhaps recalling examples from your own experience which might support that contrary view. If you turn to the notes at the end of this chapter, you will find a brief discussion of each of the statements which you may like to read now, while referring back to your own response to each item.

Theory or experience?

Most of our opinions about management derive from a mixture of theory that we have been taught or have learned about from reading or on training courses, and what we have observed or understood from our own experience. I also asked the group of managers who completed our management quiz to indicate whether their response to each question was largely based upon their experience or upon some theory or concept they were studying or had read about.

Before you read about the responses that they gave, go back through your own answers to the quiz and indicate whether your response to

each item was based largely on formal learning about management or principally on your own experience as a manager. If the opinion you expressed was based upon formal learning put L beside the answer, but if you were relying more upon your personal experience of management (either managing or being managed) then write E. Then count up the number of times that you relied upon your experience and work out the percentage(E × 5).

As you saw from the managers' responses analysed in Tables 3.1 and 3.2, there was no complete consensus about any of the statements made, but there was significant agreement as to what had influenced their views. Tables 3.3 and 3.4 show the extent to which students' views were influenced by experience or by theory. The first one shows the responses of the students who were not yet half-way through their studies. While there was no pattern to the *strength* of the views held, there was significant agreement as to the *influence* behind their views. In every case the large majority of the students indicated that their responses were based on their experience and not on the theories that they were studying or knew about.

Table 3.3   Results of management questionnaire: replies from new students

Question	Experience	Theory	Don't know
1	22	1	1
2	19	4	1
3	19	3	2
4	21	1	2
5	20	3	1
6	21	2	1
7	19	3	2
8	21	2	1
9	22	1	1
10	18	4	2
11	17	4	3
12	18	4	1
13	19	4	1
14	18	2	4
15	21	0	3
16	15	6	3
17	16	5	3
18	15	8	1
19	20	2	2
20	17	4	3

Total number of replies = 24

Table 3.4   Results of management questionnaire: replies from completing students

Question	Experience	Theory	Don't know
1			
2	33	1	2
3	29	5	2
4	27	8	1
5	26	8	2
6	26	6	4
7	27	7	2
8	18	13	5
9	29	2	5
10	30	4	2
11	26	7	3
12	20	13	3
13	23	12	1
14	22	13	1
15	22	11	3
16	24	8	4
17	20	11	4
18	25	9	2
19	23	10	3
20	17	16	3

Total number of replies = 36

Among the new students, question 18 produced the greatest number of answers based on theory (8 out of 24), but even here the answers themselves ranged from strong agreement with the statement to strong disagreement. This statement was 'A manager's main responsibility is to the shareholders'. You might expect there to be a range of opinion about this, depending upon whether the manager was used to working in the public or the private sector. However, our managers came from both the public and the private sectors and the majority of them (19 out of 24) disagreed with what is an accepted view, at least among those working in the private sector. These managers who did not agree with the statement might have argued that a manager's main responsibility is to the customer, or to their boss, or in some instances to their immediate team or colleagues. You can probably also think of circumstances where the manager's main responsibility is to their own family, and the needs of the organization have to come second.

We might expect to find theory influencing the answers of the students nearing the end of their course to a greater extent. This was in fact the case, although for only one question did anything like 50 per cent of the students feel that their view was based upon theoretical knowledge (question 20). And again the responses to this question showed that their views ranged from strong agreement to strong disagreement. These managers also demonstrated a greater tendency to have contrasting views on other statements in the quiz.

It is important to note that these were all managers who were spending a considerable amount of time studying management theories, concepts and ideas, and yet what influenced them most in their views about aspects of management was their own experience rather than theory. This was confirmed when we spoke to some of them. They said that while they could think of theories which added to their understanding of management, what really shaped their views was what they had experienced and observed as managers. A number of them said that a strong influence was also recent 'trends' in organizations, such as the development of customer charters and the move to quality standards.

You might like to compare your answers now with those of the two student groups.

The basis of your own management philosophy

It is actually a little unfair to ask you to state categorically whether it is experience rather than theory that shapes your view or the reverse. In reality it is often a mixture of both, or rather, some theory, idea or concept, or even a generally held management view which has been tested against your own experience of real management life. You probably find that most of the time you respond to management situations in an almost instinctive way. In doing so you are calling not upon what you have learnt in formal situations but on the knowledge and experience you have gained from working in organizations. This is how your own personal philosophy about management has been developed. It is no wonder that it may from time to time be at odds with that of your colleagues whose own philosophy has similarly eclectic roots, and why your common sense approach may seem 'non-sense' to them.

The question is whether your philosophy is good enough to ensure that you can manage effectively in the turbulence of today's management environment. Can you tolerate ambiguity and uncertainty or do you try to reduce the complexity by ignoring those factors which do not fit with your particular view of reality?

Do you ever *really* think about what you are doing? Do you challenge your own assumptions and do you question the 'givens' in any situation to increase your understanding? Are you noted for the *uncommon thinking* which you bring to management or do you prefer to 'go with the flow'?

Summary

The aim of this chapter was to illustrate how much experience, personal values and randomly acquired information combine in determining our view of the environment in which we manage and how we respond to it. Management as practised can never be an exact science and so it is useful to talk about approaches and philosophies rather than to look for or expect right answers. However, experience alone is rarely a sufficiently sound basis on which to build a philosophy which is robust enough to cope with the complexity which managers have to face today. Models, theories and management concepts are only helpful if they are used to extend rather than limit our thinking. Under pressure, even the most experienced managers may fall into the trap of dealing simply with the issue which presents itself, ignoring the underlying factors which relate to it and are interrelated.

So can managers ever get it right? If your philosophy is based upon firm convictions about management, it seems you may be in danger of underestimating the complexity of the issues with which you have to deal. If you spend time trying to understand the complexity, you may find it more difficult to make an effective response. What you *can* hope for is to increase your potential to arrive at appropriate ways forward and this is what the rest of this book is about.

Reading through this book and doing the related thinking and activities will encourage you to use frameworks and techniques to help you to unravel some of this complexity. By becoming aware of the particular perspective that you bring to each management situation, and of the values and assumptions upon which it is based, you will recognize its limitations. By using techniques to discover the varying perspectives of others you will gain a greater insight into what really happens in organizations. And by beginning to think in *uncommon* ways you will be able to deal more effectively with the problems and dilemmas of organizational life.

Notes on management philosophy quiz

The purpose of the quiz was to help you to recognize some of the assumptions that you bring to management. There were no right responses to the statements, but below are some comments on each of the statements which should prompt you to reflect in more depth upon the responses that you made. There are cross-references where appropriate to other chapters in this book.

1 The reference here is to Douglas McGregor and his Theory X and Theory Y. You will find this mentioned in many management texts on motivation and it is discussed in some detail in Chapter 6. The statement here relates to Theory X, which is that people need to be driven because, so this theory goes, they are naturally lazy, and left to their own devices will work as little as possible. Theory Y, on the other hand, is that people are intrinsically ready to assume responsibility and work towards organizational goals. As a manager you will possibly find that people range across the whole spectrum from X to Y. Whatever you believe and whatever your experience, there are implications for how you manage the people for whom you are responsible. There are organizational implications too. For example, according to Theory X, people would need to be controlled, cajoled, directed, rewarded and punished. Theory Y implies that people need to be given the chance to assume responsibility, or to be empowered, because they are essentially self-motivated. Management rhetoric today assumes that Theory Y applies, although a lot of practice might lead you to think that Theory X is more true! Chapter 6 examines why an understanding of this apparently simple theory can help you to construct useful management tools.

2 Charisma is undoubtedly a very useful attribute. It draws people towards a leader and in turn attracts their loyalty and support. A charismatic leader may be able to induce people to change their behaviour, to work harder, to override their particular prejudices in order to become followers. It is a question more of personality than of expertise, so unfortunately charisma cannot be acquired. However, charisma is not essential for success. For example, Bill Gates, the chairman and chief executive of the Microsoft Corporation, would probably not be described as a charismatic leader. In fact he has twice been described in *The Wall Street Journal* as a 'nerd'. Yet Microsoft is a phenomenally successful business which he co-founded at the age of 19. He is a natural leader who inspires what has been described by a senior vice president of Microsoft as 'a maniacal work ethic' in the company (Zuckerman, 1990). Charisma can also be a dangerous quality; people who fall under the spell of a charismatic leader may become blind to their faults. You might think of some world leaders, politicians and evangelists who would come into this category.

3 An organization chart only describes the formal relationships within an organization. A diagram of the organization's structure, whether it is the traditional chart or a matrix representing cross-functional working in project teams, actually reveals very little about organizational dynamics. Just as important are the informal systems and networks which spring up and which provide the means by which tasks are accomplished, initiatives are developed and communication takes place. The two major metaphors for organizations (the machine and the organism) and systems thinking as a way of understanding the real organizational dynamics are discussed in Chapters 4 and 5.

4 While it is important for organizations to focus upon quality, the procedures themselves do not necessarily guarantee that it will be achieved. If too much emphasis is placed upon the functioning of the systems and upon procedures, the outputs or outcomes can be overshadowed and this can actually inhibit the development of effective quality initiatives.

5 If the pace of life were not so fast it might be possible to establish a set of objectives which would remain unchanged until they were eventually achieved. Some planning models which you may have met run as follows;

● Agree the overall plan
● Set objectives to meet the plan within an agreed timescale
● Obtain feedback to determine how much progress has been made towards meeting the objectives

At this stage some adjustments may need to be made, for example, to the timescale in which the tasks are to be accomplished or to the resources which have been allocated. This is a very rational approach and it is discussed in Chapter 12 in relation to decision making and problem solving. However, your own experience as a manager will tell you that since the environment is unstable, you can expect change at any time, whether it is the market in which you operate, the technology with which you work or the resources (physical, financial and human) that are available to you. For this reason it is frequently necessary to revise your objectives, recognizing that you cannot possibly achieve what you first intended and that you must be prepared to sub-optimize or compromise as the only way forward. Objectives should be constantly revisited or they will ossify in a timeframe which no longer applies.

6 Some people may work harder if paid by results, others may feel that this is not a fair way of rewarding effort and commitment. This book does not review the various methods of remuneration, but the discussion of motivation theory in Chapter 6 will be helpful here. Other points to think about are the role of appraisal and whether performance can be fairly assessed if the outputs are not measurable in quantitative terms.

7 This is only one aspect of a manager's one, although there are some managers who feel it is their major role. Managers who feel that this is their most important role in respect of managing people may be more inclined to believe that McGregor's Theory X applies (see note 1 above).

8 Successful innovators are not people who dream up ideas in a detached way. They are more likely to be doers. In organizations they are people who, often frustrated by blocks to progress, use their imagination to see the possibilities for action in order to realize a project or an idea. They are often met by considerable scepticism, particularly if they happen to be working in an organization which does not have a culture of innovation. One well-known innovator in the field of business is Anita Roddick. There are many other examples of innovators, both men and women, quoted in *Managing Innovation* edited by Jane Henry and David Walker (Sage Publications, 1992). Innovators and adaptors are discussed briefly in this book in Chapter 8.

9 When things go wrong, there is rarely a simple solution. This is partly because the reasons the problem occurred are rarely simple and also because of the way in which organizations behave. A problem in one part of the organization usually casts ripples into other parts. This may be because the process concerned directly affects the work of people elsewhere in the organization, or because of the strength of the informal systems and networks through which people operate. It is helpful to think about organizations in terms of systems, each having within it a number of sub-systems, some of which may be based on work functions with others being cross-functional or social. This important idea is discussed in Chapter 5. There are creative techniques which will help you to identify the real roots of a problem and to generate ideas for solving it. Some of these are discussed in Chapters 9 and 10 and you can try them out for yourself by working through the associated activities.

10 This may be more true than we would like to think! So much of effective people management depends upon personal style and the ability to work with and through other people, even though knowledge, practical skills and under-standing are the qualities that tend to be assessed at interview. Some organizations today place a great deal of emphasis on the type of personality a job candidate has, using psychometric tests, assessment centres or sometimes graphologists in order to probe below the surface and choose the right person for the organization.

11 Managers are not expected to come complete with a crystal ball, but they do have to be tuned into the environment in which the organization is operating so that changes can be anticipated and planned for. See Chapter 11 for more about managing in times of change and increasing complexity.

12 You disregard feedback at your peril and it can come from any number of sources. Some of it you will solicit, but sometimes the most informative is the feedback that can be gathered through informal networks. However, the manager also has to keep his or her eye firmly on the ball and it would likewise be equally perilous to be so intent on information gathering that you failed to spot that you were straying off course. You may like to think of sporting analogies where taking the eye off the ball is always a recipe for a failed shot or a missed goal.

13 You only need to read through the appointments page of the national papers to recognize that this is what companies are now doing, removing older managers in favour of younger ones. Many advertisements actually specify an upper age limit up front, often with the ceiling set at forty. From what you have learned doing the quiz, you will appreciate the extent to which you rely upon experience in making management decisions. It might be possible to state the opposite case, that young dynamic organizations need managers with experience.

14 I would say that this is the one statement in the quiz which is true. Too many organizations fail to listen to their employees. Some which do still do not act upon the feedback they receive. *Maverick* by Richardo Semler (Arrow Books, 1993) is an account of the astonishing development of a company which did listen to its employees. This is an extract from the booklet which each new employee is given on joining the company. 'Our philosophy is built on participation and involvement. Don't settle down. Give opinions, seek opportunities and advancement, always say what you think. Don't be just one more person in the company. Your opinion is always interesting even if no one asked you for it.'

15 Much has been written about how to build effective teams, and there is plenty of advice about the types of people you need in order to make the team effective, how you can motivate them and lead them to become even more successful. However, this is easier said than done and requires the right organizational conditions, plus much nurturing and hard work on the part of the manager. Team building is a good example of an area of management teaching where prescriptions about what to do are rife. What we argue in this book is that prescriptions, blueprints and homilies about what you should do to improve effectiveness are generally insufficient, since they leave managers to figure out how to do this with the resources available and in the unique environment in which they have to operate.

16 Most organizations today have a mission statement. Some senior manage- ment teams deliver the company's mission statement to the unsuspecting workforce at roadshows and in newsletters, much as prophets coming down

from the mountain, after much close deliberation and sometimes with the help of a consultant to crystallize their thoughts. In other organizations, the mission statement will be communicated first to all staff in draft form so that they have an opportunity to comment. At best, the mission statement is the focus for the organization's strategic objectives, its *raison d'être*. At worst, it is a dusty and unoriginal collection of words which has very little meaning for the staff who work for the organization, serving to make them neither clearer about their own role and objectives nor about where the organization is heading. Most mission statements today will contain words such as excellence, quality and the customer. You might refresh your memory by turning up your own organization's mission statement and forming a view about the extent to which it successfully clarifies for you where the organization is heading and whether it is still on that track.

17 Some change can provide positive opportunities for some people, even if only in the medium to long term. More often than not the suggestion of change appears to herald problems rather than opportunities for many people. Some are more resistant to change than others and may be surprisingly hard to persuade even if the change proposed seems to others to be an improvement. Chapter 11 examines ways of approaching and managing within change, with reference to some of the ideas covered earlier in the book.

18 Your response to this question will reflect the culture of the organization for which you work or worked in the past. If you are more familiar with public sector organizations then you might substitute the word 'stakeholder' for 'shareholder'. This might be an interesting statement to debate with colleagues to try to determine where they see their own major responsibility lying. While some managers would agree absolutely with this statement, others would point out that they have responsibilities to customers, who may not be shareholders, to their staff, to their line manager, to themselves and to their families. It raises further interesting questions about people's different motives and motivations in coming to work in this organization with its particular culture, rather than another one where the management role might be comparable but the culture is different.

19 It is the job of everyone to look after customers (or clients if you are in the public sector). This does not just mean those that are external to the organization, it is equally important to look after internal 'customers' who depend upon the outputs or outcomes of your work in order to perform their own function effectively. It might be useful to note down those people who might regard themselves as you own internal customers. The significance of the interrelationships within organizations is discussed in Chapter 5.

20 This is a good example of the power of positive thinking. However, to concentrate solely on the strengths and opportunities in a proposal or a situation can leave you prone to ignore the weaknesses and threats. SWOT (strengths, weaknesses, opportunities, threats) analysis, usually referred to in marketing texts, is a simple but powerful analytical tool which you can use creatively in other situations to prompt you and extend your thinking. SWOT is discussed in Chapter 7.

Chapter 4
Organizations: machines or living creatures?

A number of the items in the quiz in Chapter 3 related to your beliefs about the nature of organizations. Such assumptions, particularly about your own organization, will be a major influence on how you respond to situations, and an important part of the 'common sense' which you exercise. But many of these assumptions may be only partly conscious. If so, you will be unable to exploit the model you *are* using to the full. Nor will you draw upon alternative models when appropriate. Two over-arching models are in common use. Both are based on analogy: the first views organizations as machines, the second as organisms. By exploring these, this chapter should enable you to become more aware of which you are using at present, and of the implications of this.

Either analogy is an example of the use of metaphor, the description of something if it were something else. Because metaphors are at the heart of much of our thinking, this chapter will look at the use of metaphor as model in general, as well as exploring the two specific metaphors addressed. It will also contrast unconscious and conscious use of models, and explore the difference between the use of a model as a version of what *is* with its use as a framework for deciding what *should be*. Your existing 'common sense' may well contain elements of both. But lack of clarity between the two may interfere with your ability to sort out some of the complexities which face you, or lead to conflicts with colleagues which are difficult to understand if the distinction is not appreciated.

Experiment with both metaphors as ways of describing your own organizational experience should help you develop a much clearer understanding of how your own organization operates. It should also begin to show how you might be able to use metaphors as models to advance your thinking about a range of situations, not merely as a tool for making sense of whole organizations. This theme will be developed in much greater detail in the next chapter. When you have completed this chapter, however, you should:

- Be more aware of your own unconscious use of metaphors
- See how this may be *limiting* your thinking
- Be starting instead to use the models described to *extend* your understanding
- Appreciate the design principles which follow conscious use of the machine model as an ideal
- Appreciate similar principles for the design of the 'organic' organization
- Be aware of the strengths and limitations of each model as the source of prescriptions for what *should* be.

Models and metaphors

Thus far, models, frameworks, structures, theories, assumptions and now metaphors have been referred to with somewhat gay abandon as aids to thinking, or conceptual tools to be used in the struggle to make sense of complexity. As the next two chapters look in some detail at the use of metaphor, and subsequent ones will bring in a range of other sorts of frameworks and theories, it may help at this point to attempt some degree of clarification.

Model is the term likely to be used most. It is applied to any simplified representation of a situation or important aspects of it. This is akin to the everyday use. An architect's model represents the external appearance of a building, rather than the full complexity of its structure and internal arrangements. An Underground map is a model of the relationships between stations and lines, but is not a good guide to distances between stations. Nor will it tell you anything about the frequency of trains. Most models we shall be using will represent both parts and relationships.

Models can be constructed in different ways. One way is by drawing an analogy between something complex with which you are not familiar and something which you know rather better, the use of *metaphor*, which will be explored in greater detail in what follows. While this can be a powerful way of extending understanding, it has its dangers. If the metaphor is pushed too far, and similarities assumed which do not exist, it is all too easy to be misled. Falling into this 'metaphor trap' is far more likely if the metaphor is used unconsciously than if its use is deliberate.

Another way of constructing models is to select certain aspects of the situation you are interested in, and find a way of representing precisely these aspects. This is the case of the Underground map. You will be doing something similar later, when using diagrams to represent selected aspects of situations you encounter. Graphic models can be a simple but extremely powerful tool.

Framework is used to refer to something rather more of an abstraction. For example, courses in marketing have long taught the importance of considering 'the 4 Ps' (product, price, place and promotion). Many have found this a useful starting point for thinking about marketing, but it is not really a representation of markets or the marketing process. Rather it is a possible set of headings under which to think. Many management 'theories' are frameworks of this kind. Fayol was used in Chapter 2 to provide a framework for looking at your role, and possible impacts upon it. Such lists are being used as very crude models if they are taken as a way of carving up the whole territory which you are examining.

Theory in its more general use refers to an organized model which is sufficiently specific to enable you to predict the effect of making changes, or to explain why observed changes may be taking place. In Chapter 6 you will meet a theory of motivation (expectancy theory) which genuinely deserves this label.

Models: real or ideal, conscious or unconscious?

Two distinctions are helpful to keep in mind when thinking about models. One is whether the model is being used as a representation of what is assumed to exist, or of what it is felt *should* be the case. Is it used as a basis for describing what is, or prescribing the way you feel things ought to be? For example, we used Fayol's list as a basis for looking at managers' jobs in general, that is, as a very rough model of what *is*. However, it *could* be taken as a basis for specifying what managers *should* do. It is possible (though not particularly likely) that an organization might decide to examine all managerial jobs, and rewrite the job descriptions to include all the elements, if they believed that Fayol was specifying what any manager should do in order to be effective. Both uses of model have their place, but it is important to be clear which use is being made at any one time.

The other important dimension has been referred to already, that is, the extent to which the user is *aware* of using a model. Conscious use, it has been argued, has fewer dangers and greater potential for creative thought than has unconscious. In order to help you bear these distinctions in mind, Figure 4.1 shows a 'model of model use'. Management 'theory' is full of such 2 × 2 classifications, all of which, including the one shown here, are so crude a reflection of the world as to be better described as frameworks than theories, or even models.

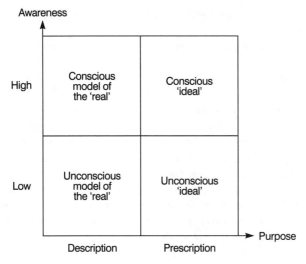

Figure 4.1 A model of model use

The unconscious machine view

Having clarified the terminology, let us examine a model that is a metaphor, but used without awareness of its existence or nature. There may be many people in your organization whose 'common sense' is driven at least in part by the unconscious assumption that organizations have, or should have, the characteristics of machines. Clues to this lie in the language used, how people are treated and expected to behave, and how the environment is viewed. The language of the machine organization may include things such as a way of operating being 'well oiled', vacancies being 'slots', or a new request seen as a 'spanner in the works'.

Listen to the language of your organization, noting down each time you hear something which is 'machine' talk, but which is used of things other than machines.

If such language is common at work, the 'machine metaphor' is probably dominant, and you will find the following associated characteristics:

- People are treated as 'components'
- They are expected to do as they are told, whatever this is, without discussion or consultation.

- The authority to tell people what to do comes from being higher in the hierarchy.
- Independent thought is a liability, to be suppressed
- The emphasis is on following specified processes exactly, rather than on results achieved

Environments are of limited importance to machines, and where the machine metaphor is the basis of thinking, little attention is normally paid to things outside the process or processes for which a manager is directly responsible. If coordination between different processes is regulated by roles and rules, there is no need to look beyond the area of immediate concern. The world outside the organization is of little importance, assumed to have no significant effect on things. There is therefore no need to investigate this world, and see what is happening there, and likely to happen, that will require a response from the organization.

If you are approaching a problem with this mindset your approach will probably be to identify any deviations from the proper process which have crept in, and then to look for ways of further spelling out procedures or strengthening controls to ensure that such deviations are removed. You are unlikely to question the goals of your part of the organization, or of the organization as a whole. You will be unable to cope with situations in which people are being 'difficult', and not following procedures, other than by firing those concerned. Such behaviour will be incomprehensible. Machine parts are not 'difficult'. Either they work or they are broken and need replacing.

If you are trying to introduce significant change into an organization where others have this mindset you can expect problems. If the changes require more than substitution of one set of rules and processes for another there is likely to be major resistance. The machine mindset is associated with avoidance of risk, conservatism, reluctance to take responsibility, and relative unconcern for organizational goals. Furthermore, in organizations which have been successfully operating with an implicit machine model for years, those who have been promoted may well be those who are most wedded to this view of the world. This difficulty in making changes in the 'machine' organization is one to which we shall return at intervals.

These examples of assumptions associated with the machine analogy show just some of the ways in which the unconscious use of the model may restrict both your thinking, and your ability to take some sorts of action. Others will become apparent from the consideration of the machine as an ideal, a template to be followed in designing or re-designing organizations.

The machine as the ideal model for organizations

For the best part of the twentieth century this view of organization seems to have been the dominant one. Indeed its origins go much further back, predating the Industrial Revolution and machinery as we now know it. The Romans appear to have organized both armies and craft guilds along lines which would meet with the approval of those teaching 'administrative management' in this century. Roman principles of military organization inspired Frederick the Great of Prussia in the eighteenth century in the reformation of his army. But Frederick also drew consciously on the mechanical inventions of his own day for inspiration, in possibly the first conscious use of the machine metaphor on any large scale.

Other major contributors to what became the dominant model in the *ideal* or blueprint sense for organization were Henri Fayol, whom you met in Chapter 2, and Max Weber. Fayol was drawing on a lifetime of management experience to formulate a set of principles of organization, while Weber was a German academic, trained as a lawyer, who prescribed a further set of principles for efficient organization of a bureaucracy. Despite the negative overtones which this word has acquired, Weber saw bureaucracy as the dominant institution of 'modern' society (he lived from 1864 to 1920). It was, he said, technically the most efficient form of organization, and he specifically likened it to a machine, contrasting it with less efficient forms which were the equivalent of using non-mechanistic means of production.

This ideal model was for a long time specifically taught as a blueprint for organization. As taught, it emphasized rationality, hierarchy, authority and procedure. The core principles embodied were:

- Top-down goal setting, with clearly specified objectives at all levels
- A clear management hierarchy, with each employee reporting to a single superior
- Vertical communication channels
- Authority to direct by virtue of managerial position
- Division of work to achieve the efficiencies of specialization
- Manageable spans of control
- Subordination of the individual's interest to that of the wider organization

As an ideal this clearly has advantages: it would not have formed the basis of the majority of large organizations for so long if it had not. Indeed, despite the rhetoric *against* such organizations, and the feeling that they are old-fashioned, the machine bureaucracy seems to be alive, well, and still probably the dominant form of organization. There are obvious practical attractions to the bureaucratic principles. If you work in an organization where it is *not* clear at any level what the goals and priorities are, or report to more than one superior who give you conflicting directions, or have felt at any time that your part of the organization, far from cooperating with other parts, was in conflict with them, the classic management model outlined above may seem indeed ideal. There are still too many 'disorganizations' which could benefit from observing the principles above. When small enterprises are successful, grow rapidly, and do not seem able to alter their structures and practices in order to cope with their larger size, such problems are all too frequent.

Consider the extent to which your organization follows the principles outlined above. Are there ways in which you feel that it follows them too slavishly? If so, think what problems this has caused you. Are there ways in which *more* 'bureaucracy' would help?

A number of *disadvantages* have been attributed to the classical bureaucratic form. These have been pointed out over the last forty years but without making much impact on the prevailing model. The problem reduces to the unsurprising finding that organizations designed on the machine model are good at the things that machines have always been good at, namely producing consistent output under constant conditions. Equally, they are bad at things that machines do not, on the whole, do. These include sensing the environment, and adapting to its changing needs. As already noted, the environment is not a feature of the machine metaphor at all.

The other major worry is that of mismatch with 'reality': people are not inanimate parts but have distinctively human characteristics. If treated as cogs in a machine organization these human attributes can be a positive disadvantage, needing to be controlled by authority and discipline. Sometimes such control is impossible. Furthermore, these attributes have the potential in a different organization to be a major asset. (This will become clearer after the discussion of motivation in Chapter 6.)

The major criticisms levelled at machine bureaucracies are therefore that they are inflexible, incapable of adaptation, with slow and risk-averse decisions as a result of rigid adherence to procedures and communication channels, and that they are wasteful of human potential, to their competitive disadvantage.

You will find an appreciation of the ideal model a useful element in your conceptual toolkit for a number of reasons. Obviously, an awareness of the potential problems will prepare you to find ways of dealing with them. It also helps to realize that the model may well be the goal of those in charge of your own organization, whether implicitly or explicitly. If so, and if your own ideal is somewhat different, and you fail to understand this difference, you may wonder why suggestions which you make sometimes fall on deaf ears. More importantly, the machine model does highlight the importance of objectives, of coordination, and of control. These aspects will be an important part of any mental models you build in trying to understand organizational situations, and will need to be considered if you are planning how to make change work.

The unconscious organic view

It is probably still the case that those who to not 'think' about organizations are unconsciously using the machine metaphor, but you may find some who have absorbed the more recent organic metaphor without being aware of it. This view sees the organization in a constant and dynamic struggle in a potentially hostile environment, needing perpetually to react to changes which are happening, or likely to happen, in that environment in order to survive. The language of this approach includes such things as 'learning', 'adaptation', 'flexibility', 'growth', 'brain', and of course 'environment'.

Listen for language around you which reflects this view, and jot down any examples. Is it being used merely because of a recent attempt to introduce such language, or does it seem to genuinely reflect a flexible organization? Is the language equally common at all levels in the organization?

The dangers of the unconscious organic view, if you have been fortunate enough to be employed in an organization where it prevails, are few. After all, organizations *do* have many things in common with organisms, if you accept the view that most of them are indeed in the business of surviving. Unconscious emphasis on adaptation and responsiveness, though within a fairly constant basic structure, is probably all to the good. Organisms exercise control too, over their processes and their behaviour. Although this tends to be more complex and dynamic than the control mechanisms in machines, criticisms that the 'organism model' lacks this strength of the machine metaphor are unjustified. Indeed, the more complex view of control implied is presumably an advantage. Perhaps the greater danger lies with the conscious use of the model, if, as is sometimes the case, it is carried to extremes.

The consciously 'organic' organization

A major challenge to the machine as a deliberate ideal came from research in Scotland in the 1950s, which suggested that such machine organizations could be contrasted to their disadvantage with a more organic form. At this time a number of traditional organizations were trying to come to terms with the then-emerging technology of electronics. A sociologist and a psychologist joined forces to research the experience of these firms, and found that for most of them success was elusive (Burns and Stalker, 1966). They were finding it almost impossible to incorporate any sort of electronics R&D function into their existing structures.

The researchers concluded that this was because of the very mechanistic structures of the unsuccessful organizations, with entrenched hierarchies and long vertical communication chains. The new R&D sections clearly needed to work closely with existing departments, but they posed many, and new, problems, and required decisions outside the traditional areas of responsibility of the managers concerned. Problems were referred upwards and upwards, resulting in overload on senior managers and impossibly slow decisions. Some organizations tried to address this problem by creating further liaison arms of the bureaucracy, or by establishing elaborate committee structures to take decisions, but neither of these strategies was at all effective.

Contrasting these unsuccessful attempts with thriving electronics concerns led the authors to suggest that a more *organismic* or *organic* form was needed in organizations facing change. They were clearly setting this up as a model in the ideal template sense, and prescribed the following characteristics:

● Rigid job definitions and hierarchies would not exist
● Tasks would be constantly redefined
● Tasks would be seen not as ends in themselves, but in the context of organizational objectives
● Groups would re-form as necessary to meet organizational needs
● Activity would no longer be restricted by specialisms or job title
● Employees would contribute specialist knowledge to tasks as required
● Responsibility would operate in all directions, up, down and sideways
● Knowledge would be recognized as existing throughout the organization, at all levels
● Networks would replace hierarchy, with authority for any purpose centred on the place where the relevant knowledge lay.

In support of this view they quoted the head of a successful electronics firm in the study as regarding the organization chart as 'a dangerous method of thinking', which precluded making full use of employees' capacities. This full use would happen only if jobs were as little defined as possible, allowing them to shape themselves to employees' special abilities. This manager who was in charge of an organization with 2000 employees, also said that written communications were actively discouraged. There was heavy reliance on personal contact between managers horizontally, among other things in order to specify their functions, as these were deliberately not defined from above.

Assess your own organization against the prescription for an organic organization outlined above. Would it be possible to make your organization more effective by a move towards the principles listed? What would be the difficulties associated with such a move?

This organismic ideal of organization, also sometimes called a 'task culture', certainly sounds attractive, and has influenced much of the subsequent writing on organizations. Gone are the rigidities of the traditional bureaucracy, replaced by a constantly changing free form of organization. But this extreme organic view would seem to underestimate the stability and control mechanisms shown by organisms! The need to coordinate will always exist in all but the smallest organizations, and coordination may be problematic under this way of operating. Control exercised at an organizational level by the allocation of projects and resources is possible only if projects can be clearly defined and are relatively self-contained. Under any other circumstances such control is much more difficult to exercise effectively.

Although a strong task focus can be very exciting for employees, they need to be committed to the enterprise in the first place, or to be able to meet their own objectives by doing something that at the same time happens to serve those of the organization. Proponents of the ideal suggest that this commitment will be a product of the structure, but not all are so convinced. With highly skilled employees operating at the forefront of their area of expertise, as was the case in the Scottish electronics company referred to earlier, commitment may be easily fostered. You may feel that in your own organization it would not necessarily follow.

The matrix as compromise

One compromise adopted in the pursuit of greater flexibility without loss of coordination has been the matrix form. This again has a strong focus on teams formed for specific purposes, but features not one but *two* lines of authority within which these operate. One may be the traditional functional hierarchy. The other, which cuts across it, may be the business area. (The dimensions may vary, depending on the nature of the organization.) Within this overall structure teams can be formed and re-formed, drawing on functional expertise as required, but with an enduring functional line of authority superimposed upon the team structure.

As an ideal model this again has both strengths and weaknesses. It is flexible, allows an organization to draw on expertise as required (provided the necessary coordination of resources can be achieved) and offers more scope for control and coordination than a pure organismic form. But there is a serious risk of 'double bureaucracy' as a result of there being two hierarchies, and there may be conflicts of priority between the two reporting lines. Unless one of these is recognized as the dominant line, in which case the matrix is described as 'slanted', such conflicts may be very difficult to resolve.

The organizational structure in which you operate, whether it is a bureaucracy, a fully organismic form or a deliberately compromised matrix, will be an important part of your working context. You need to be aware of the features associated with each of these forms as they will be an important aspect of any situation which you will encounter, and should form part of your description of it at the initial stage of diagnosing problems or planning any change.

Which ideal is ideal?

By now, you should be suspicious of questions such as these, as of any suggestion of prescription or the single 'best' model. But in case you still feel a single model would be nice, the following discussion may change your mind. The machine/organism distinction is a popular one to draw on management courses. You may well have been 'taught' the deficiencies of the one and the advantages of the other. But the case is usually somewhat overstated in order to make a point. While one of the builders of the model, Weber, *did* feel organizations should resemble machines, Fayol, the other authority usually given credit for the approach, did not see it this way at all. And the classical model of organization most often taught, and tarred with the 'machine' label, draws heavily on the principles of management which Fayol articulated in 1916.

Curiously, Fayol actually used a biological, rather than a machine metaphor. He referred to the organization as the *body* corporate (*corps social*). He justified the principle of specialization in terms of the differentiation of organs within living creatures, the principle of unity of direction in terms of the unviability of an animal with two heads, and the principle of centralization in terms of convergence of sensations upon the brain of an organism and orders sent out from there to set things in motion!

Nor are the 'weaknesses' of the machine model inherent in Fayol's original writings. Certainly he emphasized the need for vertical communications, but he explicitly addressed the danger that such communications may be disastrously slow on occasion. Indeed he suggested that where swift action was needed there should be horizontal communications, provided that this was done with the knowledge of the managers of those so communicating. He actually said that though it would be 'an error to depart needlessly from the line of authority' it would be 'an even greater one to keep to it when detriment to the business ensues'.

As well as recommending a willingness to depart from the vertical where the job demands, Fayol cautioned against 'abuse of written communications', saying that verbal communications were usually simpler, quicker, and less prone to perpetuating misunderstandings. This is strikingly similar to the electronics manager's stance quoted as an example of the organic approach!

Furthermore, Fayol specifically recognized the importance of allowing employees to exercise initiatives and take decisions, in the interests both of utilizing their capacities and of ensuring their motivation. Employees, he said, do *not* 'operate merely as a cog in a machine'. Indeed he said that planning, and then taking responsibility for the success of that plan, was one of the keenest satisfactions for an employee at any level to experience, and one of the greatest motivators.

You may by now be wondering why this digression into history. It shows, I think, a very important point, that what is taught and indeed practised may be a long way from the intentions of the originator (or in this case the co-originator – the academic Weber may be somewhat to blame in this!) so you should always treat what you are *told* about an idea with caution. Even if an original author had something sensible to say (and Fayol was drawing on years of successful management in his writings) the message may be distorted in content or in emphasis in the transmission. This realization may make you more comfortable about following one of the practices suggested as essential if you are to develop 'uncommon sense', that of questioning theories that are generally accepted, and using only those parts of them which seem to fit your experience and your context, and which *advance*, rather than limit, your thinking.

The attractions of the machine view

An even more interesting question raised by this consideration of the ideas as originally proposed is *why* the machine aspect was so attractive, when it appears that for Fayol at least the original metaphor was a biological one.

Because we frequently encounter new models, which we 'like' or discard, it is worth exploring the somewhat curious attractions of the machine view. These attractions reflect characteristics of those attracted, the academics and trainers propounding the model and the managers who are being taught it, as much as the characteristics of the view itself.

Managers seem to want at least four things of any model: simplicity, apparent validity, clear prescriptions, and reinforcement of their own position as a manager! The machine model is clearly far simpler than any biological analogy. By focusing on the rational aspects of the prescription, and de-emphasizing the need for flexibility and employee autonomy, the model becomes both simpler and more coherent and clearly focused. By downplaying Fayol's stress on the need for managers to exercise judgement all the time, based on their experience, the prescriptions are very clear. And the emphasis on the 'right to manage' which the principles concerning unity of command and the importance of managerial authority appear to justify will be attractive to any managers not quite certain of their position or status.

The emphasis on rationality and efficient organization is similarly reassuring and apparently valid. Our education has emphasized the logical and rational. The physical sciences, with their emphasis on simple cause and effect, have provided a dominant model for research for a large part of the twentieth century. We feel much more confident about our ability to operate in a rational organization, composed of rational people, than one in which people are much more intractable, or even have different views of what is rational. Above all, when faced with the complexities of management we *want* a simple set of rules that will magically turn us into brilliant managers, or transform our organizations into highly efficient ones. (It was noted earlier that popular management writers are referred to as 'gurus'.)

Management education's potential for distortion

If prescriptions are what managers want, then management education and training have been all too happy to provide them. It is far easier to teach (and to examine) lists of prescriptions than more complex formulations. It accords much more status to the teacher to offer certainties than to suggest that life is complicated, and a large part of what managers need is a sense of proportion based on experience.

Furthermore, there tends to be a 'Chinese whispers' effect in teaching. You may be taught a version of what your teacher was in turn taught, in so far as it can be remembered or reconstructed from notes. If books are used they are more likely to be people writing about what someone said, than the original source. The 'good' teacher may introduce personal examples to elaborate on points in order to increase the impact on the class. Sometimes it is the examples which are remembered, not the point they were supposed to illuminate, possibly creating another form of distortion.

Thus pressures towards examinability, impact, innovation, and enhancing the status of the teacher may well have moved the 'conventional wisdom of management' a long way from its origins, probably in the direction of simplicity, coherence, and prescriptiveness. Again this is a reason to treat conventional wisdom with caution, to work with multiple models, and to be aware always that no single model can adequately represent complex 'reality'. Because of this, prescriptions based on single and simple models are particularly to be mistrusted.

All this is not to suggest that you reject anything that you have been taught on a management course. Far from it. But it does support the position adopted here, that there are no ready-made answers that will save you from the need to do your own thinking. You need to use what courses teach you as tools, not as solutions, and to choose and modify your tools carefully to suit your needs.

Extending the use of metaphor

Thus far, we have considered the unconscious use of metaphor, as a component of 'common sense', and the danger of falling into a metaphor trap if it is used this way. This was contrasted with the conscious use of metaphor to provide an ideal template, or parts of one, generating prescriptions for organizational design. But there is another use of metaphor which is at least as important. This is the use of metaphor to generate a *range* of models that can be used in the 'experimental thinking' referred to earlier. Such models need not mimic what you think *is* the case, but be used instead in a 'what if . . .?' sense. This can be an important part of building up a rich understanding of a complex situation at the start of a change exercise intended to improve that situation in some way. It can contribute, too, to creative thinking, and the generation of potential solutions that would not otherwise have occurred to you.

Much of your most important thinking as a manager will take place when you are faced with the need to respond to rapidly changing sets of complex circumstances. And the hardest yet most crucial part of this will be the initial thinking needed to ensure that you *understand* fully what is going on. In complex situations like these you will usually find that key participants hold different views both of what is and what should be. This is, indeed, part of the complexity. Such situations are prosaically referred to by English-speaking academics as 'messes'. The French refer far more elegantly to the '*problématique*'.

To sort out the mess, or to elucidate the *problématique*, you need a range of *conceptual* models as suggested at the start of this book. For this a completely different level of use of metaphor is likely to be more useful to you than either the unconscious model or the deliberate ideal. This is the use of metaphor as the source of multiple models, each representing different but important aspects of the complexity which surrounds you. Each one will be simple enough to clarify something important. Together they will give you a far more comprehensive understanding than could any single model.

For complexity cannot be grasped in a single 'pass'. You can build up a full appreciation of a truly complex situation only by a *series* of models, each representing in a form simple enough for you to grasp it a different way of thinking about it. This is almost impossible to understand fully in the abstract, but do start to think about what it *might* mean. It should become clearer by the end of the next chapter. For although there are many metaphors which can be used to generate models, and some further ones will be introduced later, the best worked out is the systems approach to the study of complexity. This is a development by a biologist of the organic metaphor suggested by Fayol. It has been widely adopted within the social sciences, in disciplines ranging from geography to family therapy. It was not designed specifically with management in mind, but has huge potential within this area. The next chapter looks at how the approach can by used by managers to increase their understanding of the complexities of the organizations in which they operate, and of the situations which arise within them.

Summary

This chapter has explored both the unconscious and the deliberate use of machine and organic metaphors as models of organizations, and their use for both descriptive and prescriptive purposes. The machine model generated prescriptions for clear hierarchies, clear objectives set by senior management, clear procedures and managerial authority. The more organismic model sought to achieve flexibility by a changing structure based on task demands rather than hierarchy, and authority based on knowledge rather than position. You should by now have a clearer idea of the elements of both models, and the relative strengths of each.

By considering the extent to which you are using the metaphors yourself you should have become more aware of any risks you are running of falling into 'metaphor traps' because of pushing the analogy too far without being aware of this. Greater awareness should also enable you to use your less preferred metaphor when this is appropriate and to draw on all the useful aspects of whichever one you are using.

By looking at the language and behaviour of others in your organization you should also have become more aware of the metaphor which is most commonly used by colleagues, and should have an idea of how this may restrict the choices available to you, or otherwise impact upon changes which you may be considering making.

Chapter 5

Systems: perspectives and games

Systems thinking is a development of the 'organization as organism' metaphor introduced in the previous chapter. This chapter outlines the key components of a systems approach, showing how it can be used to provide a rich framework for description, applicable to parts of organizations, and different specific aspects of these as well as to the organization as a whole. The metaphor can also be used to generate models of aspects of the situation which have no obvious counterpart in reality. Used thus it can be a powerful aid to 'uncommon sense' and creativity. It helps you to escape the confines of the 'obvious' but intransigent view of a problem, and to find a different, less obvious view which may suggest a new range of possible solutions.

The systems approach was deliberately developed to overcome our intrinsic reluctance to accept and work with complexity. It uses a range of concepts, all drawn from the study of biological organisms, to highlight important aspects of that complexity. The metaphor is based on the belief that the concepts relate to features which are as important for organizations as for living creatures. These include emphasis on the *interrelationships* between parts as well as on the parts themselves, a focus on goals and control mechanisms which regulate progress towards these, and concern with the environment within which a system functions. The idea of multiple causality is also essential: apart from reflex reactions, there will usually be several determinants of an animal's behaviour. The systems approach uses these ideas as a framework for constructing multiple views of situations, views which may generate insights into what is happening that might otherwise escape you.

Using a systems framework does not imply any belief that organizations *are* living systems, merely that the two have enough in common for conscious use of the analogy to be fruitful. Because the approach makes it easy for you to model a situation as several *different* systems it makes it easier to include the multiple perspectives which may be an important aspect of situations arising in organizations. Because you are consciously exploring use of a metaphor you can play mental games with your models, breaking out of the limitations of your existing common sense. Many of these models can be represented as diagrams, making comparisons, and the working out of implications relatively easy. This chapter will introduce you to some ways of drawing organizations, or parts of them, as systems. It will demonstrate some of the ways in which the approach can contribute to the exercise of uncommon sense by enabling you to become more aware of many of your assumptions and to go beyond them.

The systems way of thinking is perhaps the most clearly worked-out approach yet to coping with the complexities which face managers. It provides the best example I know of how a mental model can be deliberately used to lift you above and beyond common sense – the intellectual equivalent of the trick of lifting yourself by your own bootstraps. Indeed, after using systems ideas and methodologies consciously for a while systems thinking may even become second nature: without being aware of it, you will be thinking *differently.*

It has been a difficult chapter to write, and will be far from easy to work through, for three reasons. The first is that, as with other chapters, several books could be written on the subject. Selectivity was a major challenge! The second difficulty lies in the need to distinguish between two uses of systems ideas. One is the straightforward use of the ideas to provide a framework for a description of an organization or problem situation which emphasizes the interrelationships between component parts and the dynamic nature of the situation. The other use is the experimental mental modelling of situations that *can* be a powerful aid to seeing situations in different ways, a precursor to creative solutions of organizational problems. The third difficulty lies in conveying an appreciation of this creative systems approach when it can only be truly appreciated by trying it. Hence the need to *work* really hard at this chapter if you are to build the approach into your personal conceptual toolkit.

By the end of this chapter you should:

- Understand the basic components of systems thinking
- Be able to use these as a framework for describing organizational situations
- Appreciate the value of diagrams as part of this description
- Understand the basic ideas of control
- See how the same situation can be described in terms of *different* systems
- Appreciate how this range of possible descriptions can lead to greater understanding of organizational situations, and make possible more creative solutions to problems

The basics of systems thinking

The ideas that constitute 'systems thinking' are deceptively simple. But applying these ideas creatively, using them to understand complex situations and to gain new insights into problems within them is a skill that you will develop fully only with years of practice. At first it is likely to feel unnatural, even uncomfortable, to go beyond the most obvious use of the framework. But because there *is* so much additional potential it is worth making the effort needed to force yourself to think in ways that very much go against the grain, and to draw, to describe, and to discuss things with colleagues or other interested parties. Because it goes against everything we have been taught, systems thinking, to begin with at least, is *hard work*. You will need to spend some time following the 'Workout!' prompts in this chapter to see for yourself just how hard – and how profitable – the approach can be.

To start with, however, the basic vocabulary of systems is unbelievably simple, as definitions of some of the central concepts demonstrate:

- *System* – a collection of parts which are interrelated in an organized way to the extent that both part and system would be changed by the removal of any of these: this collection does something of interest
- *Environment* – those things which are not in the system, but which either affect it or are affected by it
- *Boundary* – that which separates system from environment
- *Subsystem* – a part of a system which itself meets the definition of a system
- *Goal* – desired outcome or state, either ongoing or final
- *Control* – the mechanism by which feedback is used to maintain a steady state in the face of fluctuation, or to ensure movement is in the direction of a goal.

Underlying the entire approach is a belief in *holism* – the idea that you cannot fully understand the whole by understanding its constituent parts, hence the need for looking at 'the system' formed by these parts.

At their simplest, these concepts generate a useful framework for describing an organization, posing a series of relevant questions. If answered, these should give you a clear, comprehensive, though sometimes fairly obvious description of important aspects of the organization or other system with which you are concerned.

The questions are:

- What is the goal or objective of the system?
- How is achievement of this goal measured? (It might be in financial terms, and/or through a range of other measures. You might wish to question the adequacy of these measures.)

- What are the sub-systems and other components which comprise the system? (Note that sub-systems will themselves have goals and performance measures you may need to examine.)
- What are the relationships between the components of the system? (You might need, for example, to examine flows of information and resources, and authority relations.)
- Is the system you are looking at itself part of a wider system? (If so, you may need to look at the goals of the wider system, and the ways in which it influences your focal system.)
- What resources are necessary to achieve the objective, and how are these provided? (These might include finance, premises and equipment, staff and raw materials.)
- How are decisions taken? (If different people take decisions, coordination is one aspect of relationships which you will need to explore)

The more detailed discussion of systems concepts which follows will increase your ability to answer these questions. But you can already see that as a framework for a basic description of an organization, or a part of one, they provide a good starting point for understanding a situation, and that within the questions themselves are layers of other potential questions.

Beyond the basic framework

Out of the simple ideas defined above has come a total rethinking of the study of complexity which goes even beyond the framework outlined above. When the idea of 'system' as an approach to understanding complexity was introduced – by the biologist von Bertalanffy (1947, 1950) – it represented a considerable shift in outlook. Previously, social scientists were in the habit of approaching their research by separating out smaller and smaller components and then studying simple relationships between pairs of these. In this 'reductionist' approach they were using the method of the then more prestigious physical sciences. Studies of organizations seldom looked at factors outside the organization. Problems were frequently seen as purely technical, and technical solutions were sought.

Unfortunately, while the systems view has gained many converts, both in a variety of academic disciplines and among practising mangers, it is not always well understood, and not widely used in management. This may be because of its deceptive simplicity, the way it has been 'sold' or taught, or because of its real difficulty. It is still uncommon enough that two recent books expound it as a current 'solution'. It is Senge's 'Fifth Discipline', the title of his best-selling book. It integrates, he says, the other disciplines of personal mastery, mental models, building shared vision and team learning. Together these fuse into the body of theory and practice which

Senge claims is needed to build the learning organizations of the future. For Mitroff and Linstone (1993) it is the fifth way of knowing, the first four being agreement, analysis/deduction, multiple realities and conflict. They see it as essential to developing the 'Unbounded Mind', the title of their own successful book. (The association with the number 5 in both cases would seem coincidental.)

What is *not* coincidence is that both expound the power of systems ideas in coping with complexity, and thinking in the new ways that they feel the present situation demands. But in order to see why such simple ideas can be seen as so important (and I agree with both the above authors in thinking that systems thinking is one of the few approaches available today which will enable you to cope with the complexities of a rapidly changing world) it is necessary to go beneath the surface of some of the simple definitions given above.

The idea of system itself

The definition given contains a number of crucial points, the significance of which is not perhaps immediately obvious. The first is that the way in which the parts of a system are related, the *organization* of the parts, is as important as the nature of the parts themselves. Any study of complexity must include the study of relationships. This hugely increases the complexity of thought needed. We are not usually well equipped to look at multiple interrelationships and may need techniques to help us in this.

Think of some fairly obvious collection of things that could be called a 'system'. This could be a work team, a voluntary organization, or a family. What are the parts of the system? What are the relationships between parts? Try to show this as a diagram, with lines for relationships. This is easier, as you will see, than trying to describe it in words. Put in as many relationships as you can think of. These might be power relationships, flows of money, materials, information or other things.

An example of such a diagram is given in Figure 5.1. This is in no sense intended as an 'answer' against which you should check your own. It is just one possible way of representing components of something some might view as a 'system'. (If you are not convinced by the claim that diagramming is an important technique for dealing with multiple relationships, try to convey the information in your diagram, or in the one which follows, using only words. It will probably take you longer, and patterns will not be so clear.)

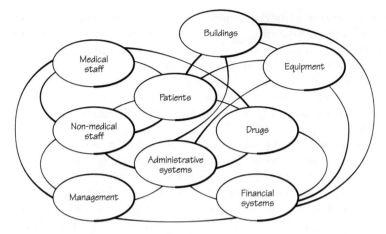

Figure 5.1   Initial relationship diagram for health care

The next important aspect of the definition of system is that it *does* something. Biological organisms are active. Using systems ideas to describe something which was static would not really make sense. Ideas of feedback and goal would be meaningless. It is the *behaviour* of systems that we are interested in. *Why* is a group of employees resisting change? *Why* is there a six-week backlog of work? *Why* is profitability in decline? *Why* did the Bhopal (or Three Mile Island, or Chernobyl) disaster happen? *What* is likely to be the effect of removing a layer of management?

These big questions may be your ultimate interest, but in looking at complex situations it may be important to look at what smaller 'systems' actually do. You might find it helpful to identify, for example, a 'system' which generated distrust among employees, a reward 'system' which encouraged poor quality work, or caused good employees to leave. It is when you turn things on their head, or look at levels below the obvious, that interesting relationships and beliefs may emerge.

Look at the system you diagrammed a few minutes ago. Try to think of at least three different titles for this system that reflect different aspects of its dynamic nature. List these below.

A system to ....

A system to ....

A system to ....

For the example given in Figure 5.1, possible titles might be 'a system to provide high-quality health care', 'a system to advance the understanding of disease and its treatment', 'a system to reduce waiting lists', or 'a system to reduce distress caused by disease as much as possible within budgetary constraints'. You can probably see which 'parts' of the system would tend to favour which of these descriptions. For example, patients, administrative staff and doctors would probably have very different perspectives and priorities.

This raises another key aspect of the definition. A system was defined as doing something *of interest*, and this immediately raises the question, '... to whom?' Out of this come the two most important points of the whole systems approach, both of which concern perspective. First, *your* perspective, as describer of the 'system', is an integral part of the description. Rather than any particular collection of components, and the relationships between them, being in any real sense a system, you are *choosing* to describe them as a system, and indeed you are probably choosing to construct several *different* descriptions of the same situation – *different* systems but closely related – in order to increase your understanding of what is happening.

Systems as a way of seeing

This point is absolutely crucial to effective systems thinking. If you want to go beyond the basic framework and use the approach to break out of preconceptions, and to gain new insights, it is essential to remember that '*Systems are in the eye of the beholder*'. You may identify a set of parts and relations that meet the definition of a system. Indeed, if you are using this approach everything you call a system *should* meet the definition. But this does not mean that it *is* a system. To think of something as *a* system, or worse, as *the* system, would be to cast this particular view of the situation in concrete. This would negate one of the major advantages of the systems approach, its ability to help you to be more flexible in your thinking, to experiment with different ways of conceptualizing the situation, and thus to break out of the confines of your pre-existing assumptions and patterns of thought and generate new insights.

The second aspect of this question 'of interest to whom?' is that your interest is not the only one likely to be important. As the above example suggested, different people involved in a situation may have different interests. Indeed different sub-groups may have different objectives, different information and thus very different perspectives on a situation. Because of the importance of relationships between parts of a system, and of system–environment relationships these different perspectives cannot be ignored. They are a vital part of the situation being investigated, and must be included in any exploration of a situation.

Try to identify two other 'stakeholders' in the 'system' you diagrammed earlier. If you can think of components and relationships that they would include but which you might have omitted, try to draw the 'system' or indeed a collection of systems as they might see it. Try also to think of possible titles that they might give the resulting systems. If you wish to concentrate on the components rather than the relationships, do this. It will still make the point that different perspectives may influence the definition of a system.

You may have been puzzled by the idea that you think of possible components of a system, and then think of a title reflecting what it does. Certainly if you were designing a system in order to achieve a particular goal you would start with the goal and then think about the parts needed to achieve that goal. But if you are not at the stage of designing anything, and instead are groping around in complexity trying to gain a better understanding of a 'mess', there is no one best starting point.

You might start with some 'behaviour' which you want to understand, and then look at possible systems which could generate that behaviour. You might equally start with what seem to be key elements in a situation and then think about what sort of system they constitute. Wherever you start, you will probably flit between the two as your understanding of the situation increases. A particular collection of things may suggest a title, this may suggest the need to include certain other things, which then suggests a refinement of a title, and so on . . . At the same time, related systems may seem worth exploring, with different titles. You may end up with diagrams of a wide range of systems and a wide range of titles.

From the above, it should be clear that the relatively innocuous definition of 'system' can produce a very different approach to looking at complexity. This approach focuses on the nature of relationships as well as the collection of parts, uses diagrams to represent this complexity, and sees what a system *does* as an integral part of its description. It also consciously strives to describe more than one 'system' relevant to any situation, these different systems representing both different perspectives which you are able to adopt, and the perspectives of other interested individuals or groups.

The environment or context

The next important idea is that systems can be understood only by looking *beyond* the system. For almost everything an organism does, the 'explanation' is likely to lie at least in part in the organism's response to its environment. The applicability of this to organizations was clear from the issues facing the managers surveyed in Chapter 2. Note that the definition above is very slightly different from everyday use: it defines the environment in terms of its relationship to the system, and it is not restricted to the physical, or 'green', environment.

Thus the environment, in systems terms, consists only of those things which affect or are affected by the system. In the case of the hospital, key features might include the relevant health authority, the government, drug companies, local GPs and characteristics of the local population. If you are focusing on part of an organization, and its financial viability, then both the wider organization and aspects of the world beyond this are likely to be significant environmental factors. This will be explored in more detail in Chapter 7. The need to look at the environment may seem so obvious as not to be worth saying. But one of the major breakthroughs in the early days of systems thinking was the coining of the term 'open system' to make the point that systems are in constant relation with their environment, and that studies of organizations which ignored the environment, as most studies at that time did, generated only very partial understanding.

There is still a need to think consciously about the environment. How often have organizations been labelled as 'producer driven', when they are working hard to do what they know they do best, without regard for whether this is what the market is demanding?

Select one of the systems which you drew before, and one of the titles you came up with. Now redraw it showing what you think are the essential components, leaving out the relationship lines, and drawing a line around all the components you have selected. Regard the space outside this line as the environment, and add those factors which you think have a significant effect on your system, or indeed are themselves significantly affected by it.

Figure 5.2 shows environmental factors for the collection of parts shown in Figure 5.1 and the first system title suggested. This form of diagram, showing system boundary, key system components and key features of the environment, is simple, but has many uses. Its main strength is that it conveys at a glance just what is being considered as a system. This is why it needs to be kept relatively simple. It is normally referred to as a systems map.

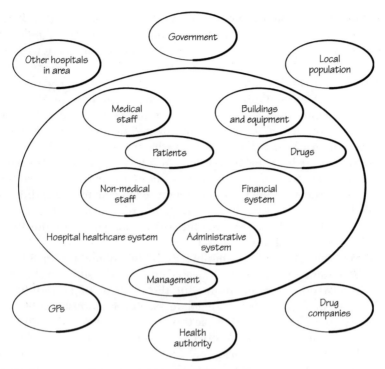

Figure 5.2 A system to provide high-quality in-patient health care (first attempt at a systems map)

In drawing your diagram it was important that you chose a single title. The title is a key part of your description of the system. It is possible to think of systems with the same components (if working at this rough initial level of description) but different titles. It is possible that the environmental factors important to each system would be different. This is another way in which your perspective is inseparable from your description, and demonstrates again that this *is a way of looking at things,* rather than the way 'things really are'.

Drawing boundaries

The line that you drew around the parts and relationships comprising your system represented your boundary. Such a dividing line between system and environment is obviously a vital part of such a diagram. In one sense, this is all that the boundary *is,* no more than a conceptual dividing line. One of the problems with the idea is that there is often a temptation to see a boundary as much more real than this – the fence around the outside of a factory, for example, or the edge of a piece of paper on which is listed a particular category of staff. Simple equations of boundary with reality will stop the fluid thinking that a systems approach aims to facilitate.

Instead of asking 'what is the boundary?' the question needs to be 'how can I decide on a boundary?' or 'what principles are guiding my decision as to whether to include this part, and relegate that part to the environment? You should by now see that where you draw the boundary is likely to depend first, on whether what it defines meets the system definition. If the system is *not* seriously affected by the removal of the part you are wondering about, if it still does whatever the title reflects without that part, then it is probably best left outside. And second, perhaps less obviously, is the system as *interesting* without the part in question? In configuring aspects of the world in systems terms you are not indulging in idle reflection. You are doing it to gain greater understanding of a situation. Which way of drawing the boundary generates the greatest insight? Why not try both ways and see!

The problem of deciding where to draw your boundary on a diagram raises important questions, and answering such questions may advance your understanding considerably. But the concept of boundary has a further use. It focuses on the need to *manage* relationships across the boundary, to interact with other parts of a wider system and negotiate for resources, compensate for the effect of changes outside your system, to network with others and form informal relationships outside the area under your control. This may sound dangerously close to accepting your work team as 'the' system. In fact there will be questions to be asked about boundary-spanning activities however you choose to draw your boundaries. The rather concrete example was chosen only to help make clear why the idea of boundary is useful.

Take one of your alternative titles, and try to draw a different but relevant boundary from that you chose previously. Think about the implications of including extra components, or excluding others. Think about how the boundary is spanned. What activities involve interacting with the environment?

This is an extended exercise, which will need to be continued over some time, rather than as an interlude while reading. Nevertheless, it is worth undertaking, both to give you a better feeling for the force of the ideas covered here and because it may help you to advance a real situation, of genuine concern to you. Identify a problem which is currently exercising your mind at work. This may be fairly recent or one of long standing. Try representing aspects of the area within which the problem lies as one or more systems, drawing systems maps to do this. Explain what you are doing to colleagues and ask them to draw their versions of relevant systems. Compare your diagrams and discuss any differences.

It is only by trying to use the systems framework, and particularly by using diagrams as part of a description of a system, that you will begin to appreciate the point of the approach. Reading about it will take you only so far. It is by *using* the ideas to describe things which you have a genuine interest in understanding better that you will find out just how helpful they can be. The extended exercise above should show you how powerful diagrams can be as a means of communication. It may have surprised you how differently you and colleagues chose to represent the situation, and how much discussion these differences prompted. It should have helped you to increase your own understanding of the situation. Above all, it should have convinced you of how important it is to look at different views of a situation if you are to come to terms with more of the complexity it contains. No worked example could achieve this.

Sub-systems and super-systems

Many systems are themselves part of wider systems, and parts of any system might usefully themselves be looked at as systems in their own right. The level at which you focus on a situation will depend upon the aspect of that situation which concerns you. For example, if you are worried about inflexibility in an organization and widespread resistance to change, you might wish to look at the structure and culture of the whole organization. If you want to know why one particular team persistently misses deadlines that are observed by all other teams, you might focus in on a much lower level. If you wish to introduce changes to a particular area you will probably start looking at systems at this level.

However, in the course of your investigations you might wish to move up or down a level, depending on what you start to find. Some part of the system on which you initially focus may start to look fascinating, and crucial to understanding what is going on. Suppose in the worked example the reason for looking at the situation was that waiting lists seemed to be *increasing*, despite the objective of reducing them. While an investigation of a 'patient admissions system' might be useful, you would almost certainly want to look at systems for allocating resources to different activities, which would be one aspect of a higher level of system than that concerned with admissions. With a problem as complex as this you would probably need to look at a number of other systems as well.

This idea of sub-system can be extremely helpful. One of the early developments in systems thinking was to draw attention to two key sub-systems in most organizations. These were the social sub-system and the technical sub-system. Traditionally all attention had been focused on the technical system. But this did not optimize the functioning of the wider system. To do this, *both* sub-systems needed to be considered, and designed with the wider system in mind. Sub-optimal solutions for each individually might combine to produce the best solution for the wider system.

Thus sending the latest technology to a developing country may be understood as an optimal solution to a 'maximize developed country exports' system. But if you were trying to make improvements to a system 'to improve living standards in the developing country' then you might need to consider social sub-systems and perhaps settle for something much simpler, but which could be maintained indefinitely with local resources.

The more you can look at sub-systems, or any systems, in non-obvious ways, the more benefit you can expect from the approach. Merely labelling existing organizational groupings as sub-systems will advance your understanding only to a limited degree. If you play games with your models, trying to think of as many possible relevant 'systems' as you can, you will start to edge into what you do *not* know about the situation, and ways of looking at it that would not have occurred to you otherwise. By looking for way-out sub-systems, 'a system to reinforce managerial authority', or 'a system to satisfy the needs of doctors to feel that they are at the forefront of medicine', or 'a system to maximize waiting lists', for example, you might identify aspects in a situation that are significant contributors to the current state of affairs. Obviously none of these things are official goals of hospitals. But if in some ways they seem to be what some system is actually achieving, it may be enlightening to explore just how things are combining to produce this result.

Goals and objectives

An important part of looking at a system was looking at what it *does*. Equally important, if you are looking at a *designed* system, is to look at what it is intended to do. The two may not be the same. To understand many problems you need to know what goals are being sought, and then compare these with what is happening in reality. It is important to remember, too, that sub-systems have goals themselves. Often these may be in conflict, either with the goals of other sub-systems or with goals of a higher system, a subject returned to in Chapter 7.

Organizational problems frequently stem from conflicts between sub-system objectives. Perhaps the budgetary control system conflicts both with the need for flexible response to problems and with the need to invest in the longer-term development of human resource capacity. Perhaps the marketing sub-system's objective of maximizing sales requires short delivery times, even on large orders, in conflict with production's need for steady production in the interests of efficiency. Your own scenario may have involved conflicts of this kind. While such conflicts are likely to be inevitable it is important to remember the point concerning sub-optimization made by the early socio-technical systems theorists referred to earlier, and the need to maximize the achievement of the goals of the system as a whole, rather than those of any sub-system at its expense.

The search for different sub-systems and the shift of focus to different levels of a hierarchy of systems enables you to describe a great variety of relevant systems. By adopting a number of perspectives on a situation, you can greatly increase your capacity to absorb key features of even complex situations. Each 'system' will represent a greatly simplified view of reality – drawing complex systems defeats the object of increasing understanding. But together they enable you to build up a greatly enriched view, and one which may escape, at least to some extent, from the confines of your preconceptions.

Feedback and control

A defining characteristic of most organisms is their ability to regulate both their chemistry and their behaviour in order to maintain a steady state. For example, warm-blooded animals will maintain a fairly steady temperature despite environmental variation. And it is not just the steady state that animals exercise regulatory mechanisms to achieve. They also pursue dynamic goals. Predators can behave in very complex ways in order to catch their prey. Whether behaviour is directed towards the steady state or a specific dynamic goal, there needs to be some way of keeping it on target, some form of control mechanism. And this is an aspect of describing things in systems terms that is likely to generate interesting insights into what is happening.

Figure 5.3 shows the basics of a control loop operating on some non-specified process which transforms some inputs into some outputs. In order to *control* this process, there needs to be some way of measuring the output (a sensor of some kind), of comparing this with the intended output (a comparator) and of taking action if the comparison shows deviation from the target. This is shown as action upon an input. For example, inputs might be two different chemicals and heat, while output might be a blend with specified properties and waste heat.

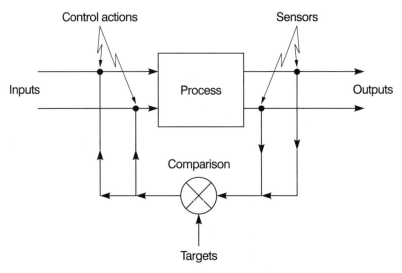

Figure 5.3 A basic control loop

Again, this is a very concrete example, which could apply equally within the machine or organism model. It highlights the necessary components of *any* control mechanism. If something is persistently behaving in a particular way, despite changes in the environment, such a mechanism can usually be identified, and knowing what it is will help your understanding. Similarly, if behaviour departs from what is desired it can be instructive to look for both existing and potential control mechanisms.

The 'model' shown in Figure 5.3 is a useful basis for this search. As with the set of systems concepts themselves, it poses a number of important questions:

- What is being 'controlled'?
- What are the important outputs?
- How are these 'sensed'?
- How good is the sensing process? (Are some important outputs not measured at all? Are some 'measures' merely indicators, correlated with the performance in some way, but not a complete *measure* of that performance?)
- What targets are being used for comparison purposes?
- How realistic are these targets? (This is explored in more detail in the next chapter, because of the impact on motivation.)
- What actions can be taken if the comparison shows a discrepancy between target and output sensed?

Workout!

If you like, this could be a further extension of the extended exercise earlier, and done with colleagues. Identify a 'system' relevant to something of concern to you at work. Title the system as 'A system to . . .'. Then think about the process which this title reflects. Identify inputs and outputs, ways in which outputs are sensed, and any targets. Some targets might be implicit, becoming apparent only when performance deviates significantly. Your job description may not *say* be polite to customers and colleagues, but if you deviate too far from politeness then control action of some kind may well be taken! Think about the sorts of control actions available. Are these on inputs, or on parts of the process? Or does 'control action' consist of revising the target to something which *can* be achieved (or in the case of overshoot is less easily achievable!). How *effective* is the control process? Is there any potential for conflict between the process you are describing and the objectives of the organization as a whole? What improvements does your analysis suggest?

The above may have taken you considerable thought, but should have provided some insight into the source of controls on the work with which you are concerned, and an idea of their effectiveness or otherwise. You may have been surprised at how partial and ineffective such controls seem to be. If so, are there other forms of control which you have not included? One such may be self-control, exercised by employees concerned, and discussed in Chapter 6.

If you identified one form of control action as resetting the targets themselves, then you may work in a more organic form of organization. One way in which such organizations achieve flexibility is through higher-order control loops, which can modify control loops below them if they are not contributing effectively to objectives at a higher level. These are discussed further shortly.

Difficulties in controlling . . .

You may have chosen an obvious system for this analysis, such as manufacturing process control or a budgetary control system, or a slightly less obvious one such as 'a system to ensure that new recruits quickly absorb the norms and assumptions, the "culture" of the organization', or even 'a system to ensure that all employees feel insecure'. Whatever you chose, the exercise above may have taken some thought, but may have helped you understand some aspects of your own situation better.

There are several common reasons for control difficulties. One is lack of clarity about targets. If no-one is clear about what is to be achieved, meaningful control is extremely difficult. Another problem is the difficulty of measuring in any reliable way many important aspects of the performance in question. In the 1970s MBO, or management by objectives, was the fashion. Something very similar is widely used today in performance appraisal and performance-related pay, with the emphasis on 'SMART', that is, specific, measurable, achievable, relevant and time-defined (rather than open-ended) objectives. The problem with MBO then, and SMART objectives now, is that while the idea is firmly based on an understanding of what is needed for control, the difficulty of measuring some key aspects of performance may be underestimated.

Because some aspects of performance *can* have SMART objectives associated with them, there is a danger that only these aspects will be seen as important. Those things which are difficult to specify, or to measure, will be quietly forgotten. This can cause serious distortions of performance, and act counter to many important organizational objectives. 'What gets measured gets done' as the saying goes. And what does not get measured may well fall off the priority list altogether.

A beautiful example of this occurred in a bank, where almost impossibly high targets for gaining new loan business were set. One branch amazed all others by meeting these targets. It transpired that the 'successful' branch had realized that the measure of performance used, the paperwork on loan proposals, could be directly manipulated. Normally such paperwork was completed only after an initial check on the loanworthiness of the applicant. If it was clear that a loan was not justified, the paperwork, which was complex and time consuming, was not undertaken. But the 'successful' branch had started to complete all the paperwork for *all* applications, regardless of whether a loan was likely to result. What was being measured was the paperwork. And the paperwork was being done! Even if half of it was a complete waste of time, and everyone knew this to be the case.

A less dramatic but common example concerns the introduction of 'response time' targets, for example in the area of customer complaints. If the target is 'a reply within 48 hours' there is likely to be a great increase in standard 'your query is being looked into' letters. In places where the postal system is a problem, this may reassure the customer. Otherwise such bland responses may make them even angrier, particularly if effort is going into writing these letters rather responding specifically to the issues raised.

One frequent problem is that financial measures, because they are highly visible and seemingly objective and relatively easy to obtain, take precedence over all others. As such measures are also time-defined, and the period is short (a year, or even a month) the resulting distortion can be considerable. It is argued that many of the ills of the UK economy are linked to the need for impressive annual accounts, and large payouts to shareholders. In Germany or Japan, where a longer-term view is taken by those investing in the organization, investment in both technology and human capital is more likely, and the longer-term prospects for the organization are therefore very much better.

Workout!

If when you were exploring a control loop earlier you failed to identify important aspects of performance *not* being sensed, see if you can find some now. If not (and not all control loops are faulty in this respect) then try to think of some relevant aspect of your own behaviour at work, or that of those you manage, which receives less emphasis than it should because there is no performance measure directly associated with it. What performance indicators might be relevant?

Economy, efficiency and effectiveness

Three particular types of measure are in common use, and worth keeping distinct in your mind. *Economy* concerns the costs of inputs to a process, *efficiency* has to do with the ratio beween inputs and outputs (a more efficient process will produce the same outputs for fewer inputs) and *effectiveness* has to do with the extent to which the outputs are what was intended and/or needed. Thus one could increase *economy* by shedding large numbers of staff. But this might well reduce effectiveness if quality or volume of outputs can no longer be maintained. It might also in the longer term reduce efficiency, as high levels of sick leave due to stress, for example, might have a disproportionate effect on outputs. Economies with capital equipment can have similar results. Because organizations have finite financial resources, economy will almost always be an important measure. But the other two measures should be considered as well, and a balance sought.

The effects of delays in the loop

Another problem you may have found was that any feedback came too late to be of much use. If you find out that the warehouse has no stock only when you go to fill a customer order which needs to be delivered immediately, and if order time for new stock is 6 weeks, you have a problem. Both the time delay before the output is sensed and the time to take corrective action will be important here. If a system does not take account of delays, it is possible for control actions to cause greater and greater swings *away* from the desired outcome. For example, each week during the 6 weeks the warehouse could be increasing its orders for stock as demand built up. Meanwhile customers could be increasingly dissatisfied, and withdrawing their orders, or placing new orders elsewhere. Suddenly there will be *increasing* stock levels, and *decreasing* orders.

The time dimension within which a control loop operates is therefore critical. When you are analysing how various important forms of control are being achieved you will need to take this aspect into consideration. For some forms of control action delays may be much longer than 6 weeks. To increase staffing if workload is increasing may take months, particularly if the staff in question need to have skills that are in short supply in the labour market, or need to be developed in-house over a lengthy period. This is often forgotten by organizations which are 'downsizing' on a purely numbers basis – a problem identified by some of the respondents in the survey described in Chapter 2.

Higher orders of control

Time is also important if you need to revise targets. In a rapidly changing context, important factors may alter so much that targets may be out of date almost as soon as they are set. If there is no mechanism for reviewing targets, they may soon cease to be meaningful, and the control loop will effectively break down. Frequently, as was mentioned earlier, the revision of targets will be carried out not within the system in question but with reference to a higher order of system in the hierarchy. In looking at this aspect of control you may like to identify such a relevant higher-order system, and look at sub-system boundary-spanning activities needed to ensure that higher orders of control are exercised effectively. Sometimes such control may be ineffective if coordination is lacking. It is all very well to increase your production targets, but if some other part of the organization supplies you with a sub-assembly, and their targets are not increased to correspond, then the 'control' exercised on you will be ineffective.

In the control loop you looked at earlier consider whether there is scope for revising targets and if there is, or should be, which 'system' would be involved in this revision. Remember, we are still talking about a system as defined by you, so think of the 'system' that helps you understand the situation best.

In the more flexible organizations sought today, the goal is to locate the control where the information is. But overall coordination of your targets with those of other sections with which you relate in some way may be important. And apart from this, you might not have the authority to take whatever action was needed to achieve those targets, or perhaps whatever action could be taken within budgetary limits. Resource provision may be a powerful constraint.

The cause *isn't . . .*

We are usually all too ready to jump in with *simple* explanations, and consequently simple solutions, when problems present themselves. This is much easier than to look for a tangled web of causes, and to untangle them enough to find an appropriate way forward. But if a situation has arisen for complex reasons, trying to improve it by changing only one of the relevant factors may make matters worse rather than better.

You might feel in the example above that in identifying weaknesses in a relevant control loop you had 'solved' a problem. But it is more than likely that this will be only part of the situation. In emphasizing the need to explore *multiple* causality, and in offering the multiple-cause diagram as a technique for doing this, the systems approach gives you a firm prod *away* from accepting simple explanations, and single 'causes'.

The essence of drawing such a diagram is to start *now* and work backwards. Many people find this surprisingly difficult. They are so used to A→B thinking that they want to start with A and look for B. Whereas with a multiple-cause diagram you start with some 'Z' and work backwards, teasing out all the factors that contributed to the state of Z. First you look at the immediate factors that contributed to Z – it happened because, say, W, X and Y happened. Perhaps the machine broke down because it was old, routine maintenance had been neglected and it was being operated too fast. You then take each of these factors and say why *they* happened. Perhaps routine maintenance was not happening because staffing had been cut to a level which no longer allowed it and/or staff were not trained or supervised in this activity. Perhaps it was a holiday period and no cover was arranged. Perhaps production pressures were such that the machine could not be spared for maintenance. For each of *these* factors you could push back a further layer to the factors which contributed to *them*, and so on. Obviously you would need to stop somewhere: it is usually fairly obvious when it is not particularly helpful to go further.

Figure 5.4 shows a generic multiple-cause diagram. You obviously need to substitute apropriate phrases for the letters when you use this diagram, and will probably have a different number of layers and of arrows at each layer, but the general shape should be something like that shown.

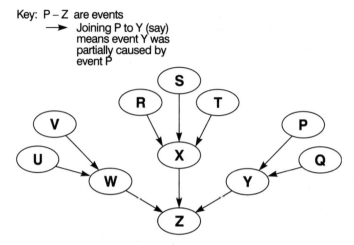

Figure 5.4   The general form of a multiple-cause diagram

Think of a situation with which you are unhappy at work, or even at home. Analyse it using a multiple-cause diagram to tease out the layers of contributory factors. Think about the implications of this enriched understanding of the situation. Does it suggest ways of improving the situation? Or does it show why 'obvious' solutions will not work?

If possible, discuss your diagram with someone who is also involved. Does it reflect their understanding of the situation? Can they add further factors? Can they see implications that you have missed? Before doing this, it might be worth checking that you have not cheated on the convention. First, are all your phrases *events* rather than *things?* Things themselves seldom contribute to situations, but events, or changes to things, do. Thus the machine did not cause the breakdown, but the fact that it had become old was a contributory factor. Maintenance staff were not a causal factor, though their failure to carry out maintenance was.

Second, did you really start at Z, rather than A? While a multiple-*effect* diagram may be of interest if you are planning something in the future, we are concerned here with understanding a present situation, the causal factors of which necessarily had to be present previously (though many of them are probably still there). All too often those new to this form of diagram start with what happened first, and then work out what followed it. It is important to do the reverse of this, and start at the end!

Third, can you read every arrow as 'B happened at least partly because A happened'? It is all too easy to put other sorts of relationships into the diagram, so that it becomes a mix of the relationship diagram which you drew earlier and an exploration of causality. This will confuse anyone to whom you show it. Even if you are not going to show it to anyone, the whole point of drawing it is to clarify your own thinking, and if you mix causes with other things you will probably still be thinking in an unclear way.

Just for interest, Figures 5.5 and 5.6 show multiple-cause analyses of very different events. These are intended to be self-explanatory, but you might like to ask yourself whether they are drawn in the way prescribed, and whether they suggest ways of modifying your own diagram.

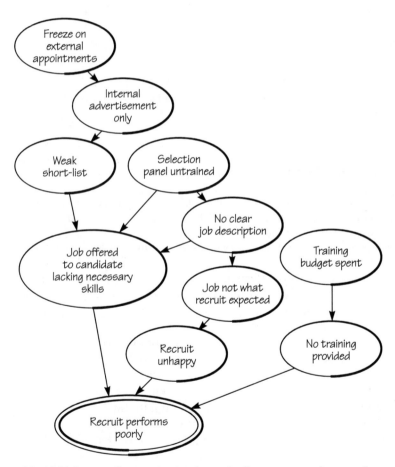

Figure 5.5 Multiple-cause diagram showing factors leading to poor performance by a recent recruit

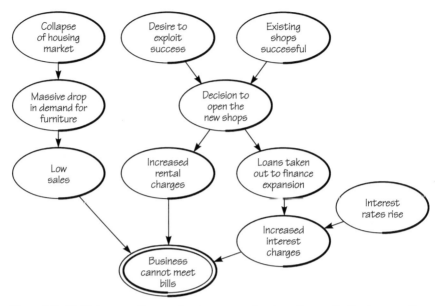

Figure 5.6   Multiple-cause diagram showing reasons for the collapse of a furniture retail business

Using a systems approach

The thinking you have done so far should have shown you that simple ideas can form a framework for useful descriptions of organizations. Furthermore, if used creatively rather than in an obvious and simplistic fashion they can advance your understanding of a situation quite considerably. To gain maximum benefit from the approach you need to use it not as a private exercise but as a framework for group working. It is much easier for a group to represent the different relevant perspectives on a situation than for you to try to imagine what these might be. And the approach emphasizes the importance of these different perspectives and of taking them into account. A group will also come up, inevitably, with a range of different models, something which is not always easy if working alone.

This helps to overcome the difficulty often found of seeing the systems you choose to describe as 'what if we look at it this way' systems, rather than as definitive descriptions of an objective reality. Those with a scientific background, trained to focus exclusively on verifiable facts, find this particularly difficult. And yet their perspective is often one which you need to include if your group is to represent all the relevant disciplines and views important to a given situation.

Systems and rationality

Perhaps the best way of justifying the apparent craziness of this kind of systems thinking is to show how it relates to the rational decision-making model with which you are probably familiar. This model suggests that you:

- Define the problem
- Establish objectives
- Generate alternative actions
- Compare options in the light of objectives
- Select the best option
- Implement your chosen solution.

While this is an eminently sensible approach to a clearly defined problem in a stable context, few of the problems you encounter will be of this kind. Defining 'the problem' may be extremely difficult, and different stakeholders, with their different perspectives, may see it very differently. It may be just as difficult to agree on objectives. Selection of best option can be only as good as the best option generated (and may not be as good as this!). If you fail to understand the problem you may not generate very good options. Or your choice between options may be based on inappropriate criteria.

The systems approach allows you to explore and then define complex problems in ways which are likely to include the different dimensions of this complexity, increasing your understanding of it in the process. Problem definition will involve identifying a variety of potentially relevant systems and using systems ideas to provide a framework for describing these in some detail, thinking carefully about their titles, diagramming them to show components and relationships, arguing with colleagues about where to draw boundaries, what to identify as sub-systems, what goals these subsystems might have, what is in the environment and what relationships are being managed across boundaries, what control loops are operating (and not operating).

By working with others to build up a range of systems models of aspects of the situation, a variety of perspectives can be incorporated into your model. The full benefits of the systems approach are realized only with group working. And diagramming will be one of the ways of communicating different perspectives within the group. The richer understanding of the whole situation gained in this process will lead to a much more complex and deeper understanding of 'the' problem, which goes beyond symptoms to root causes. Clearly, solutions which address these will have a much greater chance of success than those which address symptoms only.

Similarly, the approach will mean that you reject facile formulations of objectives. Instead realistic objectives are likely to be formulated reflecting the different objectives of people involved in the situation. A word is in order here on the topic of deciding on objectives, and on the measures which you will use to assess your options against these objectives, *before* thinking about options. This is to allow you to avoid becoming prematurely attached to a particular way forward that is for some reason immediately attractive, and slanting your comparison so that this option 'wins'. If you pay considerable attention to objectives early on, and to specifying the measures of effectiveness linked to these objectives that will be used in the modelling and comparison process, you will be more likely to avoid such bias.

The richer understanding which emerges from the 'definition in (multiple) systems terms' process at the outset will have an influence *beyond* the objective and measure definition stage, and its influence on modelling. It will also help you to generate a more creative set of options if you can treat the search for relevant systems and sub-systems as a game, playing with pictures of possible systems to see if any light dawns as a result. Systems addressing aspects of the problem of which you were initially unaware may thus emerge, giving you a wider understanding. And planning for implementation is likely to be far more realistic if the multiple relationships in the situation, and the perspectives of interested parties, are considered in the planning process. Furthermore, the involvement of those who will be affected by any 'solution' in the problem definition and subsequent stages is likely to reduce resistance to any changes which are decided upon.

Once a solution has been selected, the systems approach has further uses. In designing the implementation stage of the process, it is important that the system within which changes are taking place is fully understood, as is the potential impact on the wider system. All too often the 'knock-on' effects of a change are unexpected, and may be unwelcome. If the design has taken place with an understanding of the wider system such unwelcome surprises will be avoided.

Summary

If you have worked sufficiently hard at the exercises suggested while working through this chapter, you should by now see how a set of apparently simple ideas can be used as a framework to enable you to grasp much more of the necessary complexity in challenging situations than does normal common sense. This increase in understanding depends upon a willingness to look at situations in a multiplicity of ways yourself, and to involve a group of people with different perspectives on the situation in the process of defining the situation. Because of the emphasis on inter-relationships, and the difficulty of communicating these in prose, diagramming techniques will be an essential element in group working. So too will be exploring the implications of differences of perspective in a creative way, accepting these as important aspects of the situation, rather than something to be argued away.

It should now be clear that, far from being antagonistic to a rational approach, the apparently bizarre experimental thinking that may result from full use of a systems approach is a very necessary complement to rational methods in any situation that is complicated, and where objectives are non-obvious, or perhaps in conflict. The creative use of different 'systems' as frameworks for describing aspects of the situation should enable you to come up with ideas for action that are both more creative and more likely to be effective than the use of rational methods alone. Later chapters will offer further ideas for increasing your creativity in this context.

Even if you did think hard, as directed, you have probably gained only a faint idea of the potential benefit of a systems approach. You may be still somewhat sceptical. Don't worry if that is the case. Systems thinking is as multi-layered as an onion. Just when you think you have taken it on board you find another layer underneath, and another layer. . . . It took me about three years to move from mild scepticism to total conversion. While you may have a more agile mind, it is still likely to take considerable practice in using the approach before you stop having new insights. So even if it does seem crazy, and you hate drawing diagrams, and think that colleagues will suspect you of showing serious symptoms of stress at last, give it a fair chance. . . .

Chapter 6
Thinking about people

Many managers say that 'people problems' give them the biggest headache in their job. Engineers have been heard to mutter darkly that there would be no problems with the machines if it weren't for the operatives. You may be currently struggling with a problem of a 'personality clash' between two of your staff who need to work closely together, or worrying about how to deal with a recent recruit who has turned out to be completely without either ability or motivation, or concerned about a threatened grievance case. If so, you will be all too aware of one aspect of the need to think about how to 'manage' people.

But there is a far more significant if less obvious way in which your management of human resources is critical. This has to do not with avoiding obvious problems but with managing in such a way that your team makes a really effective contribution to the organization's goals. And it is here that your own underlying assumptions about people and those which are ingrained in your organization, and reflected in its culture and structure, may be exerting a powerful but invisible effect.

To give an example of how powerful this effect can be, some years ago one organization adopted a 'people-centred' approach to management in some of its plants. This produced such cost savings, cutting unit costs from 70 cents to 22 cents in the plants using it, that the approach, described as 'treating people as people', was designated confidential. Psychologists studying the initiative were not allowed to identify the organization concerned! Currently many organizations are publicizing their adoption of similar approaches, calling these 'empowerment', and claiming them as a major breakthrough.

It is this second aspect of managing people, and the associated ways of thinking about human beings and their motivation, both as individuals and as members of teams, that this chapter addresses. The importance of going beyond 'common sense' in this area cannot be overemphasized. People are clearly an important component of any organization. Employment costs are usually a major part of the budget. And if productivity or other measures of effectiveness can be quadrupled by more effective management, then this is highly significant. Furthermore, in a rapidly changing environment, it is the human component of the organization that holds the key to flexibility. More change initiatives have been thwarted by resistance of the employees concerned than have succeeded. A better understanding of the motivations of those concerned is essential to effective management, whether of the status quo or of change.

Because human beings are essentially social animals, and relationships with other people are an important part of almost every aspect of our life, this is an area where assumptions, both conscious and unconscious, abound. Indeed many managers pride themselves on knowing everything there is to know about 'man-management'. (This is not unconscious sexism – such managers frequently use precisely this term!) But unconscious assumptions are as likely to be wrong in this area as in any other. Paradoxically, the wealth of our past experience of social relations means that there is all the more need to *think* creatively and constructively about people, rather than accept the commonsense ideas which we all have, whether or not we are aware of them. And because social interaction is at the heart of our existence, it may feel very much that we are 'going against the grain' in querying such deeply held assumptions.

This chapter looks at some of the better-known theories of individual motivation, their strengths and weaknesses in explaining what it is that 'makes people tick', and how you can use these ideas both to improve the performance of those you manage and to prepare people to accept change. It also looks at some of the ways in which people may behave when in groups, and how such groups may be made more effective. Armed with these ideas, you should be able to think about how you can best approach any situation where you are managing other people, or working with them as part of a team. By the end of this chapter you should therefore:

● Understand why motivation is important
● Appreciate the strengths and weaknesses of some of the better-known theories of motivation at work
● Have a greater understanding of the motivation of those who work for or with you
● Appreciate the potential advantages of team working
● Be more aware of the effectiveness of teams with which you are involved, and of ways in which this might be increased.

What makes people do what they do, even if it isn't what you want?

Fayol identified the initiation and maintenance of behaviour as a key management function. Clearly, the behaviour in question needs to be *appropriate* behaviour. In some organizations considerable effort is directed towards *subverting* organizational objectives. As a middle manager you cannot expect to 'command' as Fayol did. Instead you will need to understand why people act as they do, and use that understanding to influence them to behave appropriately. For this you need to understand their motivation.

Motivating the man in the machine

For the first half of this century there was a widely held set of assumptions about what motivated people at work. There are still many organizations where the same set of assumptions forms the basis for management. Although these ideas were seldom made explicit, they were clearly reflected in the way in which work was organized in the 'machine organizations' that were predominant. This form of organization involved a high level of control. Work was designed to be done in the single approved way, this often having been worked out by 'time and motion' experts. Deciding what was to be done, and how it was to be done, was the clear prerogative of management. Those who did what was required were rewarded, often being paid on a piecework basis. Those who did not do what was required were punished, either financially or by losing their job. The assembly line was the embodiment of this approach. You can see that it is totally consistent with the principles of administrative management discussed in Chapters 2 and 4.

The other major contributor to this way of thinking, apart from Fayol and Weber, was Frederick Taylor, originally an engineer in a steel works. He was concerned by the antagonisms and inefficiencies which he observed at work. These puzzled him, as it seemed self-evident that management's interests were best served by seeking to achieve both maximum prosperity for themselves *and* maximum prosperity for those they employed. He saw the problem as resulting from a combination of employee fears that increased productivity would result in unemployment, defective systems of management, and inefficient ways of working. He advocated (first in 1903, then in more detail in 1911) a set of principles which he called 'Scientific Management'. These ideas were hugely influential for the next half-century, and still have a major impact today.

The 'science' advocated was systematic observation of work to determine the most effective methods and tools, careful selection and training of employees, and the use of incentive payments to reward high output levels. Few would argue with these principles today. More contentious is his rigid separation of 'work' and 'decision taking' which goes against modern preferences for devolved decision taking, and extreme specialization, which can be deeply stressful for the employees concerned. Even in Taylor's lifetime (he died in 1917) critics called his systems 'inhumane' and said they reduced men to the level of machines. Such criticisms would be more widespread today, and would have the added force that in a rapidly changing context, where the model of organization as machine is inadequate, the model of man as machine is even more inappropriate.

Theory X and Theory Y

In the management quiz in Chapter 3 the very first question addressed a related aspect of your own views of motivation. It was Douglas McGregor in the late 1950s who redrew attention to the set of assumptions about motivation implicit in the Fayol/Taylor approach to management. (In fact Taylor had made them fairly explicit, but by then few were reading Taylor himself, just what others said or wrote about him.) McGregor called this set of assumptions 'Theory X'. Important though his ideas are, some at least of his success must rest on this inspired title!

The 'Theory X' assumptions are that:

- The average human dislikes work and will avoid it if at all possible
- Productivity schemes are an important element in overcoming this dislike
- People need to be coerced, controlled, directed, and punished if output is to be maintained
- The average human being prefers to be directed, avoids responsibility, has little ambition, and wants security above all.

Think about the extent to which your experience of employees suggests that these assumptions are valid. Talk to others in your organization, preferably those who have not been exposed to formal management courses, and see whether there are others around you who hold this set of assumptions.

McGregor's contribution, apart from the catchy label 'Theory X', was to point out that these assumptions may be inadequate. There may be an alternative set of assumptions, 'Theory Y', which if valid would lead to a very different approach to management. He suggested that these competing assumptions are:

- Exerting effort at work is perfectly natural: work can be either satisfying or punishing depending on the circumstances

- External control is not the only form of control: self-control is also possible if the person is committed to objectives
- The most significant reward of all may be satisfaction of a person's need to 'self-actualize' (more of this later)
- The average human can learn not only to accept but also to seek responsibility
- Many more people are able to contribute creatively to solving organizational problems than actually do
- The potential of the average person at work is not fully used.

Under these assumptions, the role of the manager is to arrange conditions at work so that indivduals can satisfy their own needs by behaving in a way that furthers the organization's objectives. Thus their natural tendency to exert effort at work is harnessed in the organization's interests, while the individuals who are exerting this effort gain satisfaction from so doing. In the process, more of their potential is used, and they make a greater contribution to organizational problem solving.

The previous exercise was not an attempt to catch you out, and to show how old-fashioned and unenlightened you were if you felt that people in your experience behaved in a 'Theory X' way. Many people do. The important point that McGregor was making is that if managed under 'X' assumptions, people will behave in an 'X' way. And at the time he mooted these ideas, the machine organization was the 'ideal', so most people *were* being managed in this way. In that sort of organization, self-control is highly unlikely as people are all too aware of being seen as part of the machine, do not feel valued, gain no satisfaction from exhausting themselves by working as hard as they are able in order to further the organization's objectives, and are given no scope for creativity.

As an aside, here is a story which suggests that even under the fairly dehumanizing regime of working on an assembly line, 'human' character-istics will show themselves, and people *will* exert effort just to express their creativity. I heard it when I was working near Detroit, with organizational psychologists who had done research in automobile assembly plants there. Such plants apparently had whole departments devoted to 'man-proofing' the line, that is, to ensuring that jobs could be done *only* in the approved fashion.

Originally the cars had F O R D in individual letters. The letters had bolts on the back for fixing in different places, and the bonnet or rear part to which they were fixed arrived with pre-drilled holes in the appropriate places. Thus the 'man-proofers' had ensured that there was only one way in which the letters could be fixed. (They had had unfortunate experiences earlier, with cars leaving the line labelled F R O D, or other variants.) However, before long, the assembly-line workers were borrowing drills from other parts of the factory, drilling new holes, and deviant spellings were again rife. In desperation the company moved to a single piece of chrome, with *Ford* in joined-up writing!

There are several interesting points to emerge from this story. First, McGregor would seem to have a point in suggesting that there is untapped energy and creativity in the employee – at least the employee on the assembly line. Second, these qualities are a positive liability in the machine organization. In order to use this potential, a different sort of organization is needed. Third, we need a much better understanding of human motivation. Without this we shall be unable to align the objectives of the organization and those of employees, something both Taylor and McGregor suggested was important.

The range of human motives

Psychologists have devoted considerable attention to motivation, whether of rat or human. A central assumption was that in order to motivate, a reward must satisfy a need. Thus a thirsty rat will go to considerable lengths to obtain water, and a hungry one will do things to obtain food that it will not do when well fed. There was even a rather nasty set of experiments in which rats were interrupted in mid-copulation, and forced to traverse an electrified grid to resume their activity, in order to see how strong a shock they were prepared to endure.

The next step in 'understanding' motivation was to look at the range of needs which might be satisfied. Many rival sets of classifications were produced, but one has been adopted almost wholesale by management writers. This is Maslow's 'Theory of Motivation', propounded in the early 1940s. There were two elements to this theory. The first was that there were five categories of basic needs. The second was that these categories formed a hierarchy. Behaviour would be driven by *unsatisfied* needs, and those needs which would be active, or pre-potent, at any time would be those unsatisfied needs lowest in the hierarchy.

The categories, starting with the lowest, were:

- *Physiological needs* such as hunger, thirst or the drive for sex
- *Safety needs*, that is, the avoidance of danger or threat
- *Love needs*, for affectionate relations with people in general, both the giving and receiving of love and affection
- *Esteem needs*, both for self-respect and the respect and high regard of others, including the desire for adequacy, achievement, confidence, independence and freedom
- *Self-actualization needs*, to fulfil our potential – note this varies hugely between individuals: Maslow gives as possible examples artistic creation, athletic achievement, or being an ideal parent.

Given that Maslow's theory was intended to help with the understanding of psychopathology, it is curious that it has been so influential in management theory. The categories do not seem to be all that much better than many of the other sets of ideas. There is some doubt as to the usefulness of the idea of pre-potency. Yet you saw that McGregor was suggesting the importance of self-actualization as one of his assumptions. And if they remember nothing else from a management course covering the general area of human behaviour, students will remember Maslow's hierarchy.

So what use *can* you make of this framework in your conceptual toolkit? The first point to note is probably that physiological needs are unlikely (unless meetings run into lunchtime!) to be active in many of those with whom you work. Food and drink are therefore unlikely to be powerful motivators. You probably did not think that they would be! However, it is worth reflecting that the shift of manufacturing to less developed parts of the world has taken place precisely because such needs *are* active there, and people are prepared to work for very low wages and in conditions that would be unacceptable in the UK because their survival does depend upon it.

Second, safety needs *are* frequently threatened by restructuring and associated redundancies, and threats are *perceived*, rightly or wrongly, in most change initiatives. Maslow's suggestion that such needs will predominate over any higher ones if they are active may go far to explain why so many change initiatives fail. The emphasis in 'selling' such change may well have been on rewards which would satisfy higher-order needs. Such factors would be irrelevant if the staff in question still perceived the change as a threat to their job security. Instead, success would rest in the first place on ensuring that those who were *not* threatened by the change believed that they were secure.

Third, the most striking thing about Maslow's 'theory' is the point most often forgotten: the huge variation in human needs. By learning the five major labels, it is all too easy to feel that you 'understand' motivation. But within each of the broad categories there are many different needs, and they are complex, and modified by perceptions. A comment that you might see as demonstrating affection might be taken by someone else as patronizing, therefore as *reducing* satisfaction of esteem needs. Self-actualization for you might be totally different from self-actualization for others. Therefore any generalizations about human motivation, and assumptions about what will motivate 'people' in general are suspect.

Fourth, and perhaps why Maslow has been so widely quoted, the idea of 'higher-order' needs for self-actualization, and for esteem, is a powerful one. If lower-order needs are more or less taken care of, then these needs may become important motivators. And from an employer's point of view, it may be possible to arrange work to meet these needs without great expense, thus creating a win–win situation, where employer and employee can both satisfy their objectives at the same time.

Thus whether or not you accept Maslow's categories as 'the' way of classifying needs, and whether or not you fully accept the idea of hierarchy of needs, they provide a useful framework for starting to organize your own thoughts about what outcomes are likely to be motivating for those with whom you work, and for asking the questions needed to find out more about your particular situation. Linked with the expectancy model, which is described below, they give you one possible way of making sense of the situation in which you find yourself, and of making changes that will improve it.

Expectations and expectancy

Before looking at ways in which work might be made to satisfy higher-order needs, there is one other theory which is enormously useful. This is the expectancy theory of motivation, developed by Vroom and elaborated by many, key among them Porter and Lawler. (If this interests you, look for papers written by these authors.) The theory is a version of the control model described in the previous chapter, applied to the exercise of self-control as advocated by McGregor. It allows you to answer the question 'Under what conditions will self-control be exercised to maintain a high level of effort at work?'

Thus the process controlled is the exertion of effort by an employee, and the standard against which it is measured in order to see whether control action is needed is the extent to which the exertion of this effort produces valued rewards. Figure 6.1 shows this basic loop. The key components are E, the effort expended, O, the outcomes resulting from this effort, and C, the comparison process of the value of these outcomes with some internal 'standard' of what is appropriate. In contrast to the control loop for a simple engineering process, where too low a level of output might be expected to result in an increased input, the reverse is likely to happen here. If the effort does not produce rewards which the employee sees as justifying that effort, or if from the outset there is no belief that such outcomes will result, then the *expectancy* associated with that effort will be low. Only if the expectancy is high will the effort be expended.

At first sight this may seem like a simple argument for piece rates, or other forms of incentive payment, and indeed this may be one way of increasing expectancy. But expectancy theory is a development of the simple loop shown in Figure 6.1. A further component, P (for perform-ance), is inserted between E and O. Seldom is effort rewarded *per se*. Getting an 'A' grade for effort but a 'D' for achievement on a school report does not leave a child feeling happy. It may offer some protection against

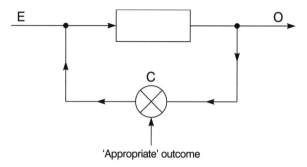

Figure 6.1   The basic effort–outcome control loop

parental wrath, but child and parent would feel far more satisfied with a reversal of the grades. It is the achievement that brings the praise, and at work it is the attainment that tends to be rewarded. Payment is by results, not by effort.

The model is further elaborated by emphasizing that it is not the actual links between effort and outcomes that are important, but the *perceived* links: subjective rather than objective probabilities are what is important. It matters little whether your efforts will actually produce rewards. It is crucial that you *believe* that they will be rewarded. Of course, if there is no real link, it may be difficult to keep believing that there is one, but the other situation, where there is a link but it is either not seen or not believed in is all too common. Figure 6.2 shows the elaborated model. Dotted lines are used to emphasize the subjective nature of the links.

You can begin now to see the advantages of a model like this over some of the simple prescriptions for increasing motivation. Admittedly, it offers no easy answers. 'Increase the expectancy of rewards associated with the efforts you want' is far from a simple prescription, persuasive though it may

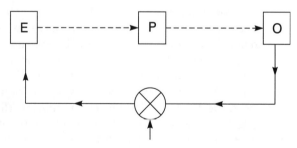

Figure 6.2   The elaborated expectancy model

be. Indeed, it raises more questions than it answers. But by exploring these questions, and coming up with answers appropriate to the situation with which you are concerned, you may be able to increase markedly the motivation of those with whom you work towards behaviour which you wish them to show, and to reduce undesirable motivation.

Identifying the right 'effort'

Look at each of the parts of the model in turn. Take 'E' first. There will be several different sorts of 'effort' that are relevant. The Ford workers going to great lengths to rearrange spellings were exerting efforts in directions which were definitely not desired by management. You may have other examples of 'effort' which are not progressing organizational objectives. Expectancy theory would suggest that for each such 'E' there will be expectations of valued outcomes associated with it. Understanding the expectancies will help you to understand the behaviour, and perhaps to direct efforts more in line with organizational objectives.

What sorts of 'E' *are* desirable in your situation? Unless you are seeking to shed staff, and have invested little in their development to date, 'not leaving' may be one important 'E'. If people are leaving, you may wish to ask them what rewards they think they will get from their new job that are lacking in the current one. The normal answer is 'more money', but it is seldom the full story: exploring perceived $E \rightarrow O$ links in more detail can be illuminating. Note that the outcomes associated with merely holding the job may sometimes be quite different from those associated with doing well in the job. If the rewards for low and high performers are identical, what would expectancy theory predict? (This situation is not all that uncommon. It occurs if jobs are secure, there are no incentive payments, and promotion either does not exist or is not linked to performance.) In this case even very low performers will feel safe. Indeed, high performance may attract hostility from colleagues who feel it 'shows them up', a negative outcome with no compensating recognition or praise from management.

The theory would suggest that in such situations very low levels of effort would be exerted in the direction of superior performance. But for those capable of achieving more there might be a realization that they could do better in a job where effort to perform *was* rewarded, and if such jobs were available those workers with the ability to perform would be those who would leave the organization. This points up the importance of distinguishing between the effort of holding down the job and the effort rather loosely specified as 'performing well'. Further distinctions will almost certainly be needed, as will become clear later. For now it is important only to remember that the question '*What* effort?' is absolutely crucial.

Making effort effective

Moving on we come to the dotted line E $--\rightarrow$ P. The question highlighted here is how the belief that effort will generate performance can be strengthened. Clearly, if effort does *not* result in the desired performance then few employees will believe for long that it does, unless there is no feedback at all or they are misinformed by their superiors. (Can you honestly say you have never been kind and told someone that something they had done was acceptable, even good, when it was not?) As it is unlikely to be in the organization's interests to encourage sub-standard performance, it is worth thinking about what is going to affect this link.

Obviously, effort will be turned into desired performance only if a number of conditions are met:

- The *ability* to perform must exist. This means that selection of people with the necessary aptitudes and ability is important, as are training and development in the necessary skills.
- The *requirements* must be clearly understood. The person must know precisely what is required - what constitutes performance.
- The *resources*, whether materials, tools, time or information, necessary to perform must be available.

Think about any weaknesses in your own ability to convert effort into desired performance. Do they fit into one of the three categories above? What about those for whom you are responsible? Is there any way in which the E $\rightarrow$ P *actual* link could be strengthened by attention to one or more of the factors described?

Improving feedback

In reflecting on your own performance you may have had difficulties because you were necessarily dealing with your *perceived* chances of performing, rather than objective probabilities. If there is little feedback on how well you perform you may *assume* that you are not doing very well. Or you may think that no news is good news and that you are doing very well indeed. Either way, you will have little basis on which to relate your efforts to your achievements.

This situation is surprisingly common despite talk of performance measurement, and the increasing use of 'performance-related' pay. And the more complex the job, the less likely is it that usable feedback will be available. If you are sewing garments together, it is very easy to see how well you have performed. The number of garments completed is a fairly good measure. If you are selling financial services some measures are fairly obvious. The volume of business done is one. But there will be other aspects which are also important. How good a relationship have you built with your clients? How appropriate is the advice you have given them, and how suitable the products which you have sold them? Both will affect your future business with them, and possibly with contacts to whom they may (or may not) recommend you. The effects will become apparent only in the longer term, and the causes may by then be difficult to trace. If you are *managing* the financial services advisors then measuring your performance will be even more difficult. Again some aspects will be fairly quantifiable, but other important ones will not.

The difficulty of measuring important aspects of many jobs is not the only reason why feedback on performance is often lacking. Many managers hate to tell subordinates how well they have performed. They may think that by conducting an annual appraisal interview, and even then mincing their words for fear of 'damaging working relationships', or even for fear of being challenged, they have given all the feedback necessary. Yet for employees to continue to improve their performance, and to become even clearer about performance requirements, and to *perceive* a close link between effort and performance, feedback is essential. And it needs to be more honest, more specific and detailed, and far, far more frequent than an annual appraisal.

Obviously, if an employee is unclear about the level of performance achieved the P $--\rightarrow$ O link is also likely to be weak. Other causes of weakness will include the absence of any such link in reality, or failure to understand such links as exist. I was once assured by a group of electricity workers that the harder they worked, the less they were paid. I never did fully understand this, but their supervisors agreed that they were right. Certainly, many bonus schemes are so complicated that they may not be fully understood, or the bonus may depend on many more things than the performance achieved by the employee earning the bonus.

The distorting potential of measures

One serious problem occurs when the valued outcome is linked to only one aspect of performance, often the one which is easily measured. This can happen at any level in an organization. To take an example from senior management, the top executives of a large US company were offered a major bonus (equal to twice their annual salaries) if stock rose 20 points and stayed there for 10 days. The 'E' exerted to achieve this measure of performance was to sack 12 000 of the 86 000 employees, freeze all salaries but their own, and cut pretty well all other spending. This allowed promises of a major payout to shareholders, and a rise in share price which lasted for the required period. These drastic actions may have seriously weakened the organization's position in future years, but in the short term they produced the 'P' that was being measured. The executives were duly rewarded.

The example of misdirected effort in banks in relation to loan applications quoted in the previous chapter was another example of the distorting power of measures. Sometimes the effect is less damaging, but improving a measure does not mean a corresponding increase in performance. One example is the way in which many hospital departments have changed procedures in order to 'improve' performance as measured. In emergency medicine, one of the Patients' Charter standards which is monitored is the time taken from booking in at reception to the time at which the patient sees a triage nurse and gives initial medical details. By allowing patients to book in at reception only after they have been triaged, 'performance' is miraculously improved. The patient may be waiting as long as ever, there may even be negative effects, as during that wait they will not be spoken to by anyone, but targets are being met 100 per cent of the time!

Rewarding performance

Clearly the P $- - \rightarrow$ O link may be a difficult one to arrange, particularly if it is difficult to measure relevant outcomes. But it is clear from the model that if it is absent, employees are unlikely to be motivated to exert their efforts in the direction desired by the organization. Of course the other important component is the outcomes themselves. Just what *are* the rewards, or indeed punishments, associated with effort, and its resulting performance? It is useful to think about two categories of outcome, normally called 'intrinsic' and 'extrinsic'.

The more obvious rewards – pay, praise, promotion – are extrinsic. They follow on performance because someone has decided to reward the performance in that way. Intrinsic rewards are those that result from the performance itself, and from the satisfaction of some of the higher-order needs Maslow suggested. When McGregor talks in his 'Theory Y' of satisfactions from self-actualization he is drawing attention to a possible intrinsic outcome. In Theory X the emphasis, in contrast, is upon negative outcomes rather than positive, and extrinsic rather than intrinsic.

What therefore needs to be done to make achieving what the *organization* requires intrinsically rewarding for the employee? What makes employees feel they have *achieved* something, by performing? What makes them feel they are developing as individuals by doing well at work? The following factors are important:

- *Feedback*, of course, on the level of performance achieved
- *Significance*, or a feeling that whatever was achieved was worth achieving

- *Use of valued skills*, rather than a feeling that anyone could have achieved as much
- *Ownership* of the performance, that is, a strong E $--\rightarrow$ P link.

These factors are more likely to be present with a fairly varied job, that has a sort of 'wholeness', in that it clearly starts at some point, produces some obvious transformation, and is then finished, that clearly contributes to organizational outcomes with which the employee is in sympathy and which are valued by society, and over which the employee has sufficient autonomy to feel that his or her own efforts and decisions produced the results in question.

Evaluating the model

From the discussion above (which even if it felt long drawn out was too brief to do justice to the theory) you should be able to see just how useful the expectancy model can be. It suggests a motivation *system*, with a set of important components, related to each other in specified ways. An appreciation of these components and relationships may not make your life easy. It offers no simple prescriptions. But such prescriptions are all too often wrong.

As an example, contrast the expectancy model with a much more popular 'theory'. This is Herzberg's (1968) 'Two-factor Theory' of job satisfaction. Herzberg asked a group of accountants and engineers to describe times when they had experienced extreme satisfaction or dissatisfaction in their job. He then classified these circumstances, and found that 81 per cent of the 'satisfiers' were associated with factors associated with higher-order needs. These factors were achievement, recognition, work itself, responsibility, advancement and growth. He called these factors 'motivators'. Sixty-nine per cent of 'dissatisfiers' were associated with factors *extrinsic* to the job, which he called 'hygiene factors'. These included company policy, supervision, interpersonal relationships, working conditions, salary, status and security.

From this, Herzberg developed the theory that to increase motivation it was important to improve the intrinsic factors, through what he called 'vertical job loading' or job enrichment. Basically this involved increasing autonomy and responsibility, improving feedback on performance and progressively increasing the challenge in jobs to the level of the employee's ability. He worked out a highly prescriptive set of steps by which this might be achieved.

These steps can be a useful starting point to increasing the intrinsic outcomes associated with performance, which according to the expectancy model is part of what may need to be done to improve performance. But because the model itself is very simple – 'hygiene factors can't motivate, only motivators can' – it led to an uncritical adoption of the prescriptions. Unfortunately, increasing responsibility will not always work. In one classic example motivation and performance were low because salesmen had not had enough training to be able to cope with the level of responsibility which they had at the outset. Applying the 'increase responsibility' formula led to near-catastrophe. If the broader expectancy model had been used as a basis for analysing the situation and considering ways of improving it, this disaster would not have happened.

From this you should be able to see that the expectancy model can provide you with one framework for *thinking* in a systematic way about why individuals in a situation are behaving in a particular way. You will become aware of information you are lacking: for example, what outcomes do staff *believe* result from performance, indeed what performance do they think is desired? And you will be able to anticipate at least some of the results of planned changes, and in consequence perhaps improve on the plans, even if this means challenging some of the assumptions made by colleagues.

Do it! Look at either the team you manage, or your own job. What *are* the relevant parts in the model? Which 'E's are important? How strong is the E → P link? What are the 'O's involved and how are they linked to 'P'? Try to draw a diagram showing the factors that are important in your specific situation. How could any of the links be strengthened to improve performance? If possible, make changes which will strengthen any weak links and see what happens!

Motivation in groups

One of the major points highlighted by the early systems thinkers was that organizations should be thought of as *socio-technical* systems, with the social sub-system being as important as the technical one. This led, in the 1960s and 1970s, to the introduction of 'autonomous working groups' as an approach to making work more satisfying, and increasing performance. Such groups had considerable freedom to manage their own work, though with specified targets. This approach has gone in and out of favour ever since, each time with a new label (high-performance teams, flexible teams, empowerment). Although the expectancy model is normally applied to individual motivation it does suggest that organizing work on a group basis may be necessary, and can be used as a framework for looking at how teams can be motivated to perform well.

Clearly, it is often easier to create *group* tasks which have the unity and identity needed for intrinsic outcomes than it is to create jobs for individuals which are complete in themselves. A relatively self-contained 'chunk' of work can be given to a group, and the *group* can be given a high degree of freedom in determining how that work should be tackled. Indeed, the group may have more of the information needed (about individual strengths and preferences, as well as about details of the process involved) to take such decisions than does higher-level management. And the group is able to manage the interdependencies between the sub-parts of the task. Thus *group* autonomy may be far easier to achieve than autonomy for individuals.

Where a visible 'chunk' of work can only be done by more than one person, it can be hard to measure individual contributions reliably. It is usually far easier in such cases to measure the performance of the *group* than of the individual. So group working is clearly a context in which key requirements for creating intrinsic motivation, namely meaningful work, autonomy and feedback, may be created.

Group working is also a context in which *social* needs can contribute to motivation, provided conditions are right. Simply working closely with people with whom you share interests may satisfy some of these needs. But just as paying wages or a salary regardless of performance is unlikely to motivate people to perform really well, the rewards of 'belongingness' alone are unlikely to be a motivating factor. Pay and company which result from merely holding a job will make people happy to continue working in that job, but will not necessarily make them work particularly effectively. In order to harness social motivations to performance, then attention has to be paid to how the group interacts and is supported.

A team or a collection of individuals?

The basic ideas of job design which result from expectancy theory apply equally to team working. The need to know what constitutes performance is just as important. Objectives for the team must be clear. Necessary skills and resources to achieve that performance must obviously be present within the team. Feedback, and linking of both intrinsic and extrinsic outcomes to performance are still crucial. These should ensure that one of the possible hazards of team working – collusion to *avoid* achieving organizational objectives (remember the FORD example) is avoided.

But if teams are to be more than a collection of individuals there are three sets of ideas that can usefully be added to these principles of job design. The first concerns the need to pay attention to managing the group *process*, as well as the task. The second concerns the need for members of groups to play a variety of different roles, and the likelihood that some individuals will have some roles which they prefer to others, and are better at. The third concerns the way in which groups need time to develop a shared understanding of how they are to work together, and may go through some fairly dramatic disagreements before reaching this. Indeed, there is always the potential for conflict within groups, and ways of managing this on a continuing basis will be important.

One difficulty in discussing group working is that there are so many different sorts of groups. A team which is assembled to solve a specific problem and then disbanded is very different from an ongoing team such as those responsible for the nursing care on a particular ward, or for running an engineering consultancy. In thinking about group working you need to bear in mind the timescale over which the group will operate, as well as the type of task which it is performing.

Managing the group process

Several writers have emphasized that the team *process* needs managing. In autonomous working groups the team itself is responsible for this, perhaps with access to skilled help in the case of difficulties. Sometimes teams have foundered because they have not had the skills needed. More attention has been paid to more traditional, non-autonomous groups, and the role of the manager with respect to process. Probably the most quoted framework for this is the 'Managerial Grid' proposed by Blake and Mouton (1964). The grid consists of two axes, each scaled from 1 to 9. The vertical axis is labelled 'concern for people', the horizontal one, 'concern for produc-tion'. This looks nicely scientific, and the labels which they apply to parts of the grid are graphic and memorable. Both features presumably contribute to the popularity of the model. Thus a manager concerned purely with 'good fellowship' and conflict avoidance would be located at 1,9 on the grid, and earn the label 'country club manager'. The manager who had no concern at all for the social process would be at 9,1 and earn the title 'task manager'. The enlightened soul who succeeded in integrating team and task requirements would be the 9,9 'team manager'.

There is considerable debate as to whether 9,9 management is appropriate whatever the context. Many writers suggest that the nature of the situation will have a major impact on the way in which it is best managed. A number of factors may influence this: the extent to which the group trusts and likes the leader; how clearly the task is defined; the urgency of the task; the power of the leader to reward and punish; the leader's preferred way of managing; the group's preferred way of being managed; the nature of the organization concerned. And does the framework offer any help to autonomous working groups which are unlikely to *have* a leader or manager in the traditional sense? The group itself may take on these functions.

Draw a grid on the lines suggested above, labelling the zones as described. Now think about your own manager, and mark the area of the grid which best describes his or her management style. Now locate your own style. How helpful is this exercise?

If you felt that it was not particularly enlightening, do not worry too much. There *is* value in highlighting the two distinct dimensions if you are a manager who focuses on one only. If this is the case then giving some thought to the neglected dimension may improve your own performance. (The exercise started with a consideration of your own manager because it is much easier to identify the shortcomings of others than to identify your own. You might even ask your team where they would place you, and compare this position with where you located yourself!)

But the grid seems to omit much of the area addressed by the consideration of motivation theory earlier, that of managing the *individual* in relation to the task, and of ensuring that performance is both achievable and rewarded if achieved. It does seem that two dimensions are inadequate, and a third at least, that of the attention paid to managing individual needs, should be added. Adair (1983) represented these three dimensions as three overlapping circles, thus avoiding the problem that pages are two-dimensional. He also pointed out that the three sets of needs are unlikely to be perfectly aligned. There will be conflict between the different sets of needs, and the manager's job (or one of the jobs the group will need to perform in an autonomous group) will be to manage this tension.

Develop your thinking about your own or your manager's style based on the grid by considering the relative importance of all three sets of needs in explaining your own efforts at work. Try to think of times when one of these sets of needs was poorly managed, and of the impact on performance. If you currently manage a team, think about how much attention you give to each circle. Is there an area which you seldom consider? If so, think about the possible needs which might be better met, or conflicts with other sets that might be resolved, and how you could exploit these possibilities to improve performance.

Mixing individual abilities

If a group is responsible for a unit of work that requires a number of different tasks to be performed, it is fairly self-evident that the skill mix within the group needs to allow for these tasks to be done well. Indeed, in the more flexible way of working that rapidly changing environments demand, it is important that the group is skilled to do not only today's mix of tasks but also those which may well be needed with very little warning in the near future. Group members may need to have a variety of skills each so that this flexibility can be achieved. This principle applies whether the abilities concern the assembly of components of consumer goods, negotiations for resources within the organization, or dealing with customers.

But as well as obvious *task* skills like these, the discussion so far suggests that *process* skills will be needed, whether possessed by a group leader or distributed between group members. These skills will be directed towards ensuring that team members:

- Are committed to the group's objective
- Have a contribution to make
- Are enabled to make that contribution
- Are noticed and valued for that contribution when made.

These factors will be important whether the task is a fairly simple operational one, or a complex strategic project intended to change the future direction of the whole organization. And they will be important whether or not the group has a formal leader, and whatever the power relationship between any leader and the group.

The above skills concern the task, group and individual needs that are probably all driving in the same direction. But Adair suggested that there would inevitably be conflicts between individual and group needs, and between both and the needs of the task. Process skills therefore need to be supported by the authority (whether given by the organization or the group) to resolve such conflicts, and if possible to do so in a way that represents a positive move forwards. You will remember from Chapter 5 that different perspectives on a situation may be valid, and that their resolution may advance understanding, provided this validity is recognized.

Group mix

One popular way of thinking about group formation, though probably one best suited to task forces rather than ongoing groups, was developed by Belbin (1981). As with much of the research on group working, this is derived from managers going through a simulation as part of a training course. Such groups provide a near-ideal source of data for management academics: they are always available, the task can be designed to suit the research, the situation is uncontaminated by pre-existing relationships or norms of behaviour, organizational culture, or complexities of competing requirements. The only worry is, of course, that these are precisely the factors which will influence the workings of real groups!

Again the popularity of the approach may be at least partly explained by the graphic labels Belbin gives to the 'types' he identified, though managers' delight in being able to label themselves as a result of a questionnaire also seems to contribute to the attractiveness of the model. The eight roles that Belbin suggested needed to be present for a team to be effective were:

- A *chairman*, who coordinates and focuses the work of the group
- A *shaper*, who is outgoing, highly committed to the task and its achievement, and spurs others to action
- A *plant*, who is more inward looking, but highly imaginative and intelligent, and the source of original ideas and proposals
- A *monitor–evaluator* who is strong on analysis and alert to faulty logic
- A *resource-investigator* who is extrovert and sociable, and though not personally creative is good at bringing in ideas and contacts from outside
- A *company worker* who is practical, good at organization, and can turn ideas into manageable tasks
- A *team worker* who holds the team together by supporting and encouraging and reconciling others
- A *finisher*, who is concerned with details, worries about schedules, and chivvies others to meet them.

It is fairly self-evident that for a team to be effective it will normally need the activities listed above to be carried out. A team that is made up exclusively of people who are continually throwing up new ideas without being concerned to work out how they can be implemented will be fairly unlikely to be effective. A team full of members obsessed with detail and meeting schedules is unlikely to come up with creative ideas.

But to what extent do different tasks require a different balance of roles? And how can different people, once they are aware of the necessary roles, escape from their labels and do what is required for the group to perform? If you are using the idea of preferred roles as a way of thinking about groups you should keep both these questions in mind.

As with task skills, it is important to consider *selection* of people, whether to the organization as a whole or to the particular group concerned, with the necessary process skills, or potential to develop them, and the development of those skills. The need will depend, again, on the nature of both task and group, and of the organizational structure within which they take place. Belbin enthusiasts would make identification of preferred role a central part of a selection process.

While this might be difficult, and some would argue about its usefulness anyway, it is important that this whole layer of complexity is realized, and steps taken to form and then develop groups with process as well as task needs in mind. Ways of working need to allow for the management of *all* categories of relevant needs. You can probably see which of the Belbin roles outlined are directed towards task needs, and which towards process needs. If all three sets of need, individual, group and task, are not recognized and taken into consideration, group working is unlikely to generate the levels of motivation, performance, flexibility and commitment that it *can* generate, and that organizations *need* if they are to remain competitive in the present climate.

If you are a member of a working group, especially one set up for a specific task, try to see how well the Belbin roles explain its successes and failures. Are there process-related tasks, for example, which are not being tackled? Are some roles being enthusiastically carried out by all members, some by none? Can you take on board some of the functions which are not receiving due emphasis, or persuade someone else to do this?

Again you may have found that this popular 'theory' was of limited usefulness. Its main value is in highlighting the things needed if a group is to be effective. The inference often drawn that people cannot develop less preferred roles may be less helpful, particularly as there is seldom much freedom in selecting task force members. The requirements for particular areas of expertise and for people who can make time at the point needed may leave little room for choice.

Developing effective groups

Given the complexities of group working, and the very powerful social forces that can be operating (being rejected by colleagues, or simply feeling that contributions made are not appreciated can be an extremely painful experience), it is not surprising that groups may take some time to become effective. People need to test out ways of working in a group, to find out how the others will react to their contribution, to see how 'safe' the situation is, how disagreement is handled, how the group *works*. These factors will be particularly important for short-term groups, but if a longer-term team gets off to a bad start it may never recover and become fully effective. Instead, negative experiences may colour people's future behaviour, making them defensive, or aggressive, or simply causing them to become uncommitted and withdraw as far as the situation allows, so that things go from bad to worse.

Again, management trainees are an admirable source of data on this, and because simulations on courses are almost inevitably short term, consideration of the stages groups go through is a popular topic for management courses. The formulation generally used is that by Tuckman (1965), which apart from its other merits provides an easy-to-remember set of labels. This identifies four stages:

- *Forming*, when the group is still a collection of individuals, seeking to establish their identity within the group, not yet sure about what the group is to achieve, and the tendency is towards politeness and superficial agreement
- *Storming*, when conflicts between individual needs surface, there may be battles for leadership if it is a leaderless group, and a lot of interpersonal hostility may be apparent, with previous agreements being overturned
- *Norming*, when norms and practices are established, and people work out how far they can trust each other
- *Performing*, which will be at a much higher level if the previous stages have been worked through satisfactorily.

The process of establishing objectives and norms may be highly obvious when a group of management trainees are thrown together and presented with a poorly defined task, or one where they are lacking vital information. (This is how trainees often see what they are asked to do!) But even if less obvious in the normal work situation, the stages may still be important.

A work group which is assembled for a particular project may *think* that objectives are clear, and that organizational norms will determine ways of working. But these assumptions may not be totally sound. Often if the time is taken to explore different perceptions of the remit, interesting differences will emerge. If these are not worked through at the outset, some important aspects of the task may be omitted, or some group members may feel excluded.

Another problem may be that ways of working in other groups may not be equally appropriate to this particular one. Even in a very hierarchical organization groups are sometimes set up to include members from all levels. If more junior staff feel they are not entitled to make an original contribution, but must 'speak only when spoken to', they may fail to fulfil the role that was intended for them by those who selected them as group members. Interpersonal aggressions may make the group a nightmare experience for all concerned if they are not worked through and resolved.

An awareness of the different stages which groups typically go through in order to become fully effective, when added to ideas about roles needed in groups, and the different sorts of outcomes that may be contingent on performance in the group situation may help you to explore group situations in a way which takes a range of relevant factors into consideration. Treat it with caution, however. If a group seems to be particularly stormy you may feel better to know that this is not uncommon. You should not, however, feel that the group *cannot* perform until it has stormed, and make trouble just to precipitate such a stage. The list of stages is merely a nicely rhyming way of describing what frequently happens, not a prescription for working in groups.

The hazards of groups

Most of the above discussion has concerned, directly or indirectly, the need to manage individual, group and task needs, and the tensions between them. Social motivations were mentioned as important, but this point was not explored in any detail. However, it is important to realize just how strong social needs can be, and the very real hazard that group needs will, because of this, become more important than task needs. The three risks are that the group may set itself up in *opposition* to organizational needs, that pressures to conform may lead to spurious agreement that is unintentionally not in the organization's best interest, and that in order for the majority of the group to feel comfortable, a scapegoat may be selected to bear the blame of the group's shortcomings.

Group and organization in conflict

As long ago as the 1920s some fascinating work was carried out into social effects at work. The most famous result was the finding that merely paying attention to groups of workers increased their output. This so-called 'Hawthorne effect', after the Hawthorne plant where the observations were made, suggests that any experimental effects need to be treated with caution. Any benefits may be the result of being treated as an experimental group, rather than the result of the particular change that has been made. This became apparent when the researchers had completed an experiment which increased the output of assembly workers by successive increases in lighting levels. When they changed the lighting back to the original level, expecting output to drop again, they were astounded to find that it increased still further.

Another finding of this study, and the one that is relevant here, is that the more cohesive groups of workers developed very strong norms of behaviour. Some of these were to do with ideas of 'a fair day's work' and resulted in the group setting output norms which group members dared not break, resulting in significant restrictions in performance of the group as a whole. The highly cohesive groups also set up a variety of ways of operating which were in violation of company policy. You can see that the social outcomes associated with various behaviours are being used *by the group* to control those behaviours. And management may find it more difficult to shift the behaviour of a group than of an individual in cases like this.

Such a finding does not mean that cohesive groups are bad. Indeed, it reinforces the importance of social motivations. But it does emphasize the need to ensure that group objectives are consistent with organizational objectives, and that the group is clear about their objectives, committed to these objectives, and that powerful rewards are associated with achieving them, rather than with behaviours which act against the interests of the organization.

Groupthink

Conformity of behaviour is obviously important, and when it is undesirable behaviour may be a problem. But conformity of thought is even more worrying. In urging in this book that you try to break out of prevailing thought patterns, both your own and those of your colleagues, we are urging an extremely difficult task. Early psychological experiments showed that when people were asked to say which of two different lines was longer, and were put in a group of 'stooges', primed by the experimenters to give the wrong answer, most would go along with the answer given by the stooges. While some were doing so for fear of looking stupid, a small minority genuinely believed that the longer line was shorter when exposed to group pressures.

This experiment used lines that were clearly different, and what should have been an easy judgement. Most management situations contain much more ambiguity, and 'answers' that can be painful to the group. Suppose that you have been putting considerable effort into a task, and vested your reputation in success. It can be very painful to accept that you are failing. In such situations the group may be very reluctant to come to this answer, and any individual even hinting at a different view may be subject to such strong disapproval from other group members that the idea is not mentioned again: it becomes quite literally unthinkable.

If this 'groupthink' prevents the group from seeing a situation clearly, and therefore from taking appropriate action, it can be extremely dangerous. In extreme situations groups of senior management have colluded in misinterpreting signals that the company was heading for disaster, even when these signals were far from ambiguous, until it was too late to do anything to save the situation. And while it may have been 'comfortable' as a group while this was happening, it became very uncomfortable for them and for everyone else in the organization very soon. You may have read about the problems faced by 'whistle blowers' who go against these pressures, but lose their jobs in consequence.

If you are developing the habits suggested in this book, of questioning assumptions, building multiple models of situations, and generally making visible, and experimenting with, your thought processes, you may have some protection against such pressures. But you will not be immune to the wish to be accepted by any group of which you are a member, so unless you can make experimental thinking a group habit, developed *before* uncomfortable situations threaten, you may still be vulnerable, and would do well to bear the hazard in mind.

Scapegoating

Another way in which the group can continue to remain comfortable is to accept that something is wrong but to not to accept the responsibility for this. Instead all the blame is put upon a single individual, often someone whose position in the group is marginal. Apart from the harm that this may unfairly cause to the scapegoat, the process is dangerous to the group. Their comfort is continued at the expense of a genuine attempt to find out the causes of the problem. And if these are not recognized and addressed, the same thing is likely to happen again.

Once more, uncommon sense, with its experimental thinking and resistance to believing in any single 'cause', should provide you with some protection against this seductive reaction. But unless you have developed this approach as part of the group norm you may again find it very difficult to resist social pressures yourself, and even harder to get the group to confront a problem, rather than avoiding the threats such confrontation brings by using a scapegoat.

Summary

Social systems are an important part of organizations: managing people is a huge and vitally important topic. The complexity of individuals, and the even greater complexity of groups, make it all too easy to rely on simplistic assumptions. However, this will risk far too narrow a perspective, failure to use employees' potential, and change exercises that have far from the desired results. A single chapter can do no more than touch on some of the ideas which may prove a useful starting point for examining your own experience and practice, taking more factors into consideration than you may have done previously. The key points which follow are, however, important.

Simple generalizations about motivation are likely to be wrong. To understand motivation, whether in the steady state or in a change situation, you need to explore the individual's *perceptions*. Key aspects of these will concern beliefs as to what is required in the job, the chances of achieving it, the rewards and punishments associated with that achievement, and the desirability of these. Rewards associated with social, esteem and self-fulfilment needs may be at least as important as the more obvious one of pay.

Group working may be necessary if the conditions for these rewards are to be created. The social process of groups adds a whole new dimension of complexity to managing people. For effective group working process skills are needed to fulfil the range of necessary roles in the group. The task being performed, and the organizational context, will both be significant influences, as will the nature of group members and of any formal leader. Simple prescriptions about the design of jobs are likely to be misleading.

Chapter 7
The organization and beyond

The central argument for 'going against the grain' in your thinking was that old habits of thought, and the common sense that they generate, are unsuited to the rapid rates of change facing you as a manager today. It was clear from the managers quoted in Chapter 2 that the issues confronting them arose from changes imposed, often with no consultation, by the organization in which they operated. These changes were driven, directly or indirectly, by changes *outside* the organization. Your ability to define any problem completely will depend upon a good understanding of the context in which it has arisen. Your ability to anticipate, where possible, and to manage changes which are imposed upon you will similarly depend upon your understanding both of the organizational context in which you work and of the environment within which that organization is operating.

You can think of the environment in which you manage as a number of 'layers'. The nearest, the one having the most immediate impact on you, is the organization within which your department or section operates. This forms the wider system, of which your part is a sub-system. Your responsibilities are determined by the organization. It provides you with the resources you need, and limits your ability to take decisions. So although as a middle manager most of the situations you encounter will require you to focus primarily on a level below that of the organization as a whole, you need to understand how you are controlled and constrained by the organization, and how you can influence these controls and constraints.

Although you may not be interacting with the wider environment directly, an understanding of how it influences the organization will help you understand, and influence, your immediate context. Also, although designed to help those with direct marketing responsibilities, some of the frameworks for thinking about markets and competitive environments can usefully be applied to your more immediate organizational environment.

In looking at your organization as context, the major focus will be upon the complex and invisible mechanisms which organizations use to coordinate and control their parts to ensure that individual and group

116

efforts are directed to organizational goals. Structure was one such mechanism dealt with earlier. Power and culture are equally important, and are explored here. In looking beyond the organization, at the market in which it operates, the discussion will necessarily be briefer. However the idea of customer is a crucial one, given the emphasis on a customer focus in many organizations today, and the importance, less often realized, of internal customers. And one approach traditionally used by those involved in marketing, SWOT analysis, also has applications in a much wider range of contexts. These concepts are therefore introduced, albeit briefly. One way of structuring your thinking about influences beyond the market, the wider environment, is also introduced.

By the end of this chapter you should be sensitive to some at least of the more important aspects of the contexts in which you are operating, and understand some of the ways in which they can influence you. In particular you should:

- Understand some of the issues concerning organizational goals, the extent to which these are shared, and some of the effects which these can have
- Appreciate some of the ways in which organizations influence, coordinate and control their sub-systems
- Be aware of major elements of the competitive environment of organizations and some of the effects these can have
- Understand some of the ways in which organizations may respond in order to adapt to changes in their environments.

What *is* an organization?

Why ask this question? Surely it is obvious that an organization is a legally defined entity, a set of parts which are designed to achieve a specified overall objective – the organization's mission. A widely quoted academic definition (Daft, 1989, p. 10) says 'Organizations are social entities that are goal-directed, deliberately structured activity systems with an identifiable boundary'.

This is the traditional view of organizations, sometimes called the 'RUGS' (for rational, unitary and goal seeking) view. This was the perspective from which Fayol was writing, and fits with the machine view of organizations described in Chapter 4. To achieve the overall goal, the organization is *differentiated* into a number of parts with manageable sub-objectives, and these parts are *integrated* by mechanisms for coordination and control.

But even Daft's unitary-sounding definition talks of a *system*. And you will remember that systems have features that are understandable only at the level of the system as a whole, so-called emergent properties. A system is *more* than the sum of its parts. This was at the heart of the rationale underpinning the approach. We have already talked of the way in which strategy can 'emerge' from the daily decisions taken by managers. There may also be a variety of goals which 'emerge' at lower levels. And there are other aspects of organizations such as their culture which might seem similarly to 'emerge' from the organization as a whole. To look at the 'deliberately structured' aspects of the system only may well be to omit much that is of crucial importance.

While you clearly need to understand the 'official' organization, you also need to be alert to less-visible *unofficial* structures which may exert an even stronger influence. As well as the official groupings shown on an organization chart there will be other groupings which are not so shown, but which nevertheless play a significant integrating or controlling role, supplementing that of official hierarchical relationships.

Organizations and their activities are complex, and simple control mechanisms are suited only to simple processes. The controlling and coordinating relationships within most organizations are far more varied than those of the management hierarchy alone. You need to understand all these relationships and how they work if your plans are to be successful. Important among such mechanisms are power, culture, reward systems and quasi-market forces. But all these need to be understood in the context of the general direction of the organization, and an understanding of organizational goals.

Do organizations *have* goals?

This may sound like a stupid question. We have already talked about the importance of organizational objectives. Daft's definition was of a *goal-directed* system, and the GS in RUGS is for goal seeking. Even the more organic metaphor had elements of control and objectives as central. There is, however, a very real question to be asked as to whether organizations, or merely the people within them, have goals. *Can* an organization have goals? Clearly, there will be some quite explicit goals both for the organization and for its component parts. These may be written into mission statements and strategic plans, and sub-objectives which need to be achieved if overall goals are to be met. They will be built into departmental objectives and objectives agreed with individuals possibly as part of the appraisal process. It is possible, however, even for some of these *official* sub-objectives to conflict with one another if planning has been poor. Even when such conflict does not exist it is possible that much of what goes on in organizations cannot be explained in terms of that organization's official goals.

You need to be aware of official goals, those which it is reasonable to describe as belonging to the organization. But the apparently stupid questioning of the existence of organizational goals should cause you to think about the extent to which official goals are what directs the behaviour of those within the organization, and about the other forces which are also operating.

Do you know what your organization's mission statement *is*? Do those you manage know? Have they thought about what it actually *means*? To what extent is their behaviour directed towards furthering organizational goals?

If this exercise sent you off to look up the mission statement, and then made you realize that it had little influence on your area of work, you are not alone. Many mission statements are so general that it is not altogether obvious what they imply, other than the vague hope of being 'best' at something, and the link between mission and an individual's goals may be far from clear. Even if people know and understand the mission and main objectives of the organization, and understand how their own objectives contribute to these, there may not be commitment to these objectives. Understanding the reasons for any lack of commitment may be an important part of defining a problem situation.

It is important, too, to be aware of any conflicts between official goals. If these have arisen because of poor planning or integration, and if those concerned are unaware of the conflict, this too may be a contributory factor in a 'mess' which is confronting you. Finding ways of aligning objectives, or at very least of minimizing the extent of conflict, may be a part of any successful way forward.

Unofficial goals and hidden agendas

By now you will be aware of the complexity of human motivation, and of the different sorts of rewards and contingencies that may influence behaviour. McGregor pointed out the importance of individual motivation and the need for management to align individual and organizational goals. Where they are not so aligned, *unofficial* goals derived from personal motives may be influencing behaviour. Sometimes this is openly recognized, sometimes such goals are not explicit and generate *hidden agendas*. Such goals and agendas may exist for groups as well as individuals, and at any level. To understand a situation you need to be alert to unofficial goals and hidden agendas. Conflicts between these and official objectives may be hard to resolve, sometimes impossible, but you may be able to contain their effects.

Sub-groups which work closely together are particularly likely to develop unofficial goals. You will remember in the discussion of teamwork that one danger of cohesive groups was that they could develop their own goals which might conflict with organizational objectives. The example there was of group limits on output. In one study of management accounting practices in a coal mine it was found that geological variations meant that output, despite the group's best efforts, varied greatly from week to week. Such variation would bring down senior officials to investigate, causing extra work for local management. The group therefore devised ways of secretly stockpiling coal from good weeks for declaration during weeks when output had been low. This enabled official records to show relatively steady output, and for local management to be left in peace. Such peace was clearly a powerful unofficial goal for this group.

When you are looking at organizational objectives as part of your investigation of a particular situation, or your planning of changes, it is important to identify both official and unofficial objectives, both of the organization as a whole and of key sub-groups and individuals within the organization who are involved with the situation. Official objectives will affect the desirability of possible options. Unofficial objectives may have a strong influence on their chance of successful implementation. You are unlikely to find it easy to identify unofficial objectives. Some you may be able to deduce from an understanding of the motives of those involved. Incorporating members of key sub-groups in any project team may also be important in order that their perspective, which includes such unofficial objectives, is built into your exploration of the situation.

Consider the group which you manage and any part of their activity that you identified earlier as not being directed towards official goals. Try to express unofficial goals which might explain that behaviour, and the rewards associated with achieving these goals. Test your understanding if possible by talking to some of the people concerned. Alternatively do this exercise for a group of which you are a member rather than leader.

The power to control. . . .

In looking at structure earlier we examined the different ways in which authority and communication lines might be arranged, and some of the implications of this. But although the idea of power is central to an understanding of organizational structure, it was not developed there. A senior manager in a major organization said that the distribution of power in the organization was the thing he had found both most difficult and most important to understand. While the distribution *may* correspond to the visible organization chart, complete congruence is unlikely. For there are many sources of power, and only one source is status. Other forms of power, with the ability to influence that they represent, are likely to be at least as important in an organization's control and coordination processes. In exploring the context of any situation which faces you, you need to be aware of where power lies, and whence it is derived.

Power derives from a number of sources, and can be exercised in a number of different ways. Handy (1993), for example, identifies five different sources:

- Physical power
- Resource power
- Position power
- Expert power
- Personal power

Physical power is frowned upon in organizations. Coercion by physical force or threat thereof would be cause for disciplinary and possibly legal action. This is not to say that it does not exist in organizations. Harder to prove but probably more common is the fear not of physical but of verbal abuse, and the power that this gives. Do you tread carefully around superiors, or even subordinates, known to be possessed of a bad temper, and agree with them rather than provoke their wrath? This can be a powerful source of influence but for the purposes of thinking about how to operate effectively when faced with the challenges of change, it may be more constructive to concentrate on other sources.

Resource power is a crucial one. The ability to give, or equally importantly to block, necessary or desired resources can give its possessor a huge degree of influence. 'Resource' does not mean the purely physical. Anything of value could be deemed a resource, be it pay, status, information, or contacts. Indeed, one of the most important 'resources' is continued employment. There are many situations where compliance is gained because staff fear that disagreement will cost them their jobs. Such fears may be the source of considerable power in many organizations. In less sinister mode, the increasing use of performance-related pay will give power to those who decide upon the level of performance achieved, if this is not objectively measurable. Indeed, control over any scarce resource can give power to the person with that control, even if they have low official status in an organization, though the sort of influence which this may enable them to influence may be restricted.

Workout!

Identify which 'resources' are important to you at work. These will include those physical resources necessary to perform your role effectively and important but less tangible factors. Now think about the control of these resources. Who derives power from having such control? How is this power exercised? What resources do *you* control, and over whom do you therefore have a degree of power?

Position is the most obvious source of power and does correspond to the organization chart. The essence of bureaucratic organizations is a clear hierarchy of authority, with rights including that to take certain decisions associated with each position. Some of these rights may be to resource power – for example, to distribute information, make decisions about promotion or bonuses, to distribute human resources between immediate subordinates. The right to *block* activity or resources may also be an important element. You will doubtless be all too aware of the extent to which your own superior has power over you. You may be less aware of its limitations, however. For example, in more bureaucratic organizations where rules and processes determine most activity there may be many areas of your behaviour over which your superior does not have control.

Expert power is that which derives from acknowledged and valued ability or expertise. It is different from the preceding two forms of power in that it is 'given' by those over whom it is exercised, rather imposed upon them. If your project team includes someone whom you all believe to know far more about one area than the rest of you, that person will be able to exert a major influence on your deliberations. You need to exercise a degree of scepticism, however. I have sometimes been impressed by colleagues who were so sure of their expertise that I bowed to their opinions on a number of occasions before realizing that their view of their own expertise was seriously inflated. This is yet another area where your own judgement is crucial. Some 'experts' may know less than you, though be far more confident about their expertise.

Personal power, Handy's final category, is interesting. In a sense it is a ragbag, the ability to exert an influence that cannot be explained by position, expertise, or control over resources. The non-experts who still manage to exert power by convincing you of their credibility may be using personal power, as may those who for no apparent reason seem to have the ear of those on high. It may be a mixture of credibility derived from other sources (past position or achievements), self-confidence, and the relevant interpersonal skills. While hard to explain, it is nevertheless potent, and identifying those who have it, and gaining their support, may be an important factor in getting a decision accepted or an initiative approved.

Using the power system

Because it is so important, it is worth spending some time identifying the sources of power in your own organization, and the individuals so empowered. While the power of those superior to you will be important, your analysis of the 'power system' in your organization will need to look at two other levels. You must become more aware of your *own* power, if you are to exploit it effectively, and also of influential colleagues on the same level as you. And you need to look at those at lower levels who have power. If you are wishing to gain acceptance of changes, these people above all will need to be convinced.

One interesting aspect is that power is essentially the *potential* to influence. Those who have it may not always choose to exert their power in order to influence. But they could do so if they saw advantage in this. For some the mere exercise of power is enough reward. These people will be easy to identify. But those who seldom use their power may be even more important as potential allies, and by thinking about sources of power you may be able to identify who they are.

Continue to develop the understanding of the power structure in your own organization which you started to work on in the previous section by including as many forms of power, at all levels, as you can identify. Think too about how you might *use* this understanding to increase your own influence.

So how useful did you find the list of sources of power as a way of thinking about this? Is it exhaustive? Did thinking about power suggest ways in which you might operate more effectively as a manager? As with the other frameworks covered, the list of sources of power is no more than a starting point. You will undoubtedly need to think quite deeply about how power is distributed in your own organization, and why. But because power is one of the most important 'invisibles' in your context it is important that you do develop your own model of the power structure of your organization, and constantly test this against your experience, expanding or revising it as appropriate. Without an understanding of this power structure, and of how you can use it to amplify your own influence by alliances with those with the relevant powers, your effectiveness as a manager may suffer.

Culture – the common sense of organizations

Power is one of the invisibles which helps organizations to control and coordinate their constituent parts. Another such invisible, and one which for many writers has power distribution as one dimension, is the idea of culture. Organizational culture has attracted a great deal of academic and business attention in recent years. Yet it has proved a slippery concept to define, and there are still major disagreements, even about such basic questions as whether you can do anything to change culture, or have to accept it as given. Despite this disagreement, there are important aspects to what is discussed under this label, and a general agreement that organizational culture can be a powerful integrating (and sometimes limiting) force. It is therefore worth teasing out some of the aspects of what people seem to mean by 'culture'.

The simplest definition of culture is 'the way we do things round here'. You will be most aware of culture when organizations merge or you start working for a different one. You may then start falling over ways of 'doing things' that are different. After a while you will absorb them, and cease to notice. Culture is thus clearly something shared by members of an organization. Intangible, it makes itself apparent indirectly, in the stories and jokes people tell, in organizational myths, in office layout, the meetings that are held and how they are conducted, and a thousand other ways. It can also be deduced from that which it would be unacceptable to say or do.

A more detailed definition, closer to the anthropological roots of the idea, refers to shared beliefs, meanings, values, ways of interacting and ways of working. You can see that this is very close to the constituents of common sense identified at the start of the book. Thus another possible definition of organizational culture might be 'that part of common sense that *is* common to members of the organization'.

There is therefore a strong reason for remaining alert to and aware of culture. It can be a powerful source of conformity, and thus a form of control. And just as the assumptions making up common sense can restrict creativity and flexibility when thinking about new and changing situations, so too can these aspects of organizations be restrictive. Some 'ways of doing things', and ways of thinking about them, can be powerfully conservative. Deviation from 'the rule' may be unacceptable action, or even thought. Some may make individuals so afraid of drawing attention to themselves that they avoid all initiative. Others may place individual needs above those of organization or customer, perhaps holding 'rules' in such scorn that gaining any kind of conformity is difficult.

There is an extensive and growing literature on culture, but what does it offer that will help you to understand relevant aspects of the organizations with which you deal? Managers find the topic fascinating, but it is not clear that they incorporate many of the ideas into their repertoire, possibly because the 'theory' that is taught on the subject tends towards the simplistic. The most quoted frameworks are extremely simple classifications of cultures. A small number (typically four to six) of different 'culture boxes' are defined and organizations are presumed to fit into these. The labels are often nicely descriptive (tough guy/macho and work hard/play hard are two of my favourites).

Possibly the most frequently quoted set of categories is that outlined in Handy (1993). Drawing on earlier work by Harrison he distinguishes between 'power', 'role', 'task' and 'person' cultures. A *power* culture is typical of a small entrepreneurial organization, with almost all the power (resource power and some personal power) located with the owner or chief executive, and all major decisions taken centrally. This sort of organization is highly responsive, though lacking checks and balances, it depends heavily on the central person's ability to decide on the appropriate response. If success leads to growth there are likely to be problems of communication and coordination, unless growth is by the spider plant method of creating almost autonomous sub-organizations, normally with finance as the connecting stalk.

In contrast to this highly centralized decision taking and power, a *role* culture, or bureaucracy, relies on a hierarchy of authority, with clearly specified roles, processes and rules. (Role is supposed to be a less pejorative term.) From earlier discussions you will be aware that such organizations offer consistency of performance, predictability and security to staff, and economies of scale, but are at risk from their lack of flexibility if their environment changes rapidly.

The *task* culture, with its net (sometimes matrix) structure, and emphasis on team working, getting the job done, and a combination of expert power and self-control was also discussed earlier. Its advantages of flexibility, responsiveness and job satisfaction have associated disadvantages of being difficult to control, and difficult to manage when there is competition for resources.

The *person* culture is focused on the individual, and rarely found in whole organizations, apart from small associations of professionals, but may exist in groups of professionals within organizations where a different culture is the norm. Universities have had a difficult time in recent years, and one senior manager likened his job of managing academics to the problem of 'herding cats': exemplifies the problems of this sort of culture or sub-culture. It works while the situation allows for individually directed activity to be advantageous to all, but if for any reason this ceases to be the case there is no-one with any effective power to take any sort of control action.

Identifying *your* culture?

Brief descriptions of the consequences of being in a particular box such as those above may be helpful in highlighting some of the ways in which culture can be exerting an influence. But as each author comes up with a different set of boxes, what conclusions are you to draw? Indeed, can you feel happy with squeezing any organization into one of a small number of categories (typically between four and six)? When culture has so many facets – beliefs, values, ways of deriving meaning from situation, ways of interacting and doing other things – all of them almost infinitely variable, how valid is such a sorting procedure likely to be? Handy points out, too, that different cultures may be appropriate in different parts of an organization, though this may present a challenge of integration.

You might well conclude that any simple categorization has to be highly dubious. As with other simple management frameworks, applying a label may give a spurious feeling of understanding. This could be counter-productive if you then stopped thinking any more about culture. If you mistakenly decided yours was 'wrong' and your organization needed to be moved into another 'culture box' the exercise might be positively dangerous. But it *is* potentially useful is to use some of the factors used in deriving the category sets, to explore where your organization sits on a number of dimensions. This may increase your awareness of some of the less obvious and intangible features of your organization influencing both what you can achieve, and how best to achieve it.

The following questions may prompt you to consider 'intangibles' which might otherwise escape your notice. You need not only to answer the question but also to think carefully about the implications of your answer. You will not come up with a neat label for your organization, but you may gain some insights into the web of beliefs and practices that contribute to producing behaviours you may wish to encourage or to change.

- How are senior managers viewed? For example, are they seen as gods, wisely directing things in everyone's best interests, demons intent on making everyone's life impossible, or remote aliens with no understanding of the organization and its employees?
- What about views of middle management? On whose 'side' are they seen as being located?
- What is it that gets people promoted? For example, is it keeping their heads down and serving their time, getting to know the right people, taking risks, technical competence and/or doing a good job?
- What are the main satisfactions employees gain from their jobs? Are they personal, or social, or derived from contributing to the organization's objectives?

- What sort of behaviour is valued and respected by colleagues? Is this the same as the behaviour which gains advancement?
- If there is a clash of priorities what comes first? For example, is it meeting deadlines, protecting staff's time or satisfaction, maintaining high quality, keeping superiors happy, meeting customer requirements?
- What sort of relationships are there between colleagues? Are they supportive, collaborative and/or competitive?
- How prevalent is team working?
- What is the balance between conforming to rules and specified processes, and taking initiatives and responding as seems appropriate to the situation?
- To what extent do individuals accept personal responsibility for their decisions, and how much feedback do they get on the results of these decisions?
- To what extent is it acceptable to make mistakes, provided you learn from them?
- What are the main sources of conflict and how are conflicts resolved? Is disagreement acceptable? Is power or negotiation more important?
- What is the power distribution in the organization, and the sources of such power? (You should know the answer to this one already!) And how great is the power difference between different levels in the organization?
- What are people most afraid of?

Use the questions to help you compare your organization with others you have worked in, or know of through friends. How can you characterize 'the way we do things round here' in your own organization? In other words, how is conformity of behaviour achieved through invisibles of beliefs, values, and agreed ways of operating? Are there additional questions which you need to add to the list above? In what ways is culture helping the organization to achieve its objectives? In what ways is it hindering?

You may well have felt that the questions gave but a small and insecure handhold on this particular conceptual rock face. If so, do not worry too much. Culture is one of the hardest of all things to grasp. We lack the vocabulary for a start. Many of the questions relate to structure and the related concept of power. They are far from the 'organizational myths' origins of the concept. Nevertheless, they offer a starting point. If you are still 'listening to the language' of your organization, as you started to do when considering whether it was mechanistic or organic, you may pick up further clues. If you keep asking yourself and colleagues what is *unsayable*, or even *undoable*, you may find further hints. Slow though the process of gaining awareness of this 'organizational common sense' may be, you need to be alert to its many dimensions, and the subtle control thus exerted.

Can you change culture?

This is clearly an important question, if these intangibles have the influence claimed for them. And from the many major initiatives directed towards changing culture it is clear that many believe it *can* be changed. But many of these initiatives fail, and this is understandable if culture is something which *emerges*, as a property of the system as a whole. This would mean that change is likely to be achieved only by changing a number of other aspects of the system. One of these aspects may be senior management! To the extent that values and beliefs of senior managers are reflected in the organization's culture, then changing these should result in cultural change. 'Corporate culture initiatives' are aimed at achieving just such uniformity, inculcating senior management's beliefs and values throughout all levels.

However, experience suggests that it is seldom this simple. Even when there is major change at the top, managers lower down in the organization, together with those they manage, often continue in the pre-existing culture. This can seriously frustrate the new 'team' who have been brought in to make changes! It is not at all uncommon for there to be quite distinct cultures at different levels and in different parts of the organization, though perhaps it is less common for this to be recognized. If culture is a form of organizational common sense, then difficulty in changing it is not surprising. You should by now be all too aware of the difficulty of changing your individual thought habits, and there has been no attempt at all to change your values! If it is so difficult for an individual, there is no reason why it should be easy for a group.

Hard though it may be, change should be possible provided enough of the things which contribute to culture are changed *in the required direction*. This means changing not merely the beliefs of senior management but of all those who work for the organization, making the desired behaviours (which are presumably what the culture change is all about) possible, and rewarding the new behaviours rather than the old.

Culture and structure

Structures will be a prime target for change. The structure–culture relationship is so strong that it is difficult to talk of culture without talking about structure. Indeed Handy (1993) illustrated the power/

role/ task/person classification by diagramming the *structures* associated with each. As you saw in Chapter 2, and indeed were probably already too well aware, organizations seem at present to be addicted to restructuring. Nor, indeed, is this a new phenomenon. Consider the following quote:

> It seemed that every time we were beginning to form up into teams we would be reorganized ... we tend to meet any new situation by reorganization. ...

You may feel that this mirrors your own experience exactly, yet the quote is from the Roman satirist, Petronius Arbiter, writing in the first century. What is more, he went on to say that such reorganization created 'the illusion of progress while producing confusion, inefficiency and demoralisation'. Does this also sound familiar?

Some of the structural considerations are obvious. Hierarchical forms of organization, as pointed out in Chapter 2, are inconsistent with a flexible responsive form of operating. Coordination by rule and process, which often accompanies hierarchies, giving the classic bureaucratic organization, is not going to allow a culture which values risk, depends upon personal responsibility, and is thus responsive and innovative. A more task-focused, flexible form of organization will be needed if a culture of responsiveness and innovation is required.

In thinking about how to change structures in order to change culture you will need to draw on the ideas in Chapter 2, and the discussion of power earlier in this chapter. Your understanding of motivation should help you to see how reward systems may also need to change if culture is to change. For unless the rewards within the organization are consistent with the 'meanings and values' and the 'ways of doing things' which the new culture is intended to incorporate, any attempt at culture change is likely to be doomed to failure. Rewards here will need to reflect social rewards and other intangibles as well as pay. And because expectancies are important, as well as the rewards themselves, employees will need to be convinced that the reward system has indeed changed.

A multiple approach to culture change

Successful culture change thus requires far more than an announcement and a video of the chief executive saying how important it is. This is unlikely to change the values held by everyone in the organization, and conservatism will be reinforced by existing organizational structures, reward systems, and beliefs about what is and is not important and acceptable. Thus you might well be sceptical of any culture change initiative failing to address all these aspects.

Culture's resistance to change does not mean you can forget it. Major change may be beyond your power, but just as strategy can emerge from a series of small decisions, culture can be affected by a series of small changes, provided that these reinforce each other. And sub-cultures may be easier to change than the culture of an entire organization. Furthermore, you need to be aware of culture just as you need to be aware of the components of your individual common sense. It is a key component in an organization's regulation of its activities, even if few are aware of it. It is therefore an extremely important part of your organizational context, and one which you need to work at understanding better if you are to work within it effectively.

The marketing environment

In deciding whether culture *needs* to be changed, the appropriateness of the existing culture to the context in which the organization operates is a major factor. If you look beyond the boundary of your organization, you can divide the environment into two further layers. The first is that which contains those factors to which the organization relates most closely, its customers, its potential customers, its competitors and its suppliers. This is sometimes called the marketing environment, though possibly with suppliers excluded. Our inclusion of suppliers is influenced by the systems approach, which often looks at a system as a way of transforming inputs into outputs. This puts suppliers of inputs on the same level as the purchasers of the outputs. Figure 7.1 shows this inner environment schematically.

Although you may not be involved in direct contacts with this inner environment, a broad understanding of its importance to your organiza-

Figure 7.1   The marketing environment

tion may be helpful. Thinking clearly about your customers, and their decision to buy, and the factors influencing this, may help you to contribute to debates within your organization. Even if not, one of the coordinating/controlling mechanisms within some organizations is the operation of a quasi-market, where you may be in competition either with other in-company suppliers or with external suppliers to provide whatever your section produces. If so, you need a clear understanding of your own internal suppliers and customers, and of the nature of the 'buying decisions' taken by the latter.

Whether your organization is operating for profit or is in the public or voluntary sector, the concept of market is relevant. Whatever the goal of the organization it will be doing something for *someone*, in exchange for the resources needed to do it. In organizations which have not traditionally thought in marketing terms, consideration of 'markets', 'customers' and 'competitors' may be a source of powerful insights.

Try to diagram your own organization's inner environment, identifying the main 'players' in each category. If you are operating in an 'internal market', try also to diagram your internal suppliers and customers. If you are having difficulty starting, think about the 'transformation' concerned and its inputs and outputs, where these come from and where they go.

Who are your customers?

In thinking about customers you should have thought about *who* they are, *what* you are providing, and *why* your own goods or services are chosen (or not chosen) in preference to those of your competitors within the industry or within your own organization. Your customers are those making this choice between you and the competition. Note that they may not be the end users or *consumers* of your product. Clearly, the more you know about your customers, the better. Information technology is now increasing the extent to which you *can* know your customers. Store 'loyalty' cards allow for highly sophisticated analysis of various characteristics of customers and their buying habits. The detailed 'consumer surveys' sent to households at regular intervals are another source. Organizations can now target their promotional materials at those most likely to respond.

But without the detailed technical knowledge which marketing pro-fessionals need for such sophisticated analyses, one or two basic ideas can help you think more clearly about how your organization is placing itself in its marketing environment, or how you are placing your own section within an internal market. The first such basic idea is the distinction between *customers* and *consumers* mentioned above. This highlights the potential separation of those taking the decision from those who actually use goods or services. This is the case whether you are supplying goods to the wholesale market or residential care to the elderly paid for by the local authority. If there is a customer/consumer split it is worth remembering that it is the nature of the customer which will have the most immediate impact on the decision to purchase. This chapter will talk in terms of customers, but if your organization has customers who are not consumers then you will need to remember both categories.

The buying decision

Almost all organizations are trying to influence some buying decision, whether 'buying' means tuning to a particular TV channel, deciding to visit an exhibition at a museum, applying to a particular university, or 'buying' a timeshare holiday apartment. The idea is equally applicable *within* organizations. If you run a training department you may be trying to encourage as many managers as possible to send their employees on the courses you provide (note that here the managers are likely to be the customers, their staff the consumers). If you run a warehouse you may need to convince senior management that it is more cost-effective to continue to use your services than to contract out the warehousing operation. Such internal buying decisions are becoming more important as organizations query the cost-effectiveness of their existing boundaries, and move towards 'contracting out' some activities.

To understand the buying decision it is important to know what is being bought. What *benefits* do you provide? The old example is that you are not selling a drill but the ability to make holes. But you might also be selling the prestige of owning the most sophisticated and most expensive drill on the market, with the status of being a star DIY practitioner. Well, maybe not, but substitute car for drill, and the importance of prestige becomes clear. Parker pens became far more successful when they realized that customers were buying gifts, not writing implements, and changed their marketing strategy accordingly.

If you do not understand what benefits the customer is *buying* it is easy to get things very wrong. If the main influence on their decision is economy, quality improvements, with associated price increases, will be a disaster. If a major benefit is prestige, it is not a good idea to aim to be the cheapest product on the market. A golf club that was struggling to increase its membership achieved this objective by putting up its prices significantly.

If you are involved with external customers, think about the benefits which they perceive themselves to be buying. Ask them to compare the benefits you offer with those offered by competitors. Identify any internal customers and ask them what they see as the main benefits you provide. Use this information to consider whether your efforts could be better directed.

This brief digression into the arena of marketing strategy should have contributed two things to the main thesis of the book. The first is a reinforcement of the importance of *perspective*. Clearly, the customer perspective is crucial if you are trying to understand customer decisions and influence these. This is true whether you are thinking of external or internal customers.

The second point to note is that a framework can be 'transported' from the situation for which it was designed and used in another. Often this can be extremely fruitful. Ideas of customer and consumer were developed as a way of looking at purchasers in the external environment, but can help you analyse your own job in terms of goods or services produced for internal customers, or non-purchasers who still provide you with the necessary resources. This may generate a different way of thinking about what you do, about priorities, and about how to 'sell' your 'product' more effectively in order to obtain the resources needed to continue producing it.

SWOT analysis

One other very simple framework is in common use when thinking about the organization's relation to its marketing environment. Again this is eminently transportable, and can be a helpful prompt to a different way of thinking about the operation of your own sub-part of the organization. SWOT analysis is therefore useful, whether or not you are involved in a marketing strategy for the whole organization.

Marketing and strategy are closely inter-related. Marketing means far more than selling: a simple definition refers to the process of identifying, anticipating and satisfying customer requirements profitably. But to do this in a competitive and changing environment requires a fine balancing act, and a continual matching of organizational capacity to market require-ments. And one of the ways of starting to think about how this can be done is to analyse the *strengths* and *weaknesses* of the organization, the *opportunities* and *threats* presented by the environment, and the relation between all these, that is, to carry out a SWOT analysis.

Strengths and weaknesses

These are features of the organization (or whatever you are considering as your system). As part of your 'system' they are things over which you potentially have some control, although your actions may well be constrained. Strengths and weaknesses are often the two sides of a single coin. This was expressed neatly as a paradox by Pugh, in his inaugural lecture on joining the Open University: organizations will have the strengths of their weaknesses, and the weaknesses of their strengths.

Thus a small and highly flexible organization may have responsiveness as a strength. The corresponding weakness may well be that it cannot offer economies of scale on large routine jobs. Conversely, the large machine bureaucracy will have major strengths if requirements are for a massive and standardized operation, but weak in meeting demands for a tailored and flexible product. Some organizations may be set up to deliver at the lowest possible cost products which are relatively unsophisticated and may vary somewhat from the specification. Others may work to very small deviations of output, but at a higher cost. For almost any strength there may be a potential weakness, of which you need to be aware. As ever, the search is for 'horses for courses'.

Identify the major strengths, as you see them, of your organization or other relevant system. Consider whether each strength has a corresponding weakness. Similarly think of your system's weaknesses. Can you express any of these in terms of their corresponding strengths?

In labelling something as a strength or weakness you were inevitably relating your own organization both to competitors and to customer demands. Strengths and weaknesses exist only in relation to what others can deliver and what the market requires. The ability to produce a wide range of mechanical calculators ceases to be a strength when the market moves on to electronic machines. Having a force of highly qualified service engineers is not a strength if others have similar forces, trained in more up-to-date techniques and able to offer a cheaper service. This is why even when looking at these more internally focused aspects of SWOT the competitive environment is important.

Opportunities and threats

The other two elements of the analysis refer firmly to the environment, though just as strengths and weaknesses made sense only because of the environment, so opportunities and threats are there because of the nature of the system in question. An opportunity for one organization might be a threat to another. Technological developments might be an opportunity for an organization with the financial resources to invest in them, and the flexible and trained staff to exploit them. To an organization lacking both they would present a threat. Opportunities and threats might develop out of changes in the inner environment, or from changes beyond this.

In trying to balance the organization's capacities with market demands, the aim has to be to exploit the potential strength of any characteristic, and minimize the impact of weaknesses, responding proactively to any opportunities and taking what defensive action is needed against threats that cannot be turned on their head, and made into opportunities. Figure 7.2 suggests the ideal path, of turning weakness into strength, using this to exploit opportunity, and ring-fencing non-exploitable threats to minimize impact. Of course, this ideal path will seldom be followed, but it is worth bearing in mind as a goal.

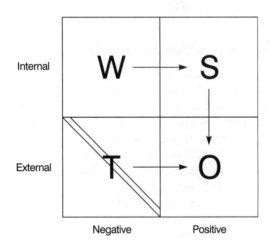

Figure 7.2   The strategic path through SWOT

Even if you are not involved in discussions about organizational strategy you can use the SWOT framework to think about your own sub-section of the organization. Here you would be looking at the wider organization, as well as the marketing environment discussed above, as a source of opportunities and threats, and restricting the consideration of strengths and weaknesses to those of your own section or department. The framework itself is again crude: you will need to do almost all the thinking yourself using the headings it provides as prompts.

Complete the SWOT analysis of your chosen system by considering its position in relation to the organization and its environment. What changes, if any, does this suggest you might make?

Suppliers

You can use your understanding of customers to look at internal or external suppliers by reversing the perspective. You become the customer taking the buying decision, and need to understand what benefits are important to you. If you know enough about suppliers to understand *their* perspective, and *their* marketing environment you may be able to identify their, and your, relative power, and exploit this knowledge in developing a mutually beneficial relationship.

The wider world in which an organization operates

Moving on to look at the environment beyond the marketing environment may seem a daunting task. Potentially you need to understand the world, and all that is in it and all that is likely to happen to it! Fortunately the systems definition of environment restricts the area of concern to those factors likely to have a significant effect upon the system, or to be significantly affected by it. This is still a potentially enormous area for many organizations, and some framework is needed as a starting point for it. A widely taught framework, which many managers find useful, suggests four major categories of factors likely to influence an organization:

- Social factors
- Technological factors
- Economic factors
- Political factors.

These are, for obvious reasons, referred to as the STEP (or PEST, depending on your preferred order or acronym) factors.

As with other simple categorizations, any attempt to fit the world into four boxes (why is it so often four?) is ambitious. It is often difficult to decide which box a factor fits into. To agonize over how to 'box' something is, however, completely to miss the point. While it may be satisfying to label something as 'an economic factor' it will not help you all that much. There is certainly a large body of economic theory. Some of it may be useful if you are dealing with the environment. But economic theory may also help you understand the likely impact of some factors labelled as social or technological or political. Categorizing is not the purpose of the exercise. The main use of the framework is to act as a prompt in identifying environmental changes likely to impact upon your own organization.

To give you some idea of some of the things which use these headings might cause you to consider, an extremely brief discussion of each follows. If the topic interests you, you will find more detail in most introductory marketing texts.

Social, or socio-cultural factors

A wide range of factors might come under this heading. Demographics, the statistics concerning the size, age and health of a population, is one. A hospital and a night club might both be affected by change in the age distribution of those living within their catchment area. Demographic factors affect both the potential number of consumers for whatever your organization produces (i.e. the marketing environment) and the pool of potential employees. Lifestyle changes such as increasing foreign travel, or most women now working outside the home, can have a huge effect. Changing values may have a major impact too. The growth of concern for the 'green' environment has affected markets as far apart as those for fur coats and washing-up liquids.

Try to identify socio-cultural influences on your own organization. What impacts have there been in the last five years, and what impacts are likely in the next five?

Technological factors

A dramatic change in recent years has been developments in information technology. As a manager these will almost certainly have had a direct impact on your own role within the organization. In some industries, for example financial services with the growth in direct banking and insurance, the impact has been huge. The possibility of whole areas of information processing work shifting to lower wage economies now exists, too, with the possibility of near-instantaneous transmission of vast amounts of data, so that jobs other than manufacturing are now shifting away from traditional locations within Europe. Even within Europe, work patterns may shift as a result of growth of interest in teleworking.

Other technologies have also changed. Biotechnology is a growing field capable of having major effects over a wide range of industries. Other new materials also continue to be developed which alter manufacturing processes or make whole new products possible.

Identify any recent ways in which technological factors have impacted on your own organization. Can you think of the most likely developments in the near future, and their likely impact?

Economic factors

Many of the economic factors likely to impact on an organization are fairly well known, and need not be detailed here. This does not always mean that changes in them are easy to predict, as both governments and organizations have found. Whether a country's economy is in a state of growth or recession will clearly affect organizations which operate in that country. Growth is likely to increase demand for goods and services, while reducing the labour available to an organization to produce them. Changes in interest rates and in inflation will impact upon an organization's finances, as well as on the market for many products. Exchange rates and taxation will also be important.

List the major economic influences on your own organization, as far as you are aware, and the direction these are likely to change over the next two years. Is your organization likely to be helped or hindered by these changes?

Political factors

Many of the managers surveyed for Chapter 2 pointed to major impacts of government action. Conservative policy with respect to the public sector, and the firm belief that market forces are the best regulator, have driven many changes. Managers referred to compulsory competitive tendering, privatization, producer–provider splits, and pressures on local authority funding. In the private sector, government policy on prescribable drugs was quoted.

It is not only national governments that influence organizations. The single market has meant that European legislation can impact on organizations throughout the European Union. Impacts of legislation will be wider than the area covered, affecting any organization for whom the area is a major market. European car manufacturers, for example, have found stringent US requirements for emission control (driven by consumer concern for health and the environment, a socio-cultural factor) a restricting factor.

There are many different forms of direct impact on organizations in the private sector, in addition to those via the effect on markets. Employment legislation may have a profound effect. The retrospective granting of pension rights to part-time employees is but one example. While some legislation may be easy to forecast (hence the major lobbying industry aimed at preventing some of it!), some may come as a complete surprise. Governments may make major changes in response to quite small issues if they perceive a tide of adverse publicity. Organizations can do no more than react, sometimes dramatically, when unanticipated legislation is introduced. Alertness to political factors may however reduce the number or surprises of this kind.

Consider whether your own organization is likely to be affected by government action in the next few years. Are you aware of planning which takes this into account?

The discussion above should have made you more aware of some at least of the factors external to your organization which may force it to make changes if it is to survive. Some of the effects of these were direct, some via impacts on the markets in which the organization operates. Unless you are a senior manager you may not need to forecast environmental changes and plan your organization's response to these in order to maintain its competitive position. But since many of the changes which you have to cope with will be driven by such environmental factors it may help you to understand better the reasons for some organizational initiatives. This understanding, if you can communicate it to your team, may help them to make a more positive response to the changes needed.

Summary

This chapter has attempted to alert you to some at least of the major influences exerted by three 'layers' of the environment in which you operate, the wider organization within which your area is located, its marketing environment, comprising customers (actual and potential) competitors and suppliers, and other factors which can influence the organization either directly or via the marketing environment.

When looking at the organization itself, structure, as discussed earlier, is one major factor. Another is culture, which can be thought of as the 'common sense of the organization'. Both will influence what you can and cannot achieve as a manager or as a change agent. Other sub-systems which you need to understand are the closely inter-related reward system and the power structure. If making changes, you will need to ensure that changes in different areas reinforce each other.

When considering the marketing environment it can be helpful to distinguish between customers and consumers, and it is essential to understand the benefits that customers value most highly, and are purchasing. Otherwise it will be impossible to understand, or to influence, the decision to purchase. Clearly, it is also important to know what benefits are offered by competitors. In order to maximize competitive advantage, this understanding must be combined with an analysis of the strengths and weaknesses of the organization, and the relationship between these and opportunities and threats presented by either the marketing or the wider environment. This 'SWOT' analysis can also be used to look at sub-systems of the organization, and to examine your role as a customer of your suppliers.

Within the far environment factors can helpfully be grouped into socio-cultural factors, technological factors, economic factors and political factors (easily remembered by the acronym STEP). These headings can usefully provide a 'shopping list' of potential factors to consider, but will take you very little further. Most of the information you need, and the ways that you process that information, will depend upon your understanding of how such factors work, in particular of those most likely to impact upon your own organization.

Chapter 8
Creativity in management

Models, definitions, prescriptions, labels, prompts and rational analytical techniques are all available to help managers manage better, but as the previous chapters have shown, they need to be used to extend your thinking rather than to limit it. It is very easy, for example, to do a simple SWOT analysis to identify the strengths, weaknesses, opportunities and threats facing you. It is much more interesting and exciting to begin to ask how to turn the threats into opportunities, to prevent the strengths from turning into weaknesses, to explore why the weaknesses are there. Other interesting questions could follow, such as 'What would a SWOT analysis of our organization look like if we asked our competitors to do it, or gave it to our customers to do, or the people in our customer services department, or on our reception desk?'

In this chapter we begin to look at creative approaches to management and management thinking. It begins with a brief examination of what is meant by creativity and creative thinking and the need for creativity in management today. It goes on to explore the question of personal style and how mindsets, prejudice and 'group think' can constrain problem solving and decision making in organizations. The chapter concludes by looking at the use of metaphors and pictures as powerful ways of communicating where words are inadequate.

By the end of this chapter you should:

- Recognize the value of creativity in management
- See that your own and others' mindsets and prejudices can be barriers to effectiveness
- Appreciate the value of metaphors and pictures as a means of understanding complexity and ambiguity.

The functions of management

If you have thought about, or studied, management (or even if you have read the first three chapters of this book!) you will be aware that there are a number of definitions of the key functions of management. You may feel that you are called upon to perform some of them rather more than others. You may also have begun to think about the fact that different managers have very different management styles; that they clearly feel comfortable in certain roles, and will perform less effectively in others.

My own feeling about management today is that it is often a fairly messy business which throws up complex situations requiring managers to possess and apply a range of management skills. It is not therefore something which can, or even should, be defined by reducing it to a number of key roles. Fayol's definition of management, for example, reflects certain fundamentals of the role as he saw it, but it seems unhelpful, in considering management effectiveness today, to restrict our understanding of what managers really do to these five broad elements. Fayol's description of the management functions which you read about in Chapter 2 may be a useful starting point for you if you have never thought about what management consists of in general terms. In this part of the book, however, you will come across metaphors and aspects of management which demonstrate the wider scope and potential of the modern manager's role.

Just as there is no such person as the 'typical manager', neither are the situations with which managers have to deal 'of a type'; mostly they are 'uncommon' in that they often have a dimension or a potential which is new. This is partly a reflection of the constantly changing and frequently chaotic environment in which management today takes place. But it is also because managers have to work with and through other individuals, each of whom has their own understanding about the nature of environment in which they work as well as particular behaviours which need to be considered. These differences need to be taken into account not because they must all be accommodated but because unless they are understood they can cause resistance and friction.

The art of management

Management is at least as much an art as a science. It has to do with crafting situations, with constructing frameworks, with orchestrating events. In a less turbulent environment it would perhaps have more to do with analysis, the application of a suitable model or formula and the careful observation of results. But, except for those managers who also have a specific professional role where these skills are used, the day-to-day experience of general management is likely to be less orderly. This is often because, if you are a busy manager, there is simply not time for such a systematic approach, even if it were appropriate. You need to rely upon other thinking skills just to get by. Clearly there *is* value in the analytical rational approach to the key tasks of management and this will be discussed further in Chapter 12 in relation to decision making. But the particular survival skills which you need are not usually those which are taught on management courses. They have to do with the way in which you approach the situations in which you find yourself, and how you think your way through them so that you can go on to deal with them effectively.

What we have argued throughout this book is that relying upon 'common sense' thinking is not enough and that the thinking has to be 'uncommon' because many of the management situations which you face each day are uncommon too. What you need to do is to think in new ways, to be ready to challenge your previously held assumptions and views so that you can become more receptive to new ideas and possibilities. Your common sense can soon become stale and overfamiliar. You can begin to react in predictable ways because you rely upon it too much *without* thinking. Think back to Figure 1.1 about what constitutes your common sense about management. This can be 'recycled' by the addition of new ideas and experiences to become the kind of sense which can cope more effectively with the uncommon situations which managers today continually face. The key to this is the ability to think creatively, so that you constantly reconstruct and expand the models that you develop to help you (Figure 8.1).

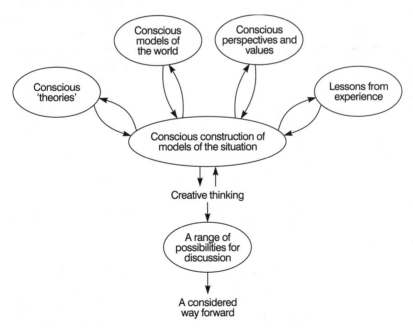

Figure 8.1   Using creative thinking

You may not think of yourself as being particularly creative and so, although you might agree that it would be useful to have some new ways of tackling management problems, you would prefer not to have to create them yourself. The creative techniques that will be introduced in this and the following chapters should help you to think in 'uncommon' ways about the kinds of situations that occur in management life. You do not need to be a creative person, you just need to be willing to 'think beyond the box' of your own existing management philosophy. By using a few very simple techniques anyone can develop their capacity to think creatively. And it is certain that in today's' management environment, with its ambiguities and uncertainties, you need more than just a 'common sense' approach. Thinking beyond whatever box we happen to be trapped in, whether it is the box of our personal philosophy, the box of our organizational culture or the box of our own self-image, takes some courage. However, failure to do so places severe limitations upon both individual and organizational effectiveness.

What is meant by creativity?

When you think about creativity or the process of being creative, it is probably those individuals working in areas of artistic endeavour who first come to mind; musicians, artists, dancers and writers, for example, where the word 'creative' is often linked with the word 'genius'. In the field of science, the creative genius would be an inventor or discoverer. Our initial thoughts about creativity in art and in science might lead us to assume that what produces creativity comes from two very different sources. In the artist it may be seen as a 'gift' or an exceptional talent. In the scientist perhaps a combination of exceptional intelligence, combined with prolonged application in a particular field of study, plus the occasional good luck in being in the right place at the right time to 'stumble' on a discovery. Our first thoughts, of course, do not discriminate, they generalize, and out of these two stereotypes has grown a kind of universal shorthand to describe people who are creative in both these fields. For example we may refer to someone as 'an arty type', and in the media, particularly the tabloid press, scientists are commonly referred to as 'boffins'. Yet within our two stereotypes of the creative individual, research has shown that there are elements of truth about what constitutes creativity.

One group of theorists has argued that creativity is the product of quite normal cognitive processes, such as recognition, reasoning and under-standing, but that what distinguishes creative individuals from others is their determined application to their particular field of work. It is clear that sudden inspiration or flashes of insight play only a small part in the creative process. So, although it is probably true to say that some individuals are by nature more inclined to be creative than others, if you disregard the view that creativity is a mysterious gift granted only to the few, it seems logical to suppose that with hard work and training, your own creativity could be developed.

Creative managers

Studies of creative people have noted that they have certain characteristics or skills in common:

- Good verbal communication skills
- A capacity for redefining problems
- The ability to ask appropriate questions
- Tolerance of ambiguity
- A willingness to take risks
- Openness to new ideas and perspectives

In the next two chapters you will be introduced to some techniques to help you to redefine problems and to generate ideas for moving beyond the problem situation but first we need to examine why it is that modern managers need to develop their creativity in order to be effective in their work.

It could be argued that, until recently, organizational life tended to preclude creativity by its managers, except possibly for those relatively few senior managers and chief executives who achieved their position because of their special entrepreneurial ability. Creativity begins by challenging assumptions and asking questions and ever more questions, and so it had no place in the machine bureaucracy. Typically, organizations were so structured that ambiguity for managers and others was minimal. Job descriptions, organization charts, procedures, regulations, checks and accountabilities, audit, appraisals, objectives and personal, team and divisional targets all determine the way in which we approach our management functions. So, although the external environment contained uncertainties, internally the organization was designed to eliminate them. They were not part of managerial life. Think of all the memos that you have received and possibly written for 'the purpose of clarification'. How often, when there was a possibility that you may have been misunderstood or misinterpreted have you sent a memo to 'cover your back'. In management life, ambiguity can be dangerous. And yet by insisting that the situation is only as you see it, that there is a reality and a certainty which can be defined, that your view should not be challenged, you immediately exclude the crucial creative question 'What if . . .?'

Risk taking

Neither was risk taking the preferred strategy for managers in traditional bureaucracies. Clearly defined objectives and established areas of responsibility and accountability ensured that managers did not take risks. Indeed, some organizations, and you may have worked in one of them, seemed driven by a collective fear of failure. Managers were typically judged and rewarded by their success in achieving objectives, not in coming up with innovative ideas, except in those organizations whose business was all about coming up with ideas, such as marketing and advertising. The focus was on past and present performance first, and future challenges second.

Today, as you have seen in Chapter 2, organizations are changing. Structures are becoming less hierarchical, work is carried out through cross-functional project teams, which form to carry out a particular task, then disband once the project is completed. Responsibilities and decision making are being devolved, employees are thus 'empowered' to act without referring up through the organizational hierarchy. The introduction of new technology has meant that we have begun to question old ways of working and look for new approaches and new alliances between groups of staff who would not normally have found themselves working together. The idea of customer service is being revived. The major UK supermarkets, for example, are competing with each other to find innovative ways of retaining customer loyalty, by offering additional services not usually associated with food retailing, or forming alliances with local bus companies to 'deliver' customers to stores which are not on normal bus routes. The external environment creates a climate of increasing change and uncertainty for organizations and individuals, and the focus has shifted to future challenges and opportunities. In this uncertain and 'risky' environment, organizations need managers who can think creatively.

Uncommon thinking

Unfortunately, the education system which most managers have experienced does not encourage uncommon thinking. Examiners award marks for producing standard responses to questions; scriptmarkers are provided with 'model answers'. The student who begins an answer by questioning the validity of the question does not succeed in the education system! Creativity is confined to certain limited subject areas, and children, for fairly obvious reasons, are not invited to question assumptions and values that are handed down either at school or at home.

We might speculate on whether this is an appropriate way of equipping young people for a future where the only real certainty is that there will be change, but that is not the business of the present book. It does seem to follow, though, that managers brought up in such an educational system may need help in developing new ways of thinking in order to manage effectively now and in the future. Charles Handy, in his book *The Age of Unreason*, calls this new kind of thinking 'creative upside-down thinking'. He goes on;

> New ways of thinking about familiar things can release new energies and make all manner of things possible. Upside-down thinking does not have to aspire to the greatness of Einstein or the all-embracing doctrines of Marx. It has its more familiar variants. . . . Upside-down thinking invites one to consider the unlikely if not the absurd.

Jay, talking about the creative manager in his book, *Management and Machiavelli,* comments that nowadays 'there seems to be a danger that managers are hiding behind the word management in order to fend off the idea of creativeness'. His point is that it is not enough to change things by copying the changes that others have made. In today's world of constant change, you have to change them before anyone else does. This, he argues, is creative change.

Creativity at work

If you are not working at a strategic level in your organization, you may be wondering what this has to do with you. Does not the kind of creative change that Jay is talking about fall into the realms of senior managers and chief executives, striving to keep one step ahead of the competition? However, all managers today are involved in change. If you think about the idea of the organization as an organism, where there is an interrelatedness between its various parts, you will recognize that even a small change in one part of the organization may disturb the equilibrium elsewhere. You will remember from the discussion in Chapter 4 that, like an organism, an organization as a whole is constantly responding and adapting to changes in its environment. It is this struggle to adapt and change which brings with it the kinds of management problems that are discussed in the next chapter, where 'traditional' management responses are no longer adequate. Managers today need to be quick-thinking, creative and flexible enough to adapt to new management situations.

It would be an overgeneralization to say that no organization in the past had the kind of in-built flexibility which seems to be the aim of organizations today. As you saw in Chapter 7, Charles Handy identified these flexible organizations as task cultures, operating in competitive environments where product life is short. Task cultures are also team cultures where individual status and objectives are less important than getting the job done or the project completed. However, most of us in the past worked in power cultures, where control is exercised from the centre by a few individuals, or role cultures (or bureaucracies) where control is exercised though rules and procedures, and position brings power. Handy likens this culture to a Greek temple, stable and long-lasting until the ground beneath it moves. And the ground is beginning to move. Chapter 2 described some of the changes which have been causing organizational earth tremors in recent years, but there will be others, unique to your organization, which will inevitably mean that the culture has to change.

As employees we tend to adapt to the culture in which we work, or move to one where we find a better fit. Since the majority of us used to work in role or power cultures it is not surprising that many managers have never been required (or allowed) to exercise their capacity to think creatively at work.

Leading with the right

But what is it that makes some people more inclined than others to think creatively? It has been thought for some time that the brain has two hemispheres which control the body's movements, the right side of the brain controls the left side of the body, while the left hemisphere controls movements on the right side. Furthermore, the two hemispheres process information in different ways, the left doing so sequentially and the right simultaneously. These two halves of the brain do not necessarily develop at the same rate, so, for example, some people become very skilled at linear, sequential analysis, while others rely upon seeing relationships and connections between ideas, and relate more to visual than verbal stimuli. More recent research has challenged this theory, but for now it is a useful means of discussing the way in which it might be possible for individuals to hone certain mental skills while neglecting others, in the same way as we can become expert at some practical skills simply through practice.

In less turbulent times, it was traditionally planning and analytical skills that were demanded and rewarded in management, even though these were only one aspect of what managers had to do. (Think back to Luthans' research discussed in Chapter 7.) Today we look for managers with 'transferable skills' because what is needed is flexibility. Planning and analysis place emphasis upon the ability to process information in an orderly and rational way. In left brain/right brain terms, the power of the right brain was not called upon in management and so was largely undeveloped. Until recently those managers who were valued were those who demonstrated that they could 'lead with the left'!

Henry Mintzberg, writing in the *Harvard Business Review,* points out that there are matters that our right hemisphere 'knows' instinctively because the thought processes involved concern the connections that can be made simultaneously and holistically in response to stimuli that our left hemisphere cannot express. If you are the type of person who is strongly intuitive, who has 'hunches' about situations and people without necessarily having any hard 'evidence' to support them, this may come as some consolation. It can be very frustrating for intuitives to try to persuade others to come to their view about a particular course of action, when the only rationale they can offer is that they 'have a hunch' about it or that they 'sense' that it is the right thing to do.

Using the whole brain

'I can't deal in facts,' a colleague of ours has cried. What he means is that at times he comes up with a possible way forward but cannot show the logical steps through which he went in order to get to that point. While he has developed strong analytical skills through years of working as a manager, largely in role cultures, his natural way of processing information is through the relationships and connections that he makes in response to a number of stimuli (often visual), plus a 'sense' of how they relate to the whole picture.

Mintzberg argues that today there is more to management than planning and that we need to appreciate more what he calls 'the relationship holistic processes'. He hypothesizes that 'the important policy processes of managing an organization rely to a considerable extent on the faculties identified with the brain's right hemisphere'.

What we argue in this book is that as management life becomes more fragmented, as the frequency of new demands made upon you in a single day increases, as technology creates the need for speedy responses rather than long deliberations, you need to develop your right brain skills. However, this does not mean that you must leave your well-developed analytical skills to wither away. As will become clearer when you go on to practise some creative techniques for problem solving in the following chapters, creative thinking is not loose thinking. It too relies upon the ability to analyse and evaluate the creative outputs to deliver effective solutions.

As a footnote to this section it is worth considering for a moment whether current trends in management training are making it more difficult to develop a personal management style. In the past the most successful managers were often characterized by their individualistic approach. Many of them were (and are) iconoclastic, some were exceptional decision makers, flamboyant risk takers who backed their hunches about situations and people; some were tyrants, riding rough-shod over the wishes and feelings of others, hiring like-minded people then firing them at will. The current move in management training is toward the development of sets of competences for managers at all levels. While the competences so far developed cover the range of management functions, the worry must be that the result could encourage the growth of identikit managers, competent on all fronts, sound and effective but managing 'within a box'.

The force of intuition

The colleague mentioned above relies heavily on intuition as he does his job. Isenberg (1984), in a study of how senior managers think, found that they use intuition in five distinct ways:

- To sense when a problem exists
- To perform well-learned behaviour rapidly and instinctively
- To synthesize isolated bits of data and experience into an integrated picture
- To check out the results of rational analysis
- To by-pass in-depth analysis and come up with a plausible solution

It is clear from this list that intuition is not just inspired guesswork, and that it does have important contributions to make to the various stages of dealing with problems, that is, recognizing that there is a problem, defining it, generating ideas, evaluating options and finding a solution.

Other researchers have suggested that there are ways of strengthening intuitive ability. They include techniques like meditation and mind-mapping. However, there appears to be no evidence yet that these techniques actually do increase intuitive powers. If you are naturally intuitive you should not feel reticent about using this ability in a management context. If you are not, then trying out some of the creative techniques described in later chapters may help you to develop related skills, such as that of seeing the patterns or relationships between ideas, which can prompt creative thinking.

Personal style

There are a number of inventories which measure personal style. One of those is the Kirton Adaption–Innovation Inventory (KAI) which measures creativity, problem solving and decision-making style. The inventory was developed by Michael J. Kirton as a result of his study of management initiative. According to his theory everyone can be placed somewhere on a continuum running from highly adaptive at one end to highly innovative at the other.

In problem solving, adaptors will tend to research a few ideas deeply, whereas innovators will range far and wide in their search for ideas. While it is not possible within the scope of this book to explore the question of personal style in depth, it is important for what follows to note that when it comes to dealing with the problems and related decisions which form the bulk of what a manager does, not everyone has the same approach. Figure 8.2 indicates some of the key differences between adaptors and innovators.

Adaptors	Innovators
Precise, reliable, methodical	Undisciplined, imprecise
Worry at resolving problems	Prefer to discover new problems to tackle
Tend to follow tried and tested routes	Query any assumptions made
Stick at tasks over long periods of time	Dislike extended periods of work on some tasks
Seen not to mind repetitive tasks	Dislike routine
Seldom challenge authority	Dislike rules
Have a capacity for absorbing details	Poor at dealing with detail
Like conformity and consensus	Tend to 'go it alone'

Figure 8.2   Some characteristics of adaptors and innovators

Read through the characteristics of each type and see if you could plot yourself on the high adaptor–high innovator continuum below. (If you wanted to find your exact KAI score you would need to take the inventory.)

High
adaptor _____ innovator

High

Now try to plot three colleagues with whom you work most closely or the individual members of your team.

It would be very surprising if you found that they could all be located on exactly the same point of the continuum as you. While clearly this is no accurate piece of research that you have carried out (it is based on your perception of them, which may well not agree with how they perceive themselves to be), it should give you an indication of why it is naive to expect that people will work comfortably together towards agreed solutions when their individual approach to what they are doing may be so radically different.

Kirton (1984) notes the differences in behaviour between adaptors and innovators and the correlation in personality characteristics between adaptors and innovators and those who are left-brain or right-brain dominated. Interestingly for those who are concerned with building teams or developing group consensus or support for a proposal, there may be a considerable amount of disharmony between the two (Figure 8.3).

To INNOVATORS adaptors can seem	To ADAPTORS innovators can seem
Slow moving	Liable to cause havoc
Stuck in a rut	Uncontrollable
Wedded to rules and systems	Uncaring about rules and procedures
Unenterprising	Arrogant
Bureaucratic	Loners
Part of the 'establishment'	Dismissive of standards of behaviour
Predictable	Unpredictable
Dependent on others	Intolerant of the views of others

Figure 8.3   Perceptions of adaptors and innovators

Prejudice and conceptual maps

It is clear from Figure 8.3 that individual behaviours have the potential to cause misunderstanding and friction in teams and organizations. We prefer to deal with people whose responses are likely to be similar to our own, who are, as Margaret Thatcher when she was the British prime minister described, 'one of us'. The selection process is not always an accurate indicator of whether someone will fit into a team. This is why an increasing number of companies are using psychometric tests as a way of finding out about a candidate's personal style. The danger, of course, of continuing to appoint 'like minds' is that friction will be eliminated completely and stagnation will occur. A certain amount of tension within a team can produce a creative energy, where ideas are critically examined and old ways of doing things are challenged.

All of us have personal prejudices about people, places and situations. These will be based upon and have been formed by our past experience. They are often irrational and we would find it difficult to justify them, but nevertheless they are very real. Legislation has been introduced in the European Union in an attempt to counter the worst types of prejudice over race, disability, gender and sexual orientation in organizational life, but prejudice can be very deep rooted. Not only may it be very difficult to eliminate a personally held prejudice, but people who have a particular prejudice may be blind to its existence. For example, while I might publicly deplore the existence of ageism, I might still find that my short-list of candidates contains no-one over the age of forty. This might be one of the 'values' components of my own 'common sense'.

Not all prejudices are so well documented as those mentioned above. They can be very personal indeed, relating to someone's accent, style of dress, or appearance. They may not always be negative. It is equally possible to be irrationally prejudiced *in favour* of some people, places or things. Our prejudices, together with our ideas, images, knowledge and understanding about the world are all part of our own personal reality. It has a particular meaning and importance for us and shapes the way in which we respond to others. Some researchers have called this a 'conceptual map' which we use in order to make sense of and interpret our experience. Conceptual maps help us to distinguish the important from the trivial, the familiar from the threatening. We rely upon conceptual maps as a speedy way of interpreting ambiguity; they provide a framework based upon our past experiences and a guide to how we should respond to new ones. We have not one map, but many, from which we can select one for use in the appropriate situation. They determine, to a great extent, the way in which we react to the events in our daily lives.

We rely upon our conceptual maps to synthesize and interpret situations we encounter, very much as we might a real map if we found ourselves in unknown territory. But, of course, personal maps offer only a very limited and subjective view of reality, since they are composed of elements of our individual experience. Conceptual maps, just like real maps, can be invaluable guides as we try to explore the ambiguities of management. However, in situations where we are under stress we are likely to put pressure on others to accept that this is the *only* view of reality. Maps help us to simplify the complexity of life, to reduce the mass of information that comes our way to that which fits in with our own personal reality. Unless we recognize that they are fallible and that they should frequently be checked and revised, they may lead to our having only a partial view of reality, seeing those things which confirm our view, rejecting or ignoring those which do not.

Mindsets

The danger is that if we do not use our experience to refine and extend our conceptual maps they can become part of a fixed and relatively limited thinking framework. Such frameworks are known as mindsets. They can apply to groups as well as individuals. For groups, it can be argued, there is value in sharing a common view of reality. It may have been reached after a considerable amount of 'storming', and once arrived at it acts as a template for the group's reaction to events and their dealings with others. New members joining the group will be ostracized if they do not rapidly conform to this view of reality. However, group mindsets, or 'group think', can be as limiting and limited as personal mindsets.

It is easy to see why busy managers, trying to deal with the complexities of management life, might be unwilling to examine and challenge their own mindsets. They are a significant part of an individual's management 'philosophy'. Their effect is that managers will tend to play down or disregard information which does not fit with their view of reality; under pressure, they select those facts which are consistent with their mindsets, focusing on what they expect to find, not what is really there.

Mindsets are often used as a convenient short-hand, as in statements like 'we all know that our finance department are a bunch of idiots' or 'there's nothing wrong with the product, its just not marketed properly'. There may be little evidence to support these particular versions of reality, but nevertheless they are used without thinking and tend not to be questioned. One of the most powerful words in the vocabulary of a *creative* thinker therefore is 'Why?'

Creative thinking has to do with discovering the possibilities in a situation, looking at it from new angles and different perspectives. Mindsets inhibit this process. They induce us to look only for the familiar and that which conforms to our notion of reality and to overlook or reject other possibilities. They imply that we look backwards rather than forwards. Gareth Morgan (1988) talks about the need to develop 'proactive mindsets' which encourage us to look ahead, to identify opportunities as well as problems, and to look for ways of reframing problems so that we discover positive avenues for development. There is more about this way of thinking in the following chapters.

Removing the mindsets

Happily, though, the *blocks* caused by mindsets can be dissolved and some of the techniques which follow will help you to do this. Sometimes simply encountering a real crisis which cannot be interpreted with reference to any previously held map or mindset will be enough to expose their limitations. However, when the ambiguity is so great that familiar patterns of understanding are no longer helpful, people become extremely stressed. This is particularly so in times of major organizational change.

Nevertheless, it never easy to change the mindsets themselves, partic-ularly when they relate to the views that we hold about our own capabilities. The first step is to recognize that they exist. This is an important point to remember, for example, when talking to people at work about their performance. It may be that the mindset is so strong that they consistently misinterpret signals and communications from colleagues in order to reinforce their view of themselves, for example as victim or hero.

List three negative opinions that you have about yourself. Now try and reframe them so that they read not as negative but as positive statements. For example, you might reframe 'I am critical' to 'I have high standards'.

Of course, if you can reframe negative statements you can also reframe positive statements so that they appear as negatives. For example, 'I always complete every task that I begin' could be reframed as ' I get bogged down in trivia and ignore the needs of others around me'. It might be worth repeating the activity above with some of the positive beliefs that you have about yourself. It may be that some of your colleagues or family have placed negative values on these.

Establishing a shared view

As a manager you need to be aware of the power of mindsets and the ways in which they can prevent creative responses in situations of ambiguity and change. First, you should recognize that your own ability to think creatively may be hampered by your personal mindsets. Second, you need to remember that the people with whom you work, both within and outside your team or your organization, will have mindsets of their own which may not accord with your own view of reality. This has huge implications for the way in which we interact with others. It means, for example that you need to spend time establishing 'the givens', that is, those areas where there is a shared vision of what is. It also means that you may need to find ways of checking out your own beliefs about yourself as a manager; what you regard as evidence of strong leadership may be seen by others as a refusal to listen to anyone else's point of view.

It is not always easy to gain an understanding about where other people are 'coming from' and what their perspective is. Taking a systems approach can be one way of exploring the range of different perspectives on a situation. Another way is through the power of images, either verbal or visual. The next section looks at how pictures and metaphors can help us to communicate about and explore management situations.

Images and pictures

It's said that a picture can paint a thousand words, but you don't need to be a Monet to convey what is in your head. A few lines can powerfully demonstrate your feelings about a situation. For example, when I am tutoring a group of students I need to know something about their experience of working in an organization. I know what *I* mean when I talk about organizations but it could be a wholly different view from theirs. My understanding was derived, in the main, from those organizations that I have been employed in, as opposed to those that I have read about and worked with. So when I speak about managers in organizations I have a specific image in my mind. By getting students to draw how they 'see' *their* organization I can begin to understand their own personal perspectives. Figure 8.4 shows some of the very different images of organizations that managers have drawn.

Draw your own picture of how you see your organization. Ask people that you work with to do the same and then discuss the similarities and the differences. Try to gain an understanding of why the 'picture' of the organization appears different to others and, where individual pictures are similar, consider in what ways this shared vision might be helpful.

Pictures can be a very effective way of reaching a group understanding of a problem or a strategy. They can act as a record of things as they are, or seem to be, and also a vision of the future in which certain components

Figure 8.4   Three images of organizations

of the picture take on a symbolic meaning for the group. A picture can generate much creative debate about what it represents to each member of the group. For example, a group working on a strategy for the future might begin with a picture of a road, as symbolizing a journey, as in Figure 8.5. There might be debate about why the road is imagined as straight and smooth, it could be winding and full of pot-holes and other hazards. The group might consider whether the road is really taking them towards a bright new future or leading them round a blind corner. The road might have junctions and turnings, which look attractive and might make the journey faster or more rewarding in other ways. And so on.

Figure 8.5   Roads to the future

Try creating a picture of a common problem with some of your colleagues. You should begin by getting each person to think about things that symbolize the situation for them and then to assemble these into a picture on a large piece of flipchart paper. The individual pictures can then be discussed among the group and the symbols explained and labelled. The group should then agree to work with one set of images to which they can all relate and to create a new picture using these, exploring each aspect of the picture to check their understanding of the causes and dimension of the problem. The result should be a shared perspective on the problem situation, which is an important first stage in problem solving.

Metaphors

Pictures can provide a very vivid and immediate impression of an individual's understanding or perception in a way that words cannot, and many people commonly use word pictures or metaphors to communicate with others. For some, metaphors are a habit of speech; these people tend to think 'visually' and so they also speak in pictures. Metaphors can be a very creative way of communicating, offering new insights into a situation or problem. The example which I remember from school is 'King John was a lion in battle'. This meant that all the attributes that a lion possesses could also be ascribed to King John. So we might think of nouns such as bravery, aggression, prowess, stature, ferocity and so on.

You have encountered the two most commonly used metaphors for organizations in the first part of this book, the organization as machine and the organization as organism. Although you will often find organizations referred to in terms of one of these two metaphors, you do not have to accept them as the *only* ways of thinking about organizations, especially your own. The importance of metaphors is that they provide insight, enabling us to see, and so understand, situations in a new way. Just as there is no single conceptual map which represents a 'true' reality, so there is no single metaphor which is right.

Metaphors are best used as tools for greater understanding, rather than as a short-hand for fast communications. There are many metaphors which have entered the language of management, often taken from military or naval life, from war or sport, but overuse has debased them so that they no longer capture or stretch the imagination. We talk about starting with a level playing field, running something past someone, giving ballpark figures, sailing close to the wind, and you will still find references to the 'captains of industry' in articles in the business press.

Using metaphors creatively

Gareth Morgan has written extensively about the creative use of metaphors in management in two books, *The Images of Organization* and *Imaginization* in which he offers his own metaphors of organizations. He makes the point that traditionally when thinking about a particular organization we do so in terms of the roles of the people within it, and if we draw this we concentrate on putting down boxes with lincs linking people and the activities that they perform. Morgan says that while this can be a useful mapping exercise, '. . . it can also be incredibly limiting, locking us into linear and rather reductive patterns of thought. As we sketch, we split and shape complex activities into neat and tidy parts, tying the process of organization to a variation of the mechanistic-bureaucratic mode.'

Morgan invites his readers instead to use the spider plant as a metaphor for their organization, noting down characteristics of this plant and parallels in their organization or unit. The point about the use of metaphor to help creative thinking is not that you should necessarily search until you find the most apt word to encapsulate your ideas. You can gain much creative insight through selecting a random word and then forcing yourself to draw parallels.

Try using a metaphor as a prompt for creative thinking. For example, you might think of your unit in terms of a fountain pen, and note down its characteristics.

Characteristics of a fountain pen   *Parallels with my team/unit*
Useful
Needs regular supplies of ink
Streamlined
Easily dismantled
Can leak
?Old fashioned
Stylish
Helps communications
Can dry up without notice

These are some of the ideas that occurred to me, but you may have others. The next step is to look for parallels with your unit. You may not find these easy to come up with, but note down any thoughts you have as you force yourself to explore your unit in terms of these characteristics. The aim is to encourage you to think in uncommon ways about, in this case, a situation which is very familiar to you. So, for example, you might wonder about the 'ink' which enables your unit to function. You might ask whether your team really is as streamlined as it might be; whether its present structure does make communications easier, and so on.

When you have completed this, try using other random words as metaphors for your own organization or unit. You may also like to try this activity with colleagues to see what insight you can gain into your work environment.

One word of warning before closing this chapter, metaphors can distort reality if you are not careful. Going back to the one I began with, that of King John as a lion, I listed only the positive attributes of a lion, but lions, of course, can also be cruel, arrogant, untrustworthy, and dangerous! King John may have been all of these things too, so it is important to make sure that you do not use word pictures which could be misinterpreted or ambiguous.

Summary

This has been a very brief examination of the need for creativity in management. While the main theme of this book is that managers today need to develop the ability to think in uncommon ways in order to survive, you need to remember that you do not work in isolation. Other people have very different, and possibly equally valid, perspectives on the situations that have to be addressed. Your personal conceptual maps help you to make sense of reality *as you see it*. They are both a strength but also a potential weakness when individuals assume that their version of reality is the only one, and forget the powerful influence that other people's prejudices and mindsets can exert.

Each of us also has a strong self image of ourselves as a manager. This needs to be confronted and possibly reframed if we are to gain a real understanding of our strengths as well as our weaknesses. This process of challenging our personal mindsets is a key part of developing our organizational effectiveness.

Pictures, both visual and verbal can help to extend our thinking and understanding, on a personal level as well as in our interactions with others. Using metaphors is just one of the techniques for pushing our thinking 'beyond the box', forcing us to challenge routine assumptions that we make about situations or people and to consider them from new angles.

In Chapter 9 you will be introduced to the kind of typical problem scenario with which any manager might be familiar and will discover why neither 'common sense' nor management theory alone provides an effective way forward. You will also be able to try out some creative problem solving techniques for yourself.

Chapter 9
Looking into problems

Few managers leave work at night and then forget about it until the next day. They are frequently preoccupied in non-work time by problems that relate to their job and the need to decide what to do about them. Even though you may not have to tackle the kinds of large-scale strategic issues which are crucial to the future of your organization, you will certainly confront, on a daily basis, situations which prevent the effective performance of that part of it for which you have management responsibility. And you will have a sense of unease until the problem situation is resolved.

However, the problem situations which are a feature of management life are often ill defined and vague. Part of the unease is that you sense that you haven't 'got to the bottom' of the problem. But there is pressure to come up with a solution fast and to make the right decision. Because problems can be such a distraction and failure to resolve them can be so destructive, it is essential that before leaping in with solutions you are certain that you are addressing the *right* problem. Sometimes you only *think* you are thinking about it when what you are doing is ignoring it and trying to find a common sense solution. A much more effective approach is to spend time defining the real problem and thinking creatively about where its roots might lie.

We have talked about a number of management functions so far in this book, but one of the key tasks for any manager which hasn't been yet been mentioned is to *formulate* problems. This may seem a perverse idea, when much of what a manager does seems to relate to resolving issues, smoothing out difficulties and trying to ensure that problems do not arise. However, truly effective managers do not wait for problems to arise. They anticipate them. They go beyond this and, focusing on a vision of the future, pose the problem 'How can we find a way forward?'

This chapter and the one that follows are about how to become smarter in your approach to dealing with problems. Some key points about the dangers of relying upon your common sense to tackle management problems are illustrated with reference to a short scenario. The chapter ends by introducing some simple creative techniques which you can use for defining problems. By the end of it you should:

- Have learnt something about your own approach to problem solving
- Understand why a common sense approach to solving problems may be inadequate
- Recognize how essential it is to address the real problem which may be different from the one on the surface
- Be ready to think creatively about problems

Difficulties and problems

Often when people talk about having a problem at work what they really mean is that they have encountered something which has unexpectedly occurred and is preventing some process from taking place or reducing its effectiveness. For example, you might say that you have a problem with the central heating at home or with your PC at work. However, not for a minute do you think that this 'problem' is unique or going to be so complex that it may be impossible to resolve it entirely. In a situation like this you will usually call in an expert and the problem will be solved. The non-performance of the central heating or the PC is a difficulty rather than a problem.

Difficulties occur every day in management life too. They create obstacles to progress and may take time to resolve, but with the help of someone who is familiar with these kinds of difficulties they can be fixed. Management *problems,* on the other hand, are complicated, sometimes seemingly intractable. They may be unique and they will almost certainly involve people. There are no obvious experts who can solve them, although you may want to discuss them and take advice from others. But because you are a manager you are expected to be an expert 'problem-solver', to find a way forward even in cases where there seems to be no obvious acceptable solution. The reality is that management problems are notoriously difficult to solve and require the right-brain thinking skills which are ignored by most management courses.

The characteristics of management problems are:

- They involve a high level of uncertainty
- There are no previous precedents to follow
- The variables are difficult to predict
- The 'facts' are not easy to ascertain
- There could be a range of possible options to take, all of which seem plausible
- There is pressure to come up with the 'right' answer swiftly.

Because a management problem is typically very complex, it is understandable that individuals try to reduce the complexity by considering only a part of it. Reducing the problem boundary reduces the intellectual demands. It limits the number of possible courses of action and makes the decision process both simpler and faster. It does not, of course, mean that we arrive at the best solution to the problem.

Bounded rationality

Herbert Simon, about whom you will read more in Chapter 12, writing in the 1950s about decision making, argued that most individuals most of the time are concerned with looking for a way forward that is 'good enough'. Only exceptionally will they be setting out to optimize. Because the human mind has a limited capacity to deal with complex problems, people do not attempt to scan all possible alternatives, they aim simply to 'satisfice', taking into account relatively few factors and thus reducing a highly complex world into something simpler and more comprehensible. The rational model, on the other hand, which is discussed in the same chapter, assumes that an individual selects from an infinite number of possibilities the best possible course of action.

Simon's theory of 'bounded rationality' was corroborated by later research into the capacity of the human brain to process information. It seems that because our brains have limited information-processing capacity we *deliberately* adopt a strategy of 'satisficing', to select the first alternative which meets a certain standard of satisfaction and then search no further. Because of the pressure upon managers to provide 'a quick fix', there is a tendency to find a solution before the problem is really understood. In addition, the emphasis on judging management performance in quantitative rather than qualitative terms makes managers 'solution-minded' rather than 'problem-minded', closing down the problem to limit the search for a solution rather than examining the full extent of the problem first.

This is highly significant in considering your approach to dealing with the complex problems that are a feature of management life. Simon's theory suggests that each of us sets out to adopt a simplified model of reality and then only manages a limited search for a way forward. This approach can lead to further problems; part of the process of simplifying can be to ignore the perspective of others, to fail to dig below the surface to investigate the root causes of the problem situation and to opt for the first course of action which suggests itself. Often you discover too late that you have been working on the wrong problem or on a very limited aspect of a much more complex one.

Presented problems

Most of us feel negative about problems because there is a sense in which they are thrust upon us; they interfere with what we are trying to achieve, they hold us back, they get in the way. Sometimes they are really only difficulties; sometimes they are very complex 'messes' indeed. These *presented problems*, handed to us by the unforgiving outside world, are only one kind of problem, but they are the ones which most reduce our feeling of being in control. They often relate to issues which are in themselves quite trivial, but they can have very deep-seated roots. Frequently these have to do with the way in which people cooperate with and respond to each other in the organizational environment.

The functioning of an organization is dependent upon people cooperating with each other. It is often something of a puzzle as to why people do cooperate as much as they do, especially when the structure of the organization or the strategy being followed seems designed to make this as difficult as possible. As organizations become less hierarchical and people are required to work in a less structured, more flexible way, there is often less certainty about what exactly is expected. Uncertainty and ambiguity can cause tensions and problems as people adjust to new ways of working. No amount of planning can prepare you for these problems. Even those managers who are closely in touch with the individual members of their team on a daily basis may not be aware of growing interpersonal conflicts. What follows is a short scenario which illustrates the kind of presented problem that can occur when working relationships start to break down. It was chosen because it is a situation which will be familiar to many managers. Read through the scenario and then try the workout which follows.

You are the manager of a team of people who are part of a small European company which sells pharmaceutical and surgical products required for use in hospitals and in general practice. The head-quarters of the company is based in the USA and there are further subsidiaries in Germany and Switzerland. Before being taken over two years ago yours was a small family firm engaged in the manufacture of one or two very specialist products. Since the take-over most of the products are made in the USA and Germany and the range has grown enormously. You run a customer support team, whose role is not just to sell the product but also to train the users so that the product then performs as specified.

There are four members of the sales team, each responsible for a geographical area. Together the whole team covers the south of the country and there is some fairly fierce competition between your team and the ones covering the north and west when it comes to sales figures.

The members of the team are as follows. John is in his late forties. He was born and brought up in the USA and worked for the parent company for the last 10 years. He is with you for a 3-year secondment. Christine, the youngest member of the team, is married and with a recent MBA. Mario joined the company just after the take-over. He took a degree in chemistry as a mature student and this is his first job as a graduate. The final and oldest member of the team is Robert. He has been with the company for 18 years. Before going into sales and marketing he was a pharmacist.

Because a significant part of the job is to provide after-sales training for customers and to keep users' skills updated, the team has to work closely together to devise and deliver in-house training programmes. Each member of the team is office-based. Robert and Christine share an office and a secretary on the first floor of the building, next to reception. Mario and John work in an office on the ground floor, near to the cloakrooms and coffee machine.

Up to now the team has worked well together and you put it down to the fact that they have compatible skills and a wide range of experience. However, when you are doing Robert's appraisal he suddenly announces that he cannot go on working in the same room as Christine any longer. It turns out that communications between them are so poor now that they either write formal memos to each other or leave messages with Paul, their secretary.

Robert tells you that Christine is trying to squeeze him out of his job. He wants to know what you are going to do about the situation and what support he can expect from you as the manager.

What action would you decide to take in the short term to satisfy Robert's expectation that something will be done? Use the space below to write down what your immediate response might be.

_____

_____

_____

_____

_____

_____

Your response to the scenario

At this stage you have no understanding about what the real problem is, so your immediate response should have been that you needed to find out more about the problem situation. Presented with a problem like this it is tempting for managers to act in accordance with their own 'common sense' and come up with a quick solution. But remember, your common sense consists of your own personal values, prejudices and assumptions. And the problem has been presented from a single perspective. If you start considering possible solutions at this stage they are unlikely to address the real underlying problem or problems.

Thinking 'uncommonly' about problem situations like the one in the scenario, however, should raise a number of questions. For example:

Whose problem is this?
What other perspectives might there be on the problem?
Are there any theoretical frameworks which might help me to think about the problem?
Are there any creative techniques which could help me to uncover the real problem?

The answers to these questions will not help you to solve the problem, but they will help you to explore some of its complexities. Now, it may seem strange to suggest that in order to be more effective you need to increase the level of complexity with which you are dealing. As Simon and others have pointed out, our aim is usually to make the complex simple so that we can comprehend it. However, problems which relate to complicated human beings with individual values, motives and needs, working in highly complex organizations are *never* really simple even though they may appear to be about a single issue. And taking a presented problem at its face value can mean that the best you can achieve may be a partial solution. You might even make the problem worse.

Getting to the roots of a problem

Presented problems, such as the one described above, have roots which cannot be seen. Think of these problems as weeds and use this metaphor to consider the nature of organizational problems. Presented problems, like weeds, spring up in places where they are often difficult to tackle; they can be tenacious and deep-rooted. Some of them grow at a rapid rate and shed seeds in all directions. Others appear small and insignificant above the surface, but they may be supported below by elaborate root systems and can quickly establish themselves elsewhere. Dealing with that part of the weed which you can see does not address the underlying roots; although it may appear as if the problem has been eradicated, those roots remain and go on producing more weeds. In fact sometimes, as you will know if you are a gardener, hacking away at the visible part of the weed above ground only serves to stimulate growth from below the surface. The result? More weeds!

If the gardening metaphor has made you think that you can use a fairly heavy-handed approach in excavating the roots of a problem then stop and give this some more thought. This approach might work in an area which is full of weeds, but the image I had in mind when writing this was of a weed growing in an otherwise healthy and productive garden. As you probe below the surface to find the roots of a problem, you are inevitably going to create some disharmony and unease. You need to be careful that, as you rush to tackle a weed, you are not in danger of destroying the delicate root system which supports a healthy plant growing alongside it. In responding to presented problems, you also need to tread warily. Remind yourself about Herzberg's Two-factor Theory, for example, and how factors such as interpersonal relationships and working conditions can become positive dissatisfiers and affect the motivation of individuals in a team.

The problem owner

You may have noticed that a curious phenomenon occurs in organizations when problems arise which relate to the way in which people work together. The first thing that happens is that one of the participants will decide to pass the problem up the line so that the manager, like mother, can 'make it better'. The manager then becomes the problem owner and is left with the unenviable and sometimes impossible job of acting as arbitrator or judge, and of raising expectations that they can make the problem go away. This is one of the management roles that you don't learn about in business schools!

One creative response to the scenario above would be to involve the whole team in resolving the problem, getting them to recognize that they are the real 'owners' of the problem. The emphasis would then shift from trying to apportion blame to reaching an understanding of each other's perspective on the situation. The team could then work together to identify the real problem area and then to generate ideas for a way forward. They may not be able to achieve this without some help and facilitation, but the way forward would stand a better chance of being accepted than one imposed by 'mother'.

The owner of the problem is not just some one or some group of people having an interest in the problem. The problem owner(s) must have the ability and the authority to implement a solution. Managers, especially middle managers, often seem to become the repository not just for problems pushed up to them from below, as in the scenario. They are also the natural home of problems delegated to them from above. One of the first tasks is in every case to identify who really is the problem owner and to involve them from the start.

The question of perspective

Often problems are presented from a single perspective and it is important to gain a range of views about each situation. The aim is not to add to the complexity but to seek clarity. Individuals have their own conceptual maps which help them to make sense of where they are. They will have prejudices and mindsets which will prevent them from 'seeing' a situation from any perspective other than their own. You will only be able to build up a 'true' picture by looking at the situation from other angles. It is essential for you to do this in order to be clear about the nature of the problem you are addressing. Sometimes the process of finding out what perspective others have on a situation can help you to recognize how your own particular prejudices and mindsets have distorted your own perspective!

There is a further reason for asking individuals for their views about a problem situation. There is a sense in which each one of us feels that we are the central character in every organizational drama. It should not surprise us therefore when people react badly if they feel they are being treated as if they were an extra and that their contribution is insignificant. Understanding this is a key to effective management. Even if you do not *share* the other person's perspective, it is important to recognize that it is valid for them to have one. Creative approaches to problem solving therefore begin with trying to extend the problem boundary by collecting as many perspectives and as much data as possible.

Learning from the scenario

Before moving on to consider problem solving it is useful to remind ourselves of the other factors which can make your thinking about problems more effective. The scenario brought together a number of themes from earlier chapters in the book and underlined the need for 'uncommon' thinking when addressing the kinds of situations which constitute so much of management life. There are three key areas of theoretical understanding which you would need to have as a framework for thinking about a problem situation such as the one described.

The organization as an organism

First, an understanding is required of how organizations behave and, in particular, of how your own organization behaves. The organization described in the scenario, for example, does not seem to operate as a hierarchy; team work is very important and individuals and teams need to have a fair amount of autonomy over their day-to-day working with clients. In an organization like this therefore any attempt to *impose* a solution or reduce the flexibility which exists would be strongly resisted. As you saw in Chapter 7, the prevailing culture of an organization influences the way in which the people working in it behave and how they respond to change. A solution that was counter-cultural would therefore be ineffective.

In thinking about a problem which involves the interrelationships between people in a team you might want to consider the particular metaphor that different individuals may have of the organization. It may, for example, be that for some people their own personal reality is the model of the organization as machine and they feel out of place in an organic flexible organization.

The organization as a system

Systems thinking should alert you to the fact that it is essential to obtain a range of views of the problem situation, so that you can understand it at various levels of complexity and obtain a better insight into what is happening. Thinking in systems terms will also lead you to conclude that it is important in dealing with the problems to consider the impact on the wider organization of any action you take, as well as the influence that failing to manage the problem would have. It is dangerous to deal with the situation as it appears on the surface without taking the time to explore the whole of the problem area. The scenario demonstrates how an apparently simple 'local' problem about the deteriorating working relationship between two people can raise a number of very fundamental organizational issues. These include:

- The effect on overall team performance
- The effect upon relationships with the wider organization
- The effect upon customers
- Possible financial consequences
- The possibility that other problems exist or could develop within the team.

People in organizations

Lastly, you need to understand how people behave. A knowledge of motivation theory is essential so that you can appreciate the human dimensions underlying presented problems and avoid demotivating any of the participants in arriving at a solution. Sometimes it is not easy to be sure about what motivates people to work, but isolating and removing the demotivators can be very effective.

An important part of our working lives is the social contact that we make with others, and yet your own experience will tell you that it is people in organizations who are at the heart of many of the problems with which managers have to deal. This is partly why management models sometimes seem to let us down. They simply do not take into account the vagaries and apparent awkwardness of people who seem bent on making life as difficult as possible for the rest of us. Carefully worked-out plans are frustratingly held up because parts of them have to be clarified and renegotiated. Timescales expand because other people fail to see the importance of keeping to our deadline. Colleagues complain, argue and fail to communicate with each other. If only people would behave rationally!

Of course, this represents only one perspective. It may be that the people who seem so intransigent to you have a legitimate reason to feel negative about a proposal that will affect them. Perhaps they fail to meet deadlines because you haven't made the task clear to them. Possibly they argue among themselves for the same reason. Perhaps they don't communicate well because others fail to communicate well with them.

Solving, anticipating and 'creating' problems

Of course the idea that managers can 'solve' problems is something of a misrepresentation. Focusing on finding a 'solution' implies that the problem situation is a wholly negative state and that the aim must be to remove the problem so that a return to the (implied) positive status quo can be achieved. From what you understand about complex organic organizations and how the people within them behave, you may consider that this is unlikely to happen. You should certainly question whether this is what *ought* to happen. The idea that a problem is something to be swept out of the way so that the organization can return to business as usual is out of tune with the notion of a dynamic organization constantly anticipating and responding to changes in its environment. As a creative manager you should be thinking about problems in uncommon ways, recognizing that in most problem situations there will be opportunities for learning and for positive change. A problem represents a kind of threat and the challenge for managers, as you saw in Chapter 7 is to identify ways in which a threat can be turned into an opportunity.

So far in this chapter we have been considering only presented problems. However, effective managers who are in touch with what is happening in both the near and the far environment will also find themselves thinking about another type of problem. These are *foreseen problems*, where the manager senses that, if things remain as they are, a problem will arise in the future. The manager in this situation will begin thinking *now* about how this circumstance can be avoided. For example, you might believe that if something is not done to limit the number of people who travel to work by car, then on-site car parking will become a major problem for your company. You will not wait until the problem becomes so real that it has to be addressed. By anticipating the problem you gain time to think creatively about how it might be solved and you may also be able to find ways in which positive outcomes can be achieved out of what, on the face of it, appears to be a negative situation.

The third kind of problem is the *constructed problem*, one which you construct or formulate for yourself. It goes beyond being 'problem minded' to being 'opportunity minded'. It begins with a feeling of dissatisfaction with the present and the desire to achieve a better future situation. The driving force is the need to innovate and change. The vision of the better future is not really a problem at all, but framing it in terms of a problem gives it a definition. The problem of how to move towards this vision of the future is the starting point for generating ideas for a possible way forward.

In Chapter 8 we referred to what Gareth Morgan described as 'proactive mindsets'. This is the frame of mind in which you actively seek problems to construct. The more you aim to foresee or construct problems, the more you will find opportunities for positive change. Figure 9.1 illustrates this idea.

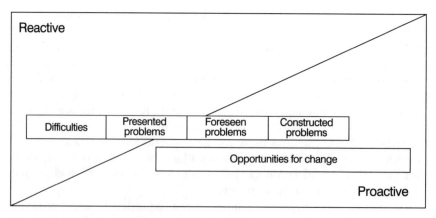

Figure 9.1 Taking a proactive approach to problem solving

Foreseen problems and constructed problems, which in a sense have no existence until we have recognized them as such, offer the most scope for creativity. While these are essentially about moving towards some vision of a better future, presented problems, on the other hand, have their roots firmly planted in the present or even, in the case of complex people problems, the none-too-recent past. However, most of the problems you meet as a manager are ones which the environment thrusts at you day after day. Tackling them requires much more than common sense. Even if you have developed a robust management philosophy and a personal style which seems to have stood you in good stead in the past, it may be because you are only viewing your performance from a single perspective – your own!

Some simple techniques for problem definition

The techniques which follow in this chapter and the next are aimed at encouraging your thinking, often using words and images as stimuli, so that you begin to consider problems in uncommon ways and actively search for fresh insights. There is a temptation, as you have seen, when faced with a problem situation to try to 'pigeonhole' it by identifying those aspects of it that are familiar to you. This immediately places a boundary around the problem and limits the extent to which you will spend time really thinking about all the issues involved in the search for a solution. To take a very simplistic example, your problem might be one of falling sales of a particular product. Last time this happened the advertising budget was increased, an enhanced sales campaign was launched and the position then improved. But is this going to be the solution every time there is a drop in sales? Perhaps the problem lies not in the expenditure on advertising but in the product itself and whether customer needs have changed.

The following techniques force you to extend the boundary around the problem and to encourage divergent, as opposed to convergent, thinking so that you explore more of its dimensions and not less. At this stage, where you are attempting to define the real problem it is often useful to work with others since, as you have seen, they will have different perspectives and information about the problem which you may not have considered.

Diagrams

There are a number of different types of diagram which can be used to identify the roots of a problem. You may be familiar with mind maps, Buzan diagrams and spider diagrams. They are similar in that you begin by writing in the centre of a large sheet of paper a brief description of the essential problem. Then you attach thoughts and ideas relating to the problem like spokes on a wheel. Other related thoughts which are triggered in the process can be recorded and linked to show their association. Figure 9.2 is based on the problem of writing this book.

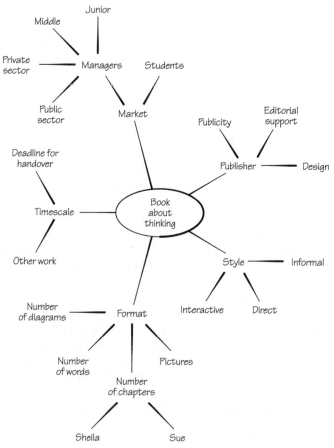

Figure 9.2 A mind map of writing this book

Another type of diagram is the fishbone diagram first developed by Professor Kaoru Ishikawa as a way of identifying all the possible roots of a problem. It is a particularly useful method when working with a group. This time the problem is the head of the fish and the 'bones' represent every possible cause of the problem. Related causes or 'sub-causes' can be shown as branches off the main bones. Once all the possible causes have been identified then the group can discuss and isolate the key underlying causes, which are the ones that will be focused on at the next stage when generating ideas for solving the problem. Figure 9.3 shows a fishbone diagram of the problem of a poor telephone answering service with causes selected for further investigation circled.

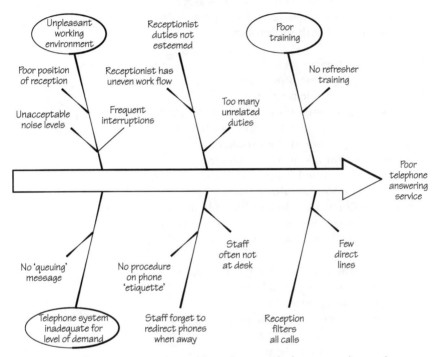

Figure 9.3 Fishbone diagram – the problem of a poor telephone-answering service

Try drawing either a mind map or fishbone diagram of a management problem of your own. You will find it helpful to involve others who have an interest in the problem, so that you get a feel for the process.

Five Ws

This is very simple technique which forces you to probe beneath the surface of the problem in order to gather more information. Again it is a useful technique to use with others. The five Ws are the questions Who? What? Where? When? and Why?

Some of the questions that might be generated are listed below, but you will be able to think of others:

Who is affected by the problem?
Who thinks there is a problem?
Who most needs the problem to be solved?
Who might be disadvantaged if the problem were solved?
Who should deal with the problem?

What effect is the problem having?
What does the problem prevent?
What does the problem change?
What is the most important aspect of the problem?
What is the least important aspect of the problem?
What annoys you about the problem?
What pleases you about the problem?
What could be gained from solving the problem?
What could be lost by solving the problem?
What real information do you have about the problem?
What assumptions are being made about the problem?
What other difficulties are being caused by the problem?

Where does the problem really lie?
Where is it causing most difficulties?
Where is it causing least difficulties?
Where might there be similar problems?

When did the problem begin?
When does it need to be dealt with?
When might the problem get worse?
When is the problem not apparent?
When do others see it as a problem?
When does it cause other difficulties?

Why is the problem important?
Why do you need to solve this problem?
Why do you not want to solve the problem?
Why could not someone else resolve it?
Why is it a problem?

These are just some of the questions you might use to start understanding more about the problem and its dimensions. There is another useful question and this is How? but it has to be used with caution otherwise it can lead you to begin to think about solutions before you have really discovered as much as you can about the nature of the problem. For example it is *not* helpful at the problem-definition stage to pose questions such as 'How might we begin to solve the problem?' However, there are other useful questions that you can ask and some of these are below:

How important is it that we solve this problem?
How does it relate to the rest of our work?
How does it affect the way that we work?
How much of our energy does it take?
How does it affect the way in which others see us?
How many people think that it is a problem?

This is a very useful technique to try with others who will have different perceptions about the size and importance of the problem as well as useful information to share.

Goal orientation

This is a technique described by Tudor Rickards in *Problem-solving through Creative Analysis*. It is a very useful way of ensuring that you are clear about what exactly it is that you want to achieve through solving the problem. It appeals to me because it has a positive sense of progression forwards rather than the somewhat negative notion that problem solving is simply a process by which an undesirable situation (the problem) is made better than it was.

The first step is to write down a general description of the problem including all relevant information. Then ask the following questions.

What do we want to accomplish?   (NEEDS)
What is stopping us from getting there?   (OBSTACLES)
What restrictions must we accept in solving the
problem?   (CONSTRAINTS)

The next step is to use these questions to arrive at new definitions of the problem. To illustrate the technique I shall use the scenario that you were working on earlier in this chapter.

The general statement of the problem is that Robert and Christine have reached a point where they can no longer work together as colleagues. Using the idea of needs, obstacles and constraints, the problem could be redefined as how to:

● Get the four individuals working together as a team (a need)
● Resolve the misunderstandings between Christine and Robert (a need)

- Review the roles and responsibilities of the four individuals concerned (a need)
- Prevent the team from becoming more fragmented (an obstacle because working relationships have deteriorated so badly)
- Change the negative feelings that Robert and Christine in particular have about each other (an obstacle preventing any fruitful discussion of a way forward at present)
- Review the physical working environment (a constraint since there are limitations on space as well as upon the budget)
- Review the way in which the team operates (a constraint because they have certain key accounts for which they are responsible and needs of the customers have to be considered)

In this way the problem can be viewed from different angles, so that new possibilities for solving it may appear.

Although this technique for problem redefinition can be used by a group, it is a very helpful one for individuals attempting to 'get their head round' a problem. Try it now with a problem that you have and see if looking at needs, obstacles and constraints leads you to think of a new way in which you might tackle it.

Summary

Management can never be an exact science. Whatever our personal understanding of what the key management functions are, broadly speaking it has to do with getting things done through and with people. As a manager you are dependent upon the inputs and outputs of others, whether in your immediate team, within the wider organization or outside it. But people, including other managers, do not share the same perspective as you do, neither will they respond in the same way to the same situation or the same stimulus. Even those whose reactions you might think you can predict can sometimes surprise you by behaviour which seems 'out of character'.

Just as people are different, organizations, made up of people trying to work within, or adapt to, the prevailing culture are also different. The environments (local, national, global) in which organizations operate are different. Even then the picture is not static. People change, the personnel within organizations change; organizations change their structure and consequently the organizational culture changes.

The nature of organizations and of people being what they are, you cannot, as a manager, expect to be dealing with common problems to which you can apply textbook solutions. However, there are *ways of thinking* which can help you to deal more effectively with the uncommon problems of management.

The starting point in problem solving is to be clear about the nature of the problem that you are trying to solve. Presented management problems often have very tenacious roots and these need to be tackled in order to eliminate effectively the problem situation which presents itself. It is also essential to remember that your perspective on the problem is not the only one and that other participants and observers may hold equally firm and, in their opinion, valid views. You ignore these at your peril.

Working on foreseen and constructed problems is very much the business of managers' today's competitive environment. This does not mean that you will not have to deal with presented problems as well – the very nature of the management environment will ensure that dealing effectively with these will be a key part of every manager's job and even apparently trivial problems can have a significant impact on the wider organization. However, you should now be thinking about them in a different, more creative, way, alert to the opportunities they may offer as well as the threats that they pose.

There are a number of creative techniques which can help you to redefine and analyse problems. Creative thinking does not imply loose or woolly thinking. The very simple techniques described in this chapter, for example, force you to explore problems from new angles, to gather even more information about them and to consider other perspectives. In fact creative thinking is actually very rigorous thinking, and the process can be quite painful, as you will have found if you have attempted any of the activities!

Once the problem has been analysed and redefined the next stage is to generate ideas for solving it. There are a number of creative techniques which can be used for idea generation and some of these will be explored in Chapter 10.

$$\textit{Chapter 10}$$
Uncovering ideas

The previous chapter ended with a brief look at four creative techniques for redefining problems. The systems approach which was discussed in Chapter 5, with its emphasis on multiple systems descriptions, is another way of understanding problems and their contexts. Time spent on this stage of problem solving is never time wasted. Once you have found out where the roots of a problem lie, and what the extent of the real problem is, possible ways of solving it will begin to suggest themselves. It may be that in the process of gathering fresh perspectives on the situation and additional information about it, it will begin to seem less of a problem and more of a potential opportunity for change.

This chapter explores the next stages of problem solving and offers some creative techniques which you can use either on your own or with groups, to generate ideas for tackling organizational problems, whether they are presented, foreseen or constructed problems. By the end of it you should:

- Recognize the value of taking a creative approach to problem solving
- Understand the process of creative problem solving
- Have applied at least one creative technique to a practical problem of your own
- Be encouraged to use creative approaches in the future.

The discipline of creative problem solving

As mentioned earlier, the notion of problem solving is something of a misnomer for two reasons. The first is that many management problems, particularly those which unexpectedly present themselves to you, do not have a single 'solution'. The steps that you take to deal with the problem situation may be complex and time consuming and sometimes are quite disproportionate to the size of the problem itself. Second, it implies that you should be solution-minded, whereas your attention ought to be directed first at understanding the problem, not finding a rapid 'solution' even if this were possible.

From your own experience you will be aware that is difficult to solve problems in organizations, to produce a win–win situation which leaves everyone feeling positive and no-one aggrieved. This is because organizations function in complex environments where financial, legislative, environmental and other constraints create restrictions, and they operate through the efforts of complex and sometimes unpredictable human beings. When you reach the stage of selecting which course of action to implement from all the ideas generated, all these constraints need to be borne in mind. (It may be that one of these constraints *is* the main problem and that you need to think creatively about how to deal with this first.) However, they should not be considered when you are generating ideas because even the wildest and seemingly impractical ideas can be scaled down, and often an 'off the wall' suggestion can contain the germ of a potential way forward.

Using creative techniques to 'solve' problems does not mean that all the things which normally upset your plans or stop you from making progress will magically disappear. You will still have to work within whatever constraints you are used to. Thinking creatively about problems does not give you any particular authority to remove these constraints, but it does give you the understanding to challenge them. Often the constraints upon what can be achieved exist largely in your own mind and those of the people with whom you work. Thinking in uncommon ways about why things are as they are and what are the real problems you need to tackle can be extremely liberating.

Recognizing assumptions

Creative problem solving is not a way of avoiding the realities of life, but a disciplined process for confronting them. Having a *realistic* view of the resources, skills and abilities available to you when you come to select the course of action which is most likely to resolve a problem is only one of the prerequisites for successful problem solving. The others are:

- The recognition that there is a gap between the present situation and what you would like it to be
- Having a realistic idea about the size of that gap
- Having the motivation to do something about it

However, it is also important to recognize that in setting out to deal with a problem, whether it is presented to you or whether it is one you have foreseen or constructed, you are making two important assumptions. The first is that it is *possible* to determine a 'vision of the future' that is attainable. Is it clear that our understanding of the present situation (of the environment as it is now and as it might become) and of the personal values, aspirations and motivations of those involved or interested in the problem are sufficient for us to arrive at a view of what the new situation might be? Lack of understanding does not prevent you from having a vision, but it does mean that you may have an unrealistic idea about the size of the gap between that point and where you are now. If you begin working on a vision which is flawed, your efforts to reduce the gap and solve the problem will be ineffective.

Once you begin to take any steps to change a situation by tackling a problem of whatever kind, you are making an intervention in a particular organizational system or systems. This brings us to the second important assumption and that is that other people will happily sign up to the vision or the goal that you are working towards. People, as you have seen in the previous chapters, will have their own personal goals and ambitions, they will have mindsets and prejudices which will be different from your own, they will have preferred ways of addressing issues, they will react differently to change. Your view of the reality now and as it might be in the future may seem a very distorted reality to others and so, in order to resolve problems, you need to try to accommodate these different views and perspectives.

This is particularly so, the more complex the problem. If the problem is one which apparently did not exist until you foresaw it or constructed it, then you will have to work especially hard at gaining the interest and motivation of others to do something about it. Even though it may be a situation which ought legitimately to be the concern of others, it will be regarded as your problem, simply because you were the one who made it exist by thinking about it. You will need to consider carefully who is likely to be helped by your intervention and, remembering systems thinking, how it is likely to bring about an improvement in the wider organization.

Some of the creative problem-solving techniques which are discussed later in this chapter are ones that you can use when working with a group of people. As in problem definition, the inputs of others at the idea-generation stage help to extend the range of possible solutions. They also create a feeling of consensus about the problem situation and a commitment to the change which will inevitably result from implementing a chosen way forward.

The iterative process of problem solving

As you might expect from what you have read so far, creative problem solving is a structured rather than a random process. It consists of three distinct stages. The Descriptive stage, as you saw in the previous chapter, consists of gathering as much information about the situation as possible in order to arrive at a redefinition of the problem. The next is the Design stage, where ideas and possible solutions to the newly defined problem are generated and developed. The final stage is the Decision stage, where potential solutions are evaluated against hoped-for outcomes and one is chosen for implementation. The first stage requires divergent thinking, as information and perspectives are sought with a view eventually to narrowing down (converging) to an agreed statement of the problem(s) to be addressed. The next stage is a further divergent process where as many ideas as possible are generated in a search for a possible solution. The final stage involves selecting from this array of ideas one course of action to be implemented. The three stages are illustrated in Figure 10.1.

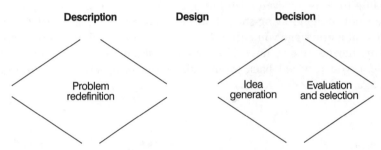

Figure 10.1   Divergent and convergent thinking in creative problem solving

Having used creative techniques to redefine the problem and generate ideas, and analysis to select a way forward, you can now proceed to implementation. If all the previous effort is not to be wasted it is important that:

● The problem owner oversees the programme of implementation
● All those who might be affected by it are briefed, consulted or participate as appropriate
● The progress of implementing the chosen solution is evaluated against the desired outcome.

If this is beginning to sound like a process for managing change it is because tackling problems, as opposed to difficulties, will involve changing old ways of doing things, old values and structures for new ones. The links between problem solving and change management are discussed further in the next chapter.

So at the implementation stage you will again need to use analytical rational thinking to plan a series of actions, to monitor progress and to evaluate the extent to which your chosen way forward is beginning to resolve the problem situation. There is always the danger that you have been addressing the wrong problem or you have not chosen the best possible solution. All too often a plan of action, once agreed, becomes, 'set in concrete' and is never changed. It may be punctiliously implemented but still fails to achieve what was intended simply because it was framed to solve yesterday's problem and today's circumstances are not the same. Typically, someone or some event has caused the goal posts to move. It may be necessary to redefine the problem yet again to reflect this, and this in turn could mean modifying the implementation programme.

You should never be so committed to a single solution that you are unwilling to revise or even abandon it if it appears not to be working. The process of problem solving should be an iterative one as Figure 10.2 shows. At the evaluation stage you either decide to continue with the implementation or, having re-examined the problem situation and redefined the problem, you proceed back around the loop, using creative techniques once again to generate ideas.

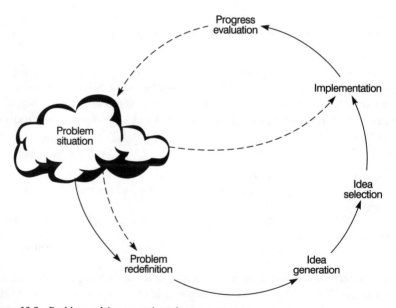

Figure 10.2   Problem solving as an iterative process

Creative problem solving therefore requires a mix of right-brain and left-brain thinking. However, the need to combine analytical, rational thinking with creativity is not confined to problem solving. Both kinds of thinking are required by managers today trying to handle complexity and ambiguity in a changing environment. We shall be going on to think about change and the limitations of rationality in the final two chapters of this book. First, the following are some techniques for you to use to generate ideas for problem solving and to evaluate them.

Design stage techniques – generating ideas

You can try any of the techniques in this section as Workouts. If you do I suggest that you avoid complex problems which are strategic in nature and apply them to problems where you are either the sole problem owner or one of the problem owners. It is also useful for you to check that you are addressing a discrete problem rather than a cluster of accumulated problems by using one or more of the techniques in the previous chapter.

The idea-generation stage begins with a clear statement of the problem, acceptable to the problem owner(s). It is useful to frame the problem as a question, for example: 'How may we increase the motivation of secretarial staff?' or 'In what ways may we improve customer care?'

It is not helpful to include terms which would limit the range of solutions at this stage. So, a problem defined as 'How may we reduce the number of customer complaints by 10 per cent in the next 6 months?' could rule out some possible solutions before they had been properly considered. A dual problem expressed as a single statement is also difficult to work with. For example, 'How may we reduce customers' complaints by 10 per cent and reduce sales overheads at the same time?' has built-in constraints upon the generation of ideas. If a problem is complex it is better to restate it as two (or more) separate questions.

Techniques to use when working alone

Very often you may not want to share the problem with others. You may be the sole owner of this problem, and although you may welcome inputs from others at the Description stage, for all kinds of reasons it may be appropriate for you to generate ideas at the Design stage alone. The following are four simple techniques which you might try.

Wishful thinking

This is a technique which many of us indulge in in an attempt to wish that a situation were other than it is. Usually our fantasizing about what might be ends at that point. However, used as a creative technique it can be a powerful way of exploring possible solutions to a problem. It works as follows:

- State the problem
- Imagine that anything is possible
- Fantasize about possible solutions by making statements such as 'If only I could ...', 'The best thing that could happen would be ...', 'The problem would be solved if only ...'

The next step is to use these fantasy statements to stimulate your thinking about the real situation by comparing them with reality and recognizing that while X is unlikely to happen, Y might be possible or while you could not really do A you might just possibly think of a way of doing B.

For example, your problem might be that a growing number of people are bringing their cars to work. On-site parking is no longer adequate and so cars are being parked in areas outside the official car park, causing delays and problems for other employees and visitors. You might state this as 'How may I dissuade my staff from bringing their cars to work?' Your fantasy answers might include;

- If only I could charge them a toll
- If only I could make them cycle to work
- The best thing that could happen would be for us to sell the car park
- The best thing that could happen would be for us to operate a fleet of buses
- The problem would be solved if we only employed people who didn't drive
- The problem would be solved if half the people came to work at night

None of these things is likely to happen, but by forcing yourself to find a fit between your fantasies and reality you might come up with solutions such as:

- Subsidize 80 per cent of the cost for people who buy and use bus passes
- Subsidize the cost of buying a bike for those who will use it to get to work

- Negotiate with a local bus company to run rush-hour services to and from key pick-up points and the company premises
- Introduce shift working and 'hot parking' so that people would share parking spaces
- Change working arrangements so that working from home could be more extensively used.

The purpose of wishful thinking is to produce unusual perspectives on a problem which may not be generated by simply considering the reality of the problem itself. Sometimes a problem may seem so intractable that logic tells you that there is no acceptable way forward. Wishful thinking encourages you to abandon logic for a moment to establish whether there may be a different perspective on the problem which could suggest a solution.

Clichés, proverbs and maxims

This is a technique developed by Van Grundy and described by him in his book, *Techniques of Structured Problem Solving*. It is another example of how forcing yourself to think of the problem in terms of other things can help to stimulate new ideas. The technique is simple to understand and use and can equally well be used with a group.

First, select a cliché which seems interesting and has no apparent connection with the problem area. There are dozens of these. Here are just a few examples:

Too many cooks spoil the broth
It never rains but it pours
A stitch in time saves nine
All's well that ends well
Beauty is in the eye of the beholder
An apple a day keeps the doctor away
Never count your chickens before they are hatched
Rome wasn't built in a day
Two wrongs don't make a right
You can't teach an old dog new tricks

Then, without having the problem in mind, write down the implications and possible interpretations of the proverb or cliché. Using these as stimuli now think about the problem and write down any ideas that suggest themselves. You can repeat the process with another proverb or cliché to derive more ideas. If you were using this technique with a group you could ask individuals to select different clichés as stimuli to obtain a broader spectrum of associations.

Morphological analysis

There are a number of (very complex) forms of this technique, but here is a simple version which you can use on your own. The first step is to select four attributes to your problem and then to find four different options for each one. It becomes too complicated if you use more than four. Every permutation of attributes and options can be considered (a total of $4 \times 4 \times 4 \times 4 = 256$), but often a number of these produce quite silly ideas which you would not wish to pursue. The technique is based on the idea of using forced relationships, that is, to consider an aspect of the problem in terms of something quite unaccustomed and it can produce some very innovative results.

For example, my problem might be 'How may our publishers best promote this book?' The four attributes that I have chosen are Places, Times, People and Methods. The options which I have selected randomly are shown in Figure 10.3.

Places	Times	People	Method
Bookshops	Daily	Students	Leaflet
Railway stations	Weekly	Managers	Poster
Supermarkets	Summer	Anyone	Announcement
Newspapers	Winter	Managing directors	Video

Figure 10.3 Morphological analysis

Two ideas produced from combining options might be:

- A winter special offer to practising managers of a free promotional video collectable from bookshops
- To hand a leaflet about the book to anyone arriving at a railway station on a particular day.

It is quite possible that I would not be able to persuade the publishers to adopt either of these strategies, but there are other ideas contained within this simple matrix which might be worth exploring with them.

Try this last technique with a problem of your own. Then get a colleague or friend to use the technique to generate ideas for solving the same problem. You will undoubtedly select different attributes and options and it should be interesting to compare your favourite solutions as well as the ideas that you both rejected.

Random words

You will have realized by now that a useful way of sparking original or creative ideas about a problem is by forcing yourself to think of it in terms which you would normally and rationally exclude from consideration. Simply choose a word at random, from the dictionary or perhaps by looking at the objects around you, and then think about your problem in terms of this unrelated word to see if it generates any new ideas.

For example, I happen to be looking at a potted plant in the room where I am writing this. So how does the problem of promoting this book relate to an indoor plant? These are the thoughts which occurred to me (which may be worth discussing with the publisher!):

It needs to focus on growth and development
It has to be firmly rooted in something
It must be eye-catching
It needs attention
It must bear fruit!
It should not be allowed to gather dust
It may need regular 'repotting'
It needs light and space

Clarifying

Before moving on to look at group techniques, a word of caution about making assumptions about the words that you use. We have stressed throughout this book that there will always be a range of perspectives on a problem and that this is why it is important to involve others in creative problem solving, both as a means of checking out the validity of your own views and as a useful source of ideas. However, just as we do not all share the same perspective, neither do we always understand what another person means, even when they are speaking the same language!

You have probably found when working with other people how difficult and open to misinterpretation even the most straightforward communications can be. We each use words and phrases that carry with them a whole collection of unspoken assumptions and prejudices which we assume will be shared by others. However, every communication we make is formed by and interpreted through the experience, ideas and connections that are unique to each individual.

In addition, the person you are addressing may be feeling unsure, dispirited, powerful, cheerful, unconcerned, angry or any one of a number of emotions as a result of something quite unrelated that has happened that day. This may colour their response in ways that you cannot be aware of and their body language may not always provide a clue. Even a perfectly innocent question may be misinterpreted. For example, if you asked someone 'Are you aware that X happened yesterday?' this might be taken to be a straightforward question to establish a fact. But it could be interpreted in any of the following ways as well:

● A put-down ('Most people know but I don't expect that you do')
● Sarcasm ('I know you know that X happened. Why didn't you take it into account?')
● A criticism ('You must have known, why didn't you tell me?')

In problem solving with a group, it is important to clarify any vague or 'fuzzy' words. In particular, you need to ensure that there is a shared understanding of the statement of the problem. For example, if your problem was expressed as 'How may we beat the competition?' you would need to check out exactly what is understood by the word 'beat'. Does it in the context in which it is being used mean 'completely dismiss', 'dominate', 'conquer' or just simply 'get ahead of' the competition? Is it clear who or what is meant by 'the competition'? Is it all competition, external and internal, or just the key players in the market? If it is just the key players, does everyone in the group know who they are? And so on. Sometimes the very process of clarification can begin to generate problem-solving ideas.

Techniques to use with groups

As mentioned earlier, it is always important to obtain a range of perspectives on a problem situation and the same is true at the idea-generation stage. The inputs of others can provide additional stimuli which can encourage creativity so long as the members of the group refrain from being judgemental or criticizing the suggestions of others. What follow are some of the less complex group techniques that can be used in a work situation. I have included among them two of the more 'wacky' techniques for you to try!

Classical brainstorming

This is one idea-generating technique which is used (and often abused) by many people. Classical brainstorming was originally developed in the late 1930s by Alex Osborn and it has led to many related techniques. It has been the subject of more research studies than any other idea-generating technique and there is some criticism of its effectiveness. However, it does produce a number of ideas in a relatively short amount of time, although it is important to remember that its usefulness is limited to fairly simple problems where all the participants have a basic awareness of the problem. They need not be 'experts', indeed using a group of experts can limit the range of ideas produced to ones which the individuals feel are of value.

The process needs a leader who will note down all of the ideas produced on a flipchart. The leader or facilitator should state at the outset the two basic rules of brainstorming. The first is that no judgement or criticism of the value of individual ideas is allowed. All ideas will be recorded no matter how outlandish they seem to others. The second rule is to go for quantity, since one idea may lead to others by association. The more ideas that are generated, the more likely it is that a solution will be found. This means that the leader should positively encourage participants to be uninhibited about contributing ideas and to 'piggy-back' on the ideas of others.

Generating ideas

The steps then are as follows. First, the leader should run a warm-up session with the group on an unrelated problem to get them into a creative frame of mind. Then he or she should:

1 Write the problem on a flipchart or board so that everyone can see.
2 Restate the rules of brainstorming.
3 Write down the ideas on the board or flipchart. (It may be quicker to have someone to help act as scribe at this stage)

The process should be stopped when ideas dry up and in any case after 30 minutes maximum.

It is important that everyone, even the most reticent, has the chance to contribute, and so rather than call for random contributions it is better to go sequentially round the group. If someone has no idea to offer when it comes to their turn they simply pass. This avoids the session being dominated by one person and one perspective.

It is also important for all the ideas to be displayed, so once one side of flipchart has been filled it should be torn off and displayed alongside the problem statement before continuing on a new sheet of paper.

The group itself can contain as many as twelve people, but with a large group it is certainly useful to have two scribes. It is also helpful to number each idea contributed. This makes it easier to group the ideas at the evaluation stage.

Evaluating ideas

This can either be done by a sub-set of the same group (or by the whole group if it is small enough) or by an entirely different group depending upon whether familiarity with the problem or objectivity is more important. The group which evaluates should consist of no more than five people and their task is to group the ideas into categories. For example, they might choose to group ideas under headings such as 'practicality', 'lowest cost', 'ease of implementation' and so on. Having done this they would then select the best ideas for further development.

Although this technique should produce a large number of ideas, its main disadvantages are the possible superficiality of many of the ideas produced and the fact that suspending judgement means that individuals do not get recognition for useful contributions.

Negative brainstorming

This is an interesting variation of brainstorming where instead of posing the problem 'How may we . . .', it is reframed as 'How may we not . . .'. This can throw up quite startling examples of things that are actually being done which could be having a negative effect on the problem situation (increasing or adding to the problem) and which could themselves be addressed as a way of solving it.

Metaplanning

This is the name of a very elaborate technique developed by a small German company called Metaplan. It is described as an 'interactional learning technique', but I have used a very scaled-down version of it with groups to generate ideas and discussion about a foreseen problem and to arrive at critical success factors. One such was a group of senior managers in a local authority and council members. The problem was how they were to become more responsive to their stakeholders.

Group size

This technique works well with groups of ten or twelve people. I have tried it with bigger groups, but the process is much more difficult to handle with large numbers. With smaller groups the number of ideas generated can be limited.

Equipment

You will need the following:

- A very large sheet of brown paper, about the size of three whiteboards
- Some means of fixing the paper to a wall
- Spray-on fixing glue, the kind which does not dry on contact but allows for repositioning
- A supply of blank cards about 20 cm × 10 cm (roughly 8 inches by 4 inches) is a good size
- A supply of marker pens, the type used to write on flipcharts

Generating ideas

First attach the sheets of paper to the wall to form a giant display board for ideas. Then write the problem statement across the top of the paper so that it is visible to everyone. Let's say the problem is 'How may we reduce sales overheads?'

Give each person in the group three blank cards each and a flipchart pen. On a separate flipchart write the statement 'I would solve this problem by . . .'.

The members of the group are asked to respond to this statement by giving their three best ideas for solving the problem, writing one on each card. Framing the statement in this way should ensure that the first word on each card is a verb. For example, responses might be 'reducing the sales team', 'outsourcing the work of the transport division' or 'redesigning our packaging'. The idea is that in this way each suggested solution is a statement about taking action of some kind. The rules are that there can be no more than ten words on a card and writing must be large enough that the cards can be read from a distance.

After allowing sufficient time for thought, the cards are collected, shuffled and then randomly positioned on the screen, using the spray-on glue to attach them. The group is then able to see all the ideas that have been generated. As with brainstorming, no comment or criticism is allowed as each card is displayed.

Grouping ideas

The next task is to look for patterns or clusters of ideas. The cards are repositioned at the group's request into idea clusters. There is usually much discussion and debate at this stage about whether a particular idea 'belongs' to one cluster or another and the originator of the idea can be called upon to clarify the idea, but cannot dictate to which cluster it should belong. The objective is for the group to reach some consensus about what the key idea clusters are, but there should be no views expressed at this stage about the relative merits of any of them.

Once agreement has been reached about how the ideas should be clustered you should draw a boundary around each group. There should be no more repositioning after this so it is important to ensure that individuals in the group are happy with the outcome. There may be ideas which do not 'fit' into any of the clusters. They may have some kind of association with one of them or they may be unique. They should not be forced to fit into a cluster but if there is a link to one of them this can be shown by a linking line. Your display board should now look something like Figure 10.4.

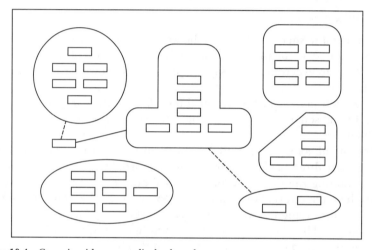

Figure 10.4   Grouping ideas on a display board

Ask the group to give each cluster of ideas a title, such as 'motivate staff', 'relocation', 'monitor performance' which broadly describes the essence of the ideas. It can be useful at this stage to get the group to try to give a short statement which encapsulates all the ideas in the cluster – a cluster definition. However, if the ideas are too wide-ranging or it is difficult to reach agreement it is possible to refer to them simply as 'the motivation cluster' or 'the relocation cluster', for example. The titles or definitions should now be listed on a clean piece of flipchart paper and displayed.

Selecting

The next step is for the group to decide which cluster of ideas is likely to contribute most towards solving the problem. It will not necessarily be the cluster containing the largest number of cards. The choice may be obvious or it may spark some heated debate. If it is clear that all the clusters are worthy of further consideration as they all have something to contribute, then you will need to prioritize.

I have done this by giving each member of the group either three or five 'votes', depending upon the number of people in the group and the number of idea clusters. The votes are represented by coloured self-adhesive dots or symbols. Each individual uses their votes to indicate which cluster or clusters contain the most important ideas in their view by sticking them against the title of the cluster on the flipchart. The votes are then counted and the ideas ranked accordingly. You should now have reached consensus about the actions which are most likely to contribute to solving the problem and which of them to explore first.

Superheroes

This is a technique for generating ideas through forced associations. Having stated the problem, each member of the group is asked to name a superhero of their own. Some commonly known superheroes are figures such as Superman, Batman or Wonder Woman, but the group may, for example, choose political figures or sports idols instead.

The name of each superhero is written down on a board as it is revealed and the nominee is asked to describe some of their key characteristics, including special skills, powers, strengths and idiosyncrasies as well as any weaknesses. The group is asked to use the information as stimuli for generating ideas. The question in every case is 'How would X solve this problem?'

Greetings cards

The final idea-generating technique is called greetings cards. It was developed by Pickens and was modified and described by Van Grundy. It is another method of generating ideas through forced associations. It is best used with a small group of between four and six people who are not actually involved in the problem area.

Each person is given a catalogue or a magazine. They are asked to cut out two or three pictures which interest them. The next step is for individuals working alone or in sub-groups of two to paste the pictures onto a piece of folded paper or card to form a greetings card for some occasion such as a birthday, anniversary or wedding or it could be a get-well or congratulations card.

Once all the cards are completed the problem is revealed and, using the theme on the cards and the pictures as stimuli, the group members are asked to generate ideas to solve the problem. The cards can be exchanged between groups to stimulate further ideas.

Decision stage techniques – selecting ideas and evaluating them

There are many techniques for evaluating and selecting ideas. Some of them are extremely complex and involve elaborate systems of screening or weighting the ideas in order to select the one which has the greatest potential. I have not included them here, because, apart from the fact that some of them are complex and may require particular training to use, unless the problem has discrete boundaries in a management environment there can be no absolute certainty that any solution will have the desired outcome. It therefore seems inappropriate to introduce such a high degree of refinement into evaluating the potential of alternative solutions to management problems.

One simple technique is to list the criteria which the chosen solution must satisfy in order to solve the problem and then to evaluate each idea against these criteria, putting a tick to indicate a positive evaluation. You can construct a table to enable you to compare the number of positive and negative 'scores' for each idea. A simple example might look like Table 10.1.

Table 10.1   An evaluation table

Criteria	Advantage	Disadvantage
Alternative A		
Ease of implementation	✓	
Technology requirements	✓	
Training/retraining		✓
Relocation costs		✓
Timing		✓
Transport logistics	✓	
Customer loyalty		✓
Alternative B		
Ease of implementation		✓
Technology requirements		✓
Training/requirements	✓	
Relocation costs		✓
Timing	✓	
Transport logistics	✓	
Customer loyalty	✓	

This is a very easy technique and you can construct a table which is appropriate to the problem and to your needs, and which allows you to examine, for example, costs versus benefits, advantages compared with disadvantages, positive contributions against negative effects and so on. The technique does not work well with large numbers of ideas because it becomes too cumbersome, and so you would probably want to do some initial screening, perhaps by asking members of the group to choose, say their ten favoured solutions and then to rank them in order to find the ten which have the most support among the group. Sticking dots, as used in the metaplanning technique described earlier, is another useful way of selecting the most popular idea or ideas.

Playfulness

It will be clear to you from some of the group techniques that one of the prerequisites for creativity is that those who are participating have a 'playful' attitude to what they are doing. This means leaving aside inhibitions about having to contribute worthy and well-formed ideas, as well as worries about having your ideas and responses judged against the inputs of others. It is this notion of playfulness which makes critics of creative techniques dismiss them as wacky or unrealistic.

Just as before you embark on strenuous physical exercise it is advisable to do some warm-up exercises, the same is true for mental work-outs. Before you begin a creative problem-solving session, warm up the participants with a simple exercise. A brainstorming session on a non-work problem is one idea, using a question of no importance such as 'How many uses might there be for a box of paper clips?'

Remember to choose a suitable and relaxing environment, away from the workplace if possible. This is important as it helps people to leave aside their accustomed literal, analytical approach to management problem solving and be willing to suspend judgement. For some people, creative techniques will seem to be entirely inappropriate in a work situation and they will be uncomfortable with being involved in thinking 'games'. But just as essential as playfulness is the need for people to have an open frame of mind which does not immediately condemn new ways of doing things simply because they are new. If you can encourage this as a manager then people are likely to involve themselves in creative problem-solving sessions, feeling that whatever the outcome it is an opportunity to learn.

Summary

This chapter has further examined the process of creative problem solving and some of the assumptions that managers tackling problems commonly make. Using creative techniques for problem solving will require an amalgam of right- and left-brain thinking, both playfulness and discipline, openness to ideas and new perspectives as well as rigour in the search for data, and the evaluation and selection of ideas. At the idea-generation stage consideration of the constraints surrounding the problem situation should be ignored, since reflecting on them could hinder creativity. However, at the evaluation and selection stage, the constraints need to be borne in mind so that the option which is most likely to be successfully implemented is chosen.

This chapter has shown you some simple creative problem-solving techniques that you can use when working alone or with a group. There are many more, and you can read about them, for example, in Van Grundy's book, *Techniques of Structured Problem Solving*, which covers a range of techniques for problem redefinition and analysis, idea generation, evaluation and implementation.

You should now be ready to explore other creative techniques and to include these in your management toolkit. You will probably decide that some techniques are too elaborate or time consuming to use in a work environment. The ones introduced in this book are all useful and usable in a management context. They are designed to encourage unbounded thinking about the uncommon problems of management life.

Chapter 11
Thinking about change

The previous two chapters looked at problem solving and we noted how the most effective managers, anxious to bring about a change for the better, spend time proactively constructing problems. Those among us who are innovators have a natural disinclination to accept things as they are and actually prefer to look for problems to solve. This does not mean that they are necessarily the most successful change agents. Adaptors can also develop what Gareth Morgan describes as a 'proactive mindset', but the way in which they approach the change process will be different. Their preoccupation will be with examining all the possible options in detail before deciding which one to implement. Highly innovative people, on the other hand, will come up with many creative ideas but may not be good at the detailed analysis and planning required to select the best possible way forward and implement it.

For both innovators and adaptors, seeking to make changes can be a high-risk strategy in many organizations, because it implies that they have a dissatisfaction with 'the way we do things around here'. Often the organizational culture does not welcome people who do not 'go with the flow' because they appear to challenge the accepted notions of where power and control should lie. And yet, in order to survive, organizations must seek to change before they are forced to change, and this means encouraging all managers not only to question the organizational myths and traditions but also to come up with creative ideas for moving towards a better future.

However, in some organizations, constructing problems and taking a creative approach to change means that often you have to work 'against the grain' and this image seemed to be an apt title for this book. In woodwork, it is easier to follow the natural grain of the wood rather than to try to work against it. Working *against* the grain, therefore, conveys an image of someone whose creative efforts are not limited by the structure and composition of the material with which they are working. Although it may take more effort to produce a result, the outcome can be both original and effective.

The notion of going against the grain is the very opposite of 'going with the flow' or letting yourself be carried along by events. In a context of change it also implies that you should not take what seems to be the obvious or common sense approach before you have considered the creative possibilities of doing things differently.

By the end of this chapter you will:

- Have thought some more about the complex nature of change
- Understand more about the role of the manager in relation to change
- Recognize why traditional change models have limitations
- Appreciate the extent to which rational and creative approaches are complementary

Why creativity is overlooked in organizations

You will rarely hear someone described as being a really creative manager. The word 'creative' in conjunction with the word 'manager' produces an uneasy picture in some minds of one who has flashes of inspiration but is inconsistent, who is a bit of a maverick and cannot be bothered with detail and the routines of organizational life. The reason may lie in the nature and strength of organizational cultures. Gerry Johnson (1988), writing about the process of managing strategic change, reminds us of how unlikely it is that an individual entering an organization can do other than conform to the prevailing cultural norms:

> Managers hold a set of core beliefs and assumptions, specific and relevant to the organization in which they work. Whilst individual managers may hold quite varying sets of beliefs about many different aspects of that organizational world, there is likely to exist at some level a core set of beliefs and assumptions held relatively commonly by the managers ... Most organizations are essentially cautious and managers are not encouraged to be risk-takers. They are encouraged to conform rapidly to 'the way we do things around here'.

So there are positive disbenefits in being the one to advocate change. To understand why this might be we need to refer back to the traditional organizational metaphor, the machine, with its implicit idea of control and order. Organizations functioned because there were in place sets of rules to be complied with. Those who did not conform were suppressed. Alongside the notion of control was the view that it was possible to predict the future and to plan for it. In the traditional organizational culture caution, order, predictability and reliability were espoused while notions of autonomy, free thinking and risk taking were rejected. Since organizations are where managers spend much of their lives it is no wonder that they have such a profound influence on our behaviour and why some managers have not developed proactive mindsets. And yet, as you are aware, organizations today operate in an environment of constant change, so how can managers deal effectively with the challenges that this offers, if the prevailing culture is one of caution?

Change strategies, change and problems

Before moving on to look more specifically at what you can do to manage change successfully in your organization, we need to be clear about the various levels of change which can occur in organizations. First, there is strategic change. Most books about change management focus upon strategic-level change. While it is interesting to read accounts of how a multinational organization was turned around through the efforts of one farsighted individual, they do not have much advice to offer to the average manager struggling to achieve results in a much smaller operation. And despite the numerous books about the successful management of strategic change there is much discussion among management writers about its nature.

Some observers have noted that rather than having an all-embracing strategic plan, business strategy is in fact developed in stages as one decision builds upon another. It has been argued that managers *consciously* take such an approach as a way of coping with complexity. This is known as logical incrementalism. Other writers say that to describe such incrementalism as logical is just an attempt to find a rational explanation for processes which might be explained in other ways.

We shall leave them to their debate. What is important for you as a practising manager is to recognize that you have to try to manage within this context of incremental strategic change. And, of course, incrementalism implies layer upon layer of change, as frequent adjustments are made to the strategic plan. This means that in charting your own course through all this, to use a sailing metaphor, you need to tack first in one direction and then in another, as the prevailing wind changes. You have to be alert to the adjustments that have to be made and you have to make sure that your team understands *why* they have to be made, what the new objective is and exactly what is expected of them.

The spin-off from strategic change may require you to make a number of significant *operational changes* as the overall strategy develops and evolves. These can be perceived as opportunities for you to develop (along with others) a vision of where you want (or need) to be in the future or they may present themselves as problems to be solved. In all probability you will find that there is a combination of both of these, opportunities and problems.

However, if you find that you are dealing only with problems, you may need to consider whether it is sufficient to be managing in such an adaptive, responsive way or whether you might take a more creative, albeit risk-taking, approach.

Other kinds of change occur quite independently of the deliberate implementation of the strategic plan, although they should be in line with the overall mission of the organization. Change may occur at any level in the organization because an opportunity for improvement is spotted and is seized upon. Change may also take place because a problem is identified and dealt with. The difference between a change situation and a problem was suggested in Chapter 9 when discussing constructed problems. But if you are still confused then one way of thinking about the difference between a change situation and a problem is to think in terms of its boundaries.

A difficulty can be resolved fairly easily given the skills and resources required. It tends to have discrete boundaries in terms of

Who is involved
The extent to which it can be treated as a single entity
The timescale in which it must be solved
The information that is known about it
The information that needs to be gathered
Whether it is capable of resolution.

A change situation, on the other hand, is much less easy to define. It is less clear

Who should be involved
How it can be treated as a single issue
How long it might take to effect a change
How much is known about the situation
What else needs to be known
Whether it is an opportunity for change or a series of problems to be solved.

Somewhere in between the two are problems, presented, anticipated or constructed as was shown earlier in Figure 9.1.

What is change?

Because *any* intervention that is made in a system produces a change of some kind, we need to be clear what we mean when we talk about change in management. Perhaps better, since I am trying to put forward my own perspective, I need to explain what I mean when writing about change in the context of this book.

It seems that the word 'change' is used indiscriminately in management to mean at least two different things. First, it is used to describe a *state* of being, as in 'the management environment today is one of complex change', indicating that the environment is variable, unstable and subject to transformation. The state of change, therefore, occurs when internal or external factors cause instability in the environment. Second, the word 'change' is used to describe the *process* by which an organization or a person or a part of an organization moves from their current situation to a new one. It is the way in which an organization responds to or anticipates instability in its environment. It may involve establishing, abandoning or reforming sub-systems, functions or procedures, and in theory you can identify the point at which the change process begins and when it is completed.

These are two equally valid meanings, but the essential difference is that the *state* of change cannot be 'managed' in the way in which we commonly think of management. Managing the *process* of change, on the other hand, requires the use of what we might think of as traditional management skills, plus uncommon thinking. It is because the environment in which managers work is so dynamic (affected by the outcomes of so many change processes both within and outside their organization) that traditional models, strategies and frameworks for managing change on their own are insufficient. In this dynamic environment, as we know, things may not always be as they first seem and systems (human and functional) do not necessarily behave as they might. So in order to manage the process of change in organizations today managers need to have more than just the ability to plan, forecast, coordinate, control and so on. They must be able to think in uncommon or creative ways and be encouraged to do so.

Managing in a state of change

The changes taking place in the external environment (sociological, technological, political, legislative and economic change, for example) which were discussed in Chapter 7 affect not only organizations but also the people who work in them. Organizations respond to these external changes in ways that produce internal changes in, for example, their structure, culture, traditional working practices and relationships.

These internal changes in turn affect the way in which people behave. Their roles change, they need to acquire new skills and new ways of thinking. Jobs may be under threat, social sub-systems, which can be a very important motivating factor, may begin to break down, and people, not unreasonably, begin to ask not 'How can we work together to move the business forward?' but 'What's in it for me?'

So the reality for many managers is that while change is a key factor in the organization in which they work, they themselves are not the ones *driving* the change. The state of change results from various shifts in strategy, and strategic decisions sometimes pay little attention to the emotional commitment to change of the people whose working lives they will affect. Also, of course, the effects of strategic change today can have a very significant impact indeed if implementation involves 'downsizing' and the outsourcing of work formerly carried out in-house.

Working in an organization which is in a 'state of change' makes it difficult for you to manage as you would like to, because there are fewer certainties and in a sense every judgement that you make and every decision that you take may contain an element of risk. You have to begin to think in uncommon ways. This was not true in the past where a manager could be guided by experience, learned behaviours and theoretical models to 'get things right'.

The manager's role

In this uncertain environment when the only certainty is change, your management role is crucial, but it is a very different one from the role where you are driving or managing a process of change. How to manage effectively in this environment should be a major preoccupation for managers today, but it is one which is overlooked by writers on change management, who focus on managing the process of change.

The major contribution that you can make when your organization is in a *state* of change is to concentrate on sustaining your team. It requires a great deal of energy and thought, as well as an understanding of how the environment, especially the internal environment, is changing and how this is perceived by the people in your team. The teams themselves will change as people are seconded out to other projects and others take their place. People's motivation will change as tasks and goals change. Social and other sub-systems will alter and new allegiances and networks will be formed. All the while the manager needs to keep the momentum going, acting as a coach, adviser, counsellor and guide.

You will need to rely on your understanding of the subtle and complex relationships that can exist between an individual and those with whom he or she works. You can increase your understanding by being in tune with what is happening, observing, listening and thinking about the far-reaching effects of seemingly trivial events. Keeping in mind the idea of the organization as an organism will prevent you from mistakenly assuming that a small disturbance to the equilibrium in one part of the organization will have no effect elsewhere.

Sustaining your team through the effects of strategic change, making sure that individuals are prepared to adapt and comply with change, keeping them motivated and committed seems a somewhat passive role. So is there really scope for the kind of uncommon thinking that we are advocating in this book? Managing against the grain implies that you never let yourself relax into the comfort of an adaptive/reactive mode. You will always be looking for the opportunities in every change situation. You will not be content to go with the flow, even when the change process is being driven from elsewhere. Your concern will be to create a climate where others are encouraged to contribute ideas and suggestions about how to take advantage of emerging opportunities as the environment transforms, so that they feel involved rather than passive players in some complex organizational drama.

You may feel that this is very vague advice, but in a sense the whole of this book has been about how you as a manager approach this key role. It does mean that you cannot make assumptions. It does mean that you have to challenge your own strongly held convictions and prejudices from time to time. And it does mean that you need think in uncommon ways about *how* you manage. Really thinking about what you do, reflecting upon and learning from your day-to-day experience of managing, can make you a far more effective manager in a context of change than relying upon management models.

The psychological contract

If you *really* think about what is going on in your organization you will make interesting discoveries about the nature of the unwritten contract between individuals and the organization. Each individual makes their own psychological contract with their organization, which is basically a set of expectations. We have an expectation that the results produced by the organization will satisfy certain of our needs. Based on this expectation, we are willing to expend our energy and are motivated to work. The organization, in fulfilling its part of the psychological contract, will provide payments and other rewards in return for certain expected results. If the rewards, whatever they are (and they are not necessarily financial ones), are diminished in the view of the individual, then the motivation to contribute the same amount of effort will also become less.

What you ask people to do, how you reward them, how you add to or reduce their area of responsibility can all affect the psychological contract, and this is something that managers need to consider very carefully in times of change. If the contract becomes 'out of balance' then people may lose their commitment and motivation. You also need to remember that the psychological contract for each individual is different. For example, while one person may welcome the 'empowerment' that comes with changes in the way an organization is structured, others may find it stressful and threatening.

I once asked a manager working in the National Health Service, whose unit was about to become an NHS trust, what she had noticed most about the way in which change was being implemented. 'The amount of deliberate sabotage which is going on' was her immediate reply. People who were feeling disempowered by all the change, and for whom the psychological contract had been broken, were reacting in the only way they could.

Managing the change process

The kind of management role described above, which is largely about sustaining people in a climate of change, seems very unlike Fayol's model with its emphasis on functions such as controlling, coordinating, planning and forecasting. Managing a change process, on the other hand, would seem to require the use of these more traditional management skills and places the manager firmly back in the driving seat.

Many writers have offered change-management models, based upon rational analytical techniques. Two of these models will be examined in detail in the next chapter. A common approach is to establish the gap between the present situation and where you want to be. This is a useful starting point but it can mean that managers get locked into the negative idea that a change process is all about escaping from an unsatisfactory present situation. If you are 'solution minded' then the gap can begin to look like a chasm, a huge 'problem' to be solved, and you focus upon finding an acceptable solution rather than upon working towards a better future.

Peter Senge, writing in 1990, describes this gap as generating a 'creative tension', which can be a source of energy by which organizations can move from a current reality towards a vision of the future. This idea of the future vision underlines the essential difference between managing change and problem solving. The difficulty with many approaches to change management is that they look suspiciously like problem solving writ large.

Change treated as problem solving tends to bring with it an unease about the future and a nostalgia for the past. Change *management*, on the other hand, should be all about working towards a better future. Managing change is not primarily about unearthing short-term problems and solving them, although this may need to happen if blocks to progress are identified. It is about working to realize a *shared* vision of the future and it should continue to focus upon the future as the implementation of the change process proceeds.

This is easier said than done, of course, but as a manager you can begin by encouraging idea generation and discussion, and establishing a culture in your own team where a certain amount of risk taking is allowed. Ideas for change need not be connected with the big strategic issues of organizational life, but should relate to areas and issues which matter to the individuals themselves or to their team, and where they have the responsibility to initiate and champion future change.

The confusion between solving problems and managing change goes some of the way towards explaining why change is so often perceived as a threat rather than an opportunity, leaving those affected by change disheartened or demotivated. Where change is always seen as a necessary reaction to some current or impending problem, the risk of failure is that the problem will remain and may even become worse. On the other hand, in organizations where the drive for change becomes internalized into a search for a brighter future, failure to achieve the future vision might just mean that the vision itself was flawed. Nothing is lost and much may be learnt in the attempt.

The starting point for change

If we pursue the idea for the moment that change is about establishing the gap between where you are now and where you would like to be and then doing something about it, the first question is, do you actually know where you are now? What do you really know about your organization, for example?

You will probably have your own organizational metaphor; it may not be either a machine or an organism, but it should be an image that helps you to keep in mind the interrelatedness of apparently separate organizational entities. This image is fine when talking about organizations in general or for conjuring up an ideal picture of how they might function. However, the real image which you have of your own organization, or that part of it in which you work and have an interest, is unlikely to be any of these. It is unlikely even to be identical to that of your colleagues or other stakeholders in the organization. Each individual will be influenced by the culture and mythologies which may have grown up about how the organization does things, for better or for worse, but each will have an image of that organization, based on their own unique perception.

You cannot, therefore, assume that your personal image of the organization is correct or even that it is understood by others. One of the reasons change management often proves so difficult is that the vision of the future which the change is intended to achieve is not a shared vision, and the starting point for change, which should be a feeling of unease about the current situation, is not commonly understood.

In Chapter 8 you saw examples of how different people 'saw' their own organization. A very powerful way of discovering the unique interpretation which individuals make of their *experience* of organizational life is to ask them a different question. Try inviting colleagues or members of your team to describe through a picture how it feels *to them* to work in your organization, using an image that is meaningful to them. Alternatively, ask them to find a metaphor which offers an insight into their perspective on the organization. It is helpful if they can illustrate this, because often pictures are a more powerful means of communicating than words. I have used this technique with groups of managers from different organizations, working together for the first time, as a way of emphasizing that they cannot assume that, when discussing organizational life, everyone is talking the same 'language'.

Figure 11.1 shows a selection of responses to the question, 'What does it feel like to be a manager in your organization?' Can you guess which of these people worked in the Scientific Civil Service?

These images can be a very useful way of exploring the differences as well as the areas of understanding between colleagues. For example, each of the managers in Figure 11.1 seems to share a feeling that they are without power in their organization, and in one case the individual clearly feels threatened. In three of the examples the manager is expressing a sense of being very much alone, and possibly out of step. These are the kinds of points which might be explored in discussion.

One of the managers had an image of herself trying to row in the opposite direction to her colleagues. This seems to invite a definite managerial response. She clearly feels personally disempowered by whatever is happening in her organization and needs some kind of support. Does her drawing indicate that she feels she is out of line or are the others in the boat her own staff whom she needs to motivate to follow her direction? What does the image tell us about her? About her staff or colleagues? About her organization? If she were asked to include her customers or clients in this picture how would she represent them? As a threat (sharks, perhaps, or gunboats)? What about suppliers, senior management other departments or colleagues? What is the environment like? Is the sea calm or choppy? Is the boat on a lake or a river? Where is the river going? And so on. By using prompts and questions like these you can extend the image and gain a greater understanding of where that person 'is coming from'.

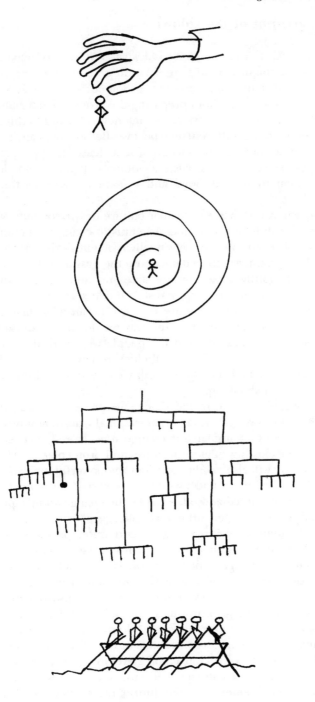

Figure 11.1   Images of working in organizations

Taking account of the culture

An activity such as the one above is a very useful way of making sure that there is no ambiguity or misunderstanding about the current situation, which is the starting point for change. Sometimes enthusiastic managers embark upon change without preparing the ground first. Change requires people to develop in new ways, to assume new roles and to think about the organization from a different perspective. Before this can happen there needs to be a common perspective (or at least an appreciation of the differences between individuals), a common language to describe the current (soon to be old) ways and a common view of the prevailing culture.

Each organization has a particular culture or 'personality' which grows and changes subtly through time. Attempts to change the culture bring a degree of uncertainty and ambiguity which people find difficult to tolerate. Think of the pain which accompanies the privatization of services or industries previously owned by the state and how those involved in the change, both internal and external stakeholders, react.

A strong organizational culture may not be an advantage in times of change. A firm commitment to the way we do things around here can mean that the organization and the people who work there may not be open to considering any other possibilities. It may not see that its business might be threatened by an organization whose culture encourages innovation and risk taking.

As a manager trying to manage a change process you will need to take into account the strength of the organizational culture and how this might affect your ability to implement change quickly and successfully. Quite apart from the existing rules, procedures and protocols with which you will be familiar, you will also need to consider the powerful lobbying which may take place via the informal sub-systems that exist. You will need not only to work with those immediately affected by the change you propose but also to sell your ideas to other influential colleagues.

The time that you will need to spend upon preparing the ground should not be underestimated when considering how long it might take to implement a change process. If you work in an organization which has not encouraged 'bottom-up change' you may need to begin to influence the culture which exists within your own team. You could begin by encouraging individuals to express their own feelings of dissatisfaction with the present ways of doing things, so that communications are not seen as necessarily being in one direction but start to flow upwards as well as down. You could develop the practice of constantly 'reviewing what we are doing', with the focus on looking forward to continuous improvements in the future rather than on revisiting the past.

Creating a vision

The next step in managing a change process is to establish a vision of where you want to be. This is an extremely difficult task since it requires you to make certain assumptions about the environment and how it might change in the future. However, it is never safe to assume that your vision of the future is shared by others and, as you saw in the previous chapter, it is essential to arrive at an accommodation between different value positions if you are going to get commitment to change. Here is one way of doing this.

You saw earlier how pictures can give a very powerful insight into someone else's perception of a situation. Imaging or visioning can also be used to reach a clear view of where you want to be. The following technique can be used with a single team which is trying to refocus or develop a strategic vision. (It could also be used to develop a future vision for a department or for an entire organization.) You will need lots of flipchart paper and coloured pens.

Let us suppose that the desire is to engender greater customer awareness in the organization. The first task is to be clear about 'the old story', which is the situation today. Each member of the group is invited to draw a picture of how they believe that the company appears to customers. The individual pictures are then discussed in sub-groups and the one which seems to capture the situation most accurately is selected for further work.

A second stage might then be to ask individuals to draw what it feels like to them to work in the organization. Again the pictures are discussed in sub-groups and either a composite picture is drawn which represents the feelings of the group or one of the individual pictures is chosen for further development.

The next task is for the whole group, or two or three sub-groups together if numbers are very large, to assemble the selected images into a single picture which they feel 'tells the story' of the current situation. You may want to end the session at this point and run the next activities after a break or the following day.

The next task is to develop 'the new story'. You will repeat the previous steps but this time individuals are asked to draw how customers might see the changed organization and then how they would feel to work in this new organization. The final step is for the group or collections of sub-groups to draw a composite picture of the new organization. Having done this and discussed the outcomes you are ready to pose the question 'How do we get from where we are now to where we want to be?'

What you have done here, through working to create a shared vision, is to arrive at a constructed 'problem'. Of course, having a vision alone is not enough, the question 'How do we get there?' is a very big question indeed. One positive thing that you can do is to identify those factors which are favourable to change, that will help you to achieve the vision. They may have to do with the culture of the organization, the timing of the change, or the likely support of other colleagues, for example, or it may be that social or technological change has created a favourable environment. You will also need to spend time considering the constraints which could hold you back. Once they have been identified, these constraints can also be described in terms of 'problems' to be 'solved', expressed as 'How may we . . .?' which is the prompt for creative thinking. In this way you can begin to break down the change scenario into smaller manageable pieces, the solution of each 'problem' being one positive step towards achieving the desired change.

Why change strategies don't work

Most change strategies, as I said earlier, are based upon rational analytical models, but it is precisely because we are trained to think rationally and analytically that we fail to really think about how to manage change successfully. Rational techniques, as the next chapter will show, are simply not sufficient to cope with the 'unknowable complexity' of management life.

If you have ever been responsible for initiating a change process you will know how frustrating it can become. Rarely is the perfect realization of your plans achieved. Some of the reasons why this might be will probably have occurred to you while you have been reading this book, since they have to do with how organizations and people behave as well as with your own personal approach as a manager. But also in our determination to behave rationally we tend to make false assumptions.

That time stands still

A typical rational change model might involve the following steps:

1 Analyse the situation
2 Establish the objectives
3 Generate options for change
4 Choose the option which is likely to give the most satisfactory results
5 Implement it
6 Evaluate

While this is going on the effective manager would be communicating with staff, encouraging their participation and motivating them to feel positive about the change. They would be alert to possible areas of resistance to change and have made contingency plans in case the implementation of the change fails to progress as scheduled.

In a different world, where time stood still, this might be an effective way forward, but this leisurely rationalism bears little relationship to the experience of real managers working in real organizations today. Time does not stand still to allow the completion of a step-by-step change process. Other problems and other pressures for change cut across it. And even if by some miracle the process was implemented as planned and the change was effected, it would be a change which had relevance in the situation that *was* and could not account for the dynamics of the present environment.

That all change is a problem

If the change model I have just described was familiar to you that is because you met something similar earlier in this book when considering problem solving. Much advice about how to manage change explicitly confuses it with problem solving, recommending, for example, that you identify the 'problem owner'. It is important to be clear about the difference. Solving a problem will inevitably *lead to* a change of some kind, otherwise the status quo (and the problem) would remain as it was. But it is crucial to remember that at the heart of a change process there is not a problem but a vision of the future.

That organizations are easy to understand

Another reason change programmes do not succeed in the way that we should like can be because we have forgotten how organizations behave. Whether you prefer to think of an organization as an organism or as a machine, either way it is true to say that for it to remain in a healthy state all parts of it need to be functioning in harmony. A change which affects one of its components will inevitably affect other functions as well since they are interdependent. So a change strategy which does not recognize the complexity and power of the systems and sub-systems within an organization will inevitably create disharmony and dysfunction.

I imagine organizational life as a kaleidoscope of patterns. Some patterns are more pleasing than others. Some are rich and complex while others are stark and simple. However, you cannot change one part of the pattern without changing the whole of it, no matter how subtly you try to move the individual pieces. You can change the total picture by shaking the kaleidoscope violently, but there will still be some pattern there with a structure and logic of its own, even though the individual pieces have either been moved or have disappeared.

Clearly, different kinds of organization will be more responsive to change than others. This is partly dependent upon the prevailing culture of the organization, but it is also a feature of its structure. The mechanistic organization, with its hierarchy of responsibilities and roles, accompanied by written procedures and records, operates most effectively in a stable environment where there is infrequent change. On the other hand, the organic organization should 'theoretically' be able to respond more rapidly to its environment, since there is no strong bureaucracy and work is much more likely to be carried out through flexible teams. I say theoretically because it does not always follow that organic organizations respond readily to change. There may be many factors which inhibit change, such as internal reporting lines which do not mirror the way in which people actually work together in teams, informal control systems exercised by certain power groups which can subvert change and the influence of strong internal networks and social sub-systems.

That communicating is easy

Many books on change management mention the importance of communicating with those people who are going to be affected by change.

List all the ways in which you have been given information about a change that is going to affect your own job in some way. Your list might include:

Mass gatherings of people in a large conference venue
Information 'cascaded' down the line in team briefings
Newsletters
A 'personal' letter from the chief executive to every member of staff
Videos featuring the chief executive and senior team

In whatever way the news of a change is communicated it is rarely seen as good news. Even if the message refers to mission statements and visions of the future this is still interpreted by individuals as spelling bad news. This is partly because most people find the prospect of change is unsettling. It is also because change is often explained as being necessary because of a huge problem which is facing the organization. It is represented as an escape from the unsatisfactory present which the organization has to make in order to stay competitive. Often those working at the sharp end of the organization do not even believe that the problem that has been identified is the *real* problem. They can point to many other problems in the organization which affect its performance, but these 'second-order' problems never seem to be addressed. It is no wonder that the prospect of change makes people disillusioned and demotivated.

Creative thinking and change

Even though it is unlikely that rational change models on their own will be sufficient in today's complex organizational environment, they need not be rejected out of hand as long as you avoid making the kinds of false assumptions mentioned above. But you are likely to be a more effective manager of change if you use an amalgam of creative and rational techniques. For example, you could use creative techniques to arrive at a vision of where you want to be, getting your team to work together to devise the 'new story' as described above. Having identified where you want to be, the next step is to rephrase this as a question, or a series of questions beginning 'How may we . . .?' You can then use one of the techniques outlined in Chapter 10 to generate ideas for 'solving' the 'problem'.

You can even use traditional change models as a prompt for creative thinking. Here is just one example. Lewin's Force Field Analysis is a useful tool for describing the forces which are driving change and identifying those which are resistant to change. A very simple force field diagram might look like Figure 11.2. By reducing the resistance to or increasing the impetus for change you can move out of the state of equilibrium.

The model is typically used by management students to summarize or describe an existing situation and they may then conclude that, for example, staff need to be motivated to change, or new technology is needed to effect change. However, the creative manager might be prompted by the diagram to ask more questions rather than arrive at solutions such as ' How may we reduce our reliance on technology?' or 'How may we persuade our customers to change their purchasing habits?' You could also use the model to generate ideas for

● Reducing the effect of a negative force
● Strengthening the effect of a driving force
● Discovering a new driving force

Once you have selected the most promising option from a range of ideas, using some analytical technique, you can begin to devise the implementation process. At this stage you will be concerned with planning

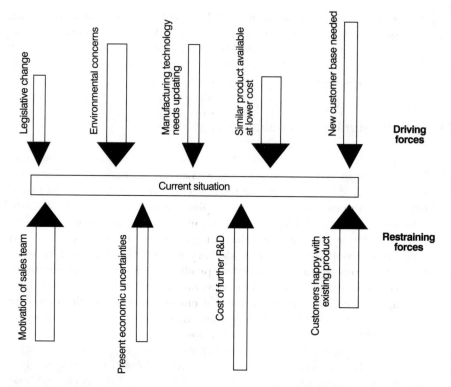

Figure 11.2   Force Field diagram showing restraining forces and driving forces for introducing a new product range

and, later, with collecting data so that you can monitor progress and evaluate how close you are getting towards the future vision. As mentioned earlier, this is an essentially rational, analytical approach which will require many iterations as the environment changes and you have to go back and reconsider whether the 'new story' is still appropriate.

Mines and pitfalls

As you proceed with the implementation of change, unexpected mines and pitfalls will inevitably be uncovered and they have to be dealt with in order to progress. Perversely, this can be because implementation plans are too well drawn and assume a rationality in human and organizational behaviour that does not necessarily exist.

One of the major difficulties can lie with the change driver, who having set off along a particular track believes that there can be no going back. In a sense this attitude is a product of how we are taught to think about management. We are encouraged to believe that successful managers are those who always get it right, who have the answers and whose judgement cannot fail. There is plenty of advice about how to be an effective manager, much of it in the form of prescriptions to follow if you want to be a success. It is no wonder that we end up believing that management mistakes constitute a failure and not an opportunity to learn. And it is not surprising that, having decided upon one course of action, managers are inclined to stick to it rather than to admit that their plans may need to be revisited and revised.

Although a change programme may begin with a clear vision of the future, it may also flounder or struggle because the full implications of the change only become clear as the implementation proceeds. When this happens those affected begin to question again the need for change, to extol the old ways of doing things as being the right way, to suffer stress and anxiety. The old cultural norms are very powerful. Any change process, even at a purely operational level, will produce a 'state of change' in which uncertainties and ambiguities exist and individual psychological contracts may appear to be threatened. It is not enough to concentrate upon the implementation process without at the same time having a strategy for sustaining people so that they remain positive.

When not to change

The imperative for change seems constant. But because change in organizations is disruptive, unsettling and even threatening to some people you should not overlook the value of retaining the status quo. Now this will seem a strangely uncreative thought in a book which is arguing for an 'uncommon approach' to organizational dilemmas. However, such is the current vogue for change of all kinds that for a manager to suggest refraining from change would certainly be going against the grain.

Because the effects of change can send damaging shock waves through organizations sometimes the imperative for change should be resisted. If your environmental scanning tells you that there are even greater pressures for change on the horizon it may be a better tactic to conserve resources and energy. Change is costly to implement in terms of human as well as other resources. It makes sense to examine the costs and benefits both of making a change and of *not* changing before moving towards implementation. You will only be in a position to do this once options for change have been generated. One of the options should always be to retain the equilibrium position, so long as this option is a viable one and not simply an excuse for inactivity.

Going against the flow

This chapter has been about the kind of management approach which refuses to go with the flow, which does not see all change as a potential problem and which encourages others to develop proactive mindsets. As we have seen, this approach can often appear to be counter-cultural and so it does take some courage.

A good example of the courage it takes literally to stop going with the flow is found in a management game that is often used in team building. The team is given a piece of metal pipe which has a number of holes bored in it. Inside the pipe is a small boat. The other piece of equipment is a small jug. The object is to fill the pipe with water so that the boat floats to the top.

What usually happens is that one member of the team is deployed to carry water to fill up the level in the pipe, while the others plug the holes in the pipe with their fingers. Inevitably, the water leaks out and despite the furious efforts of the water carrier the level barely rises. The water carrier blames the others for not covering the holes effectively, they in turn berate the water carrier for not fetching the water quickly enough. Teams can become locked in to this circular argument for some time, becoming angrier with each other, the wetter they get, until one of them realizes that they will never succeed in their task because the greater the volume of water, the greater the pressure and the faster the pipe will leak. All that is needed now is for this person to stop 'going with the flow' and persuade the others that the solution is to give up the attempt!

Summary

The world of organizations today is not one where change occurs as a single episode or event. It is one where organizations are constantly addressing change, reshaping and adjusting to their environment. There is no calm unruffled surface and very little opportunity to relax in a steady state. Change is the current reality. We cannot therefore rely upon models, prescriptions or frameworks to 'get change right'. What we can rely upon is our own ability to think in 'uncommon ways'.

The traditional approaches to the management of organizational complexity are now being challenged. A number of management writers are questioning the idea of strategic planning, for example, and are arguing that what is needed is not formulae, models and extensive data analysis but non-linear thinking. What writers such as Henry Mintzberg are calling for are new kinds of thinking by managers. Whereas in traditional bureaucracies it was the planners and the policy makers who did the thinking, today managers need to think as well as act, helping to create an organizational vision with which others can identify.

What I have been describing in this chapter is a different kind of manager, one who can sustain individuals working in an environment of change, as well as manage the process of change in an effective way; one who encourages the inputs of others and considers their perspective and is willing to question his or her own prejudices in order to 'think beyond the box'.

Such a manager recognizes that while some people thrive on change, others see it only as a threat, particularly in times of uncertainty. This manager looks for the opportunities in change. He or she is at times reflective and at times actively engaged in and encouraging discussion and debate to stimulate new ideas.

Yet one of the most difficult tasks for a manager is to create a climate where questioning what is done and being open to change is normal. For many people this means that they have to begin to think about their work and their role in a totally different way. A sense of shared values and a robust organizational culture can be an organizational strength. It can also be a weakness if challenging the myths and questioning the values are not condoned. Using creative techniques can help individuals to become aware of the potential opportunities for changing 'the way we do things' and to focus beyond the operational to the strategic.

Successful managers will use both rational and creative techniques to alert themselves to the relevance of external change for the organization and how this might affect the way things are done in the future. They will think in terms of an incremental approach to change, knowing that the process of affecting change will require many iterations as the environment itself transforms.

Chapter 12
More than rational

I recently had a conversation with someone who wanted to know what my job entailed. I described what I had been doing that morning, much of which had been spent with a member of my team who needed reassurance about her future and her confidence boosting after a particularly difficult few months at work. 'Oh, I see,' came the reply, 'You're in Personnel. I thought you were a manager.'

At the beginning of this book we asked the question 'What is a manager?' and looked the way in which Fayol had described the manager's role. However, we have stressed throughout that managers today are called upon to perform a variety of roles, depending upon the situation in which they find themselves. What Fayol had in mind was a very rational model of management which drew upon his experience of managing at a time when roles and responsibilities were much more narrowly defined than they are today, and the management environment was not subject to the kind of turbulent change which you experience.

Many of the management models which you will come across (and some of them have been mentioned in this book) are based upon rational techniques. The question is whether these are adequate to cope with the demands of managing today. This chapter argues that decision making is at the heart of *everything* that a manager does and goes on to look at the limitations of the rational model as the basis of decision making and managing change. By the end of it you should:

- Have considered the nature and impact of the decisions which you make
- Have examined whether the decisions which you make at work really are rational
- Have considered the limitations of a rational approach to problem solving, decision making and managing change
- Understand the need to enhance the rational analytical model with different ways of thinking.

What is rationality?

In the previous chapter, two models for managing change were mentioned. They are summarized in Figure 12.1 and they are both essentially rational models.

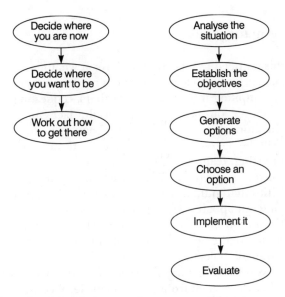

Figure 12.1   Two rational models for managing a process of change

But what do we mean when we talk about rationality? The minute that you begin to analyse a situation, to look for alternative courses of action towards a determined objective, to evaluate them and eventually select one to implement, you are moving towards a rational approach. It involves a way of thinking which is systematic and rigorous rather than subjective and idiosyncratic. The *Oxford English Dictionary* describes being rational as ' able to reason, sensible, sane . . . not foolish or absurd or extreme . . . rejecting what is unreasonable or cannot be tested by reason'. In terms of planning and decision making rationality has to do with the methods for achieving future goals. Economists, on the other hand, would think of rationality as being about selecting from alternative courses of action the one which is most likely to maximize output for a given input.

We noted in discussing creative problem-solving techniques that at a certain stage your thinking needs to switch from right brain to left brain as you set about evaluating the ideas generated and selecting the one most likely to solve the problem. The point at which models for managing change and for creative problem solving meet, therefore, is the stage at which you need to make a decision about the optimum way forward.

But, of course, managers do not spend all their time dealing with problems or managing change, so how important is the idea of rationality in management?

Redefining management

To answer this we need to take another look at what managers do at work. Much of a manager's time each day is spent reading information on screen or on paper, compiling information for others, requesting or exchanging information, either on paper, electronically, face to face or through telecommunications. If a manager has line management responsibility for staff, time will be taken up with managing those people, motivating, leading, supporting, team building and so on.

What managers *actually* do in an average day at work will certainly include activities that in themselves are quite trivial. Some of the time they will be carrying out apparently routine or repetitive activities with the help of or in collaboration with others, and it may be unclear how these various tasks contribute to the management of the organization or indeed to meeting its strategic objectives.

However, if you list *all* management activities that you carry out at work you will see that they range from the strategic-level contributions that you make (either directly or indirectly, through the operational tasks which you organize and carry out in order to implement strategy) down to the routine administrative tasks that relate to the way in which you organize your work and your time. The proportion of time you spend on tasks at each level will vary depending on your role and the extent to which you are operating at a strategic level in the organization. However, behind each of these tasks is a decision about the timing, the manner and the nature of the actions you are taking, whom to involve, whom to exclude and so on.

Management as decision making

Let us consider the idea that, whatever the *nature* of the task, what a manager is actually doing at work is making decisions. Now Fayol did not list decision making as one of his key management activities, yet the need to make decisions is implicit in all of them. For example, we can take one of Fayol's five elements of management, *coordination*. Fayol believed that since an organization performs a wide variety of tasks one of the jobs of a manager is to ensure that the work of one individual or a team is in line with that of others and that they all contribute to the overall aims of the organization. He referred to it as 'binding together, unifying and harmonizing all activity'. In order to do this the manager needs a clear sense of the whole picture and how all the individual efforts contribute. But he or she also has to decide whether more effort is required in certain areas, whether current resources are sufficient, which individuals might need additional training or support, whom to deploy on which task, whom to recruit, whether timescales are adequate, what management information is required and so on. There are numerous opportunities here for sound management decisions.

Other activities on Fayol's list are forecasting and planning. As will be shown later, forecasting and planning are essential parts of the rational decision-making process. It is clearly not enough for managers to think just in terms of the day to day. They must 'assess the future and make provision for it'. However, forecasting is not the sole province of those who make major business decisions. Each of us makes forecasts of some sort every day. On a minor level, for example, we might try to predict what the reaction of the team might be if we decide to introduce a new procedure. On a more strategic level we will take into account the possibility of an imposed structure change before deciding to invest energy in further team building. It is essential to the process of decision making that we have a view about how things might turn out if a certain course of action is taken.

Herbert Simon and his colleagues have carried out a great deal of research into the process of decision making over a number of years. For him management is all about decision making. The larger strategic-level decisions about policy create a series of occasions for further decisions as the higher-order decisions have to be implemented. Even apparently routine management activities are based upon decisions which involve some measure of forecasting and evaluation, such as the decision to telephone someone rather than use e-mail, to schedule a meeting at one particular time rather than another, to deal with this task before attending to that one even though they are both apparently equally urgent.

It is the *consequences* of these decisions, either individual or cumulative, which distinguish the effective manager. However, because many of the decisions in themselves are apparently fairly routine or low level, it may not be obvious how they contribute to the overall performance of the organization. But what is significant in management terms is not simply *what* those decisions are, but also *how, why* and *when* they were taken. This is why it is important to look at the way in which decisions are made, whether the process is based on rationality or on some purely personal common sense. While the outcomes of effective management decisions may not be immediately visible and may only really become evident over time, the effects of poor management decisions are often apparent all too quickly!

Programmed and non-programmed decisions

Simon further distinguished between programmed and non-programmed decisions. *Programmed decisions* are those which really require little thought. They are routine and often part of a recognized procedure. *Non-programmed decisions* are those which are new and non-routine, where the situation has not occurred previously and there are no precedents upon which to rely as in change situation. A programmed decision might be the way in which you handle someone's request to take a day's annual leave. A non-programmed decision might be related to the need to restructure your team. The more responsibility a manager takes on, the fewer non-programmed decisions they are likely to make.

Consider your most recent day at work (or at home if you are not presently working) and list and number the more important decisions that you had to make. Stop when you reach twenty! Plot them along the continuum below, according to whether they tended to be programmed or non-programmed.

Highly   Highly
programmed _____ unprogrammed

You will probably find that most of your decisions were of the non-programmed kind and this will reflect the nature of organizational life today and the way in which the role of the manager has changed since Simon was writing in the late 1950s. Because they relate to events and situations which are non-routine and often very complex, you really do need to give them some uncommon thought. And even though you might believe that making programmed decisions is just a matter of common sense, the really effective managers will also from time to time question the procedures of which such decisions are a part, asking 'why *do* we do things this way around here?'

The organizational impact of your decisions

Now consider the impact that your individual non-strategic decisions can make upon the organization. For example, suppose that you decide to speak to one of your team about a problem with their current performance which is affecting the motivation of the team. This is a non-programmed decision in that it is not part of a formal disciplinary process where there is a procedure to follow. However, it is not *highly* unprogrammed since the decision to handle the problem by talking to the person concerned is part of a recognized process for managing teams. The people affected by your decision, either directly or indirectly might include:

- The individual
- Others in the team, whether or not they feel your action is justified
- Others outside the team whose own work was suffering because of the team's reduced effectiveness
- Others outside the team who were aware that there was a problem
- The individual's partner or family
- Customers or stakeholders in the organization

Take one or two of the non-programmed decisions on your list and make a note of those people who were *directly* affected by it and then those who were *indirectly* affected by it in some way.

You may have been surprised at how far-reaching are the effects of some of the day-to-day management decisions that you make. Because they were non-programmed decisions you could not rely upon procedure and precedent. So how did you reach those decisions? Were you trying to follow a rational process, or were you using 'common sense'? Would they have appeared sensible, sane and reasonable to those who were affected by them? Or might they have seemed illogical and idiosyncratic? Given the environment in which managers have to make decisions, it is worth examining whether it is possible to be rational and what the rational model has to offer.

Decision making as a rational process

There are five basic stages to the rational decision-making model. It is taken from the area of planning and policy making and it is very similar to the more complex change management model shown in Figure 12.1:

1 Define the problem or the situation and identify objectives
2 List all possible ways of achieving the objectives
3 Predict the possible outcomes from each alternative strategy
4 Compare the possible outcomes with the original objectives
5 Select the strategy or course of action which most closely meets the objectives and solves the problem.

It differs in that it emphasizes the need to forecast the future (step 3) and it does not go beyond analysis into implementation.

While we might accept the logic of this approach to decision making, the *application* of the model raises a number of difficulties. So before we go on to consider how this relates to the need for uncommon or creative thinking, we should first look at its limitations as a model.

Rational analytical models were especially valued in the fields of policy making and resource allocation, for example, where the need to obtain 'value for money' and for accountability in relation to government spending programmes led to an increase in the use of analytical and quantitative techniques. They were particularly useful in those areas of public policy making where, for social and political reasons, it was important to obtain a thorough understanding of the likely outcomes of policy decisions. However, the widespread use of these techniques produced criticism and controversy. Much of the criticism pointed to the fact that the process of evaluating or weighing alternative courses of action could be distorted by personal prejudices or values in order to favour one option above another. Furthermore, the sheer volume of data that was produced as every option was researched and costed tended to hinder rather than help the decision-making process, producing the charge of 'paralysis through analysis'.

The main limitation is that it is an *ideal* model. It makes a number of assumptions. It assumes that it is possible to make accurate forecasts about the future, to fully understand and analyse the implications of alternative courses of action in an objective way, and that, once a decision has been made, the action taken will meet the objectives described. Of course, we do not live or work in an ideal world. We should not expect therefore that by relying upon a technique which is essentially rational we shall alight upon the one course of action that will completely meet our objectives and solve a problem or bring about a change. But this does not mean that we should reject it out of hand, particularly since the decisions that we do make are often made with very little reference to any type of analysis at all. They are made on the basis of 'common sense', and, as you have seen, the patterns which make up our common sense may not necessarily be the most reliable. So why do we find it so difficult to be rational?

Old friends

Simon and his colleagues, in carrying out research into artificial intelligence, found that human beings are not good at processing large amounts of new data and information. In other words, as you saw earlier, we are not naturally able to cope with the analysis of complex situations and large numbers of possibilities for action. Instead of mentally constructing decision trees to help us to evaluate alternative courses of action, we rely upon recognizing patterns in situations and comparing these with ones we have met previously.

Simon calls these patterns, built up through experience as well as formal education, 'old friends'. What in this book we have called 'common sense' contains patterns put together from and modified by our experience, and we refer to them unconsciously in our instinctive reaction to the management situations in which we find ourselves. The implications of Simon's research might lead us to assume that all we need to do to become better at the business of management is to gain more experience and to learn from it. And this is partly so. But the problem remains that the experience itself may not always be a reliable guide. Sometimes you will get away with relying on common sense. More often you will find that the decision which you thought was effective in one set of circumstances is not so in different ones. There will certainly be occasions where following your instinct or trusting in 'hunches' about the future may appear to be a very *irrational* way to behave. And sometimes we even manage to convince ourselves that we are being rational when the truth is that we are being anything but rational as the short case study below illustrates.

Applied rationality

The simple three-stage model for managing change shown in Figure 12.1 was discussed in the previous chapter. You may also have come across it in relation to decision making:

Decide where you are now
Decide where it is you want to be
Work out how to get there.

I tried this simple rational approach in making a decision about a small problem of my own, which will be common to most people at a certain time of the year. The problem was the need to get down to some serious Christmas shopping. It is included here as a small case study to demonstrate how easy it is for people to fool themselves into thinking they are behaving rationally when in fact they are following some perverted logic of their own. Does this thinking process seem familiar to you?

A. *Description: Where I am now*
Time – Saturday at end of November
Achievements to date – three presents
Constraints – other demands on time
Environmental factors – cold and starting to rain
B. *Objective: Where I want to be*
Twenty-five presents bought and wrapped
Deadline – 12 December
C. *Options for how to get from A to B plus predicted outcome*
Go shopping today for 2 hours – minimal time, could concentrate my mind, still leaves time to do other things
Go shopping all day today – guarantees I shall get it all done, more time means better decisions made, leaves next Saturdays free
Go shopping today and next Saturday – today would enable browsing, leaving next Saturday for focused buying
Leave all shopping to last minute but spend time making a list – really concentrates the mind and means no time is wasted
The decision
Each of these options had disadvantages as well as advantages, and so I was able to complete a rough cost–benefit analysis of all of them in terms of benefits gained compared with costs incurred. These related to things like increasing crowds in shops as Christmas approached, cost of parking if I spent a day shopping, the opportunity cost of neglecting other things I had to do while shopping for presents and so on.

   After weighing all the various options I decided to go for the first one. This was based on a forecast that it would be easier to park in November than on one of the Saturdays closer to Christmas, that the shops would be less crowded, that without a list to constrain my thinking I would easily find presents for everyone in less time than it might take if I took a more systematic approach a week or so later.
The result
The outcome of this decision was that after twice as many hours spent shopping on that Saturday in November as I had originally planned, I achieved five presents and so was some 80 per cent away from my target.

Rational or not?

As a *rational* process, the steps that I had taken were satisfactory. I was clear about where I was starting from and about what I wanted to achieve and in what timescale, but as an *effective* process, it was a failure. So what went wrong?

First, my forecasting was sadly flawed. Based on previous experience I should have known that shopping for Christmas presents is a process that cannot be completed at a single attempt. Why was my forecasting so poor?

● I had not learnt from experience.
● I had underestimated the constraints (time and energy, difficulty in parking).
● I had not properly anticipated the environment in which the implementation of my plan would take place.

What else was wrong with my thinking? While I limited the number of options I might consider to ones which it was worth investigating (comprehensive rationality would have included all possible options), my evaluation of the options was logically flawed. And although I *thought* that I was being objective, in fact I had already effectively made up my mind about which option I would take.

So, from the beginning, what I pretended was a rational process of comparing one option against another and weighing the relative merits of each was actually an attempt at *post hoc* rationalization because I had already made a decision based on largely non-rational, emotional reasons. I know that I have behaved in exactly the same way in making management decisions. I would be surprised if anyone reading this book has never done the same.

Learning from this case study

Although this was a very simple example of decision making in action, it does underline some important points about the danger of relying (or rather believing that we are relying) upon some model of rationality when we are actually following our own brand of common sense. It also emphasizes the need for the kind of uncommon thinking which was described in the first chapter of this book.

The first point is the extent to which your personal values and prejudices can distort your attempts to behave rationally, whether you are making a non-programmed decision or managing a change process. The pull of your own 'common sense' can be so strong that it can persuade you to leave out of your analysis any facts which do not confirm this common-sense view. In Chapter 1 we stressed how important it is to learn from your experience rather than to allow past experience to become a limitation. In my case, I had ignored what my experience told me because it cast doubt upon the logic of what I wanted to do. As a result, the forecasts that I made about possible outcomes were also flawed. If I had *really* thought about my past experience in similar situations, evaluated it and reflected upon it, I would have had a more reliable guide to the future.

Another common tendency is for enthusiastic decision makers, or those innovators who are easily bored by detailed analysis, to underestimate the constraints which might prevent them from achieving their goals. If you want your decisions to be effective you must understand the environment in which they are being made. In my case I had ignored this because, without real analysis, I had reached a decision about what action I wanted to take (although I had devised a fall-back position in case it did not succeed!). I had consequently dismissed any signals the left part of my brain might have tried to give me.

Finally, in the example above, deciding where I wanted to be was relatively simple. Both the timeframe and the objective were to some extent predetermined by two assumptions. The first was that Christmas Day will fall as usual on 25 December and that there were a certain number of people for whom I would need to buy a present. However, if you are a creative thinker you should already be challenging this kind of pro-grammed thinking. If I had been using creative techniques, for example, I might begin by asking myself how *not* to get my Christmas shopping done in time for Christmas as one route into devising a plan for ensuring that I did!

Are *you* being rational?

If, while reading this, you have been considering the kinds of decisions that you take each day at work and *how* you decide what to do, you will probably have concluded that for the most part very little actual thought goes into them. Because most managers today work under considerable pressure, there simply is not the time to spend examining all the possible courses of action and evaluating them so that you achieve the best possible outcome. You rely upon 'common sense' to help you decide swiftly.

Although you may think you are being rational, you may be, as I was, acting almost instinctively. However, it is very hard to justify decisions based upon common sense, particularly as our brand of common sense might appear to be anything but sense to others. What we might regard (and subsequently defend) as a logical and rational decision might seem 'off beam' or irrational to someone with a different view of the situation. The more experienced a manager you are, the more likely you are to act instinctively. If decision making really is at the heart of management activity we should be relying upon something more than common sense to point the way forward. Yet, as you have seen, it can be very difficult to follow a rational approach. The reasons for this lie in the limitations of the rational model when applying it to real life.

There's no time to be rational!

As you saw earlier, most of the decisions that you take each day are not the large-scale strategic ones but the host of non-programmed decisions which constitute the *practice* of management. It would be true to say that there is less chance of your adopting a rational approach to decision taking at this level than at the strategic level and more chance that you will rely upon common sense. This is because unlike most of the decisions which you have to make each day, those relating to strategic issues are on the organizational agenda. Time is therefore set aside, or found, for the information gathering and discussions that precede those decisions which are clearly going to have a major impact upon the organization.

The decisions which managers have to make every day often relate to presented problems and situations which are not part of the organizational agenda. They often relate to situations which if not corrected, would frustrate the endeavours of others and adversely affect the performance of the organization in some way. These decisions characterize the way in which a manager reacts to current events and circumstances rather than how he or she engages in the process of planning for the future. The time to gather information and discuss possible scenarios is not available. The advice to speculate about where you want to be in the future probably seems unhelpful in circumstances where your immediate response is likely to be 'Not here'.

Fortunately, management life is not all about firefighting. The problem is that the firefighting approach becomes a habit. In this frame of mind, every new situation is seen as a potential problem, to be tackled swiftly so that we can return to the business in hand. However, if you can reframe your thinking, perhaps by using some creative techniques to help you, you may find that you *are* able to plan, to innovate and to turn some of the perceived problems into opportunities for change. If this means that you can make considered decisions instead of taking them 'on the run' in firefighting mode, it is worth looking at what the rational decision-making model has to offer.

Understanding where you are

As you saw in the previous chapter, just as you have no sound basis from which to embark upon a change process unless you are clear about where you are starting from, the same is true about decision making. Your decisions will be less than effective if you only include half of the picture or you have a distorted view of reality. This does not mean that every time you make a decision you have to spend time carrying out a systematic environmental analysis. If you are an effective manager you will be in touch with what is happening in both the near and the far environments and you will keep adding to that understanding by thinking and reflection.

It is worth examining whether you really do know where you are starting from. For example, do you *really* understand where your organization is positioned in its market? What its strategic plans are for the short and medium term? Do you know how committed the individual members of your team are? Do you know what the views of your colleagues are? What are the issues on their personal agendas? Are your personal networks within and outside the organization strong? Do you really understand what is required of you in your present role? How supportive of you is your own immediate manager and what are her or his plans for the future?

From what you have read in this book about how organizations and people behave, you should already be answering these questions for yourself. Your understanding of systems thinking, for example, will have reminded you of the power of the informal systems which are present in organizations and of how necessary it is to understand the present situation from a range of perspectives. Your understanding of motivation theory, while it will not tell you why particular individuals behave as they do, will prompt you to think more deeply about their behaviour as well as your own. You should be less likely to rely on your 'common sense' and more determined to ask the kinds of questions which challenge common assumptions about how things are. You should be ready to use creative techniques to probe beneath the surface of situations as they present themselves to find out how things really are and whether there are only problems or also opportunities for positive change.

Understanding where you are now sounds deceptively simple but, among other things, it includes taking account of the activity of other people who share your environment and the fact that they might have competing objectives. It also means remembering that your present environment is constantly changing and that the individuals within it and affected by change will respond in different ways.

One reason my own attempt to follow the rational decision-making model was less than effective was that when I was describing where I was starting out from, I ignored the fact that other people were starting out at exactly the same point and that their intentions might adversely affect my plans.

Knowing where you are going

The rational approach suggests that it is possible to know where you are aiming for, but this implies that it is possible to understand and forecast the future. In management situations, of course, knowing where you want to be can be fraught with all kinds of difficulties, many of these being related to the fact that the environment in which organizations and people operate is full of uncertainties, and so assumptions about timescales and the continuing validity of today's objectives in the future cannot easily be made. The simple three-stage decision-making model focuses on reaching a view of where you want to be, whereas the planning model focuses on analysis. Whichever you try to follow, you need to remember to check that you actually are making progress in the right direction.

If you work at reaching a consensus view of a what better future might look like, as was suggested in the previous chapter, this in a sense can form the overall framework into which your decisions should fit. You will need to review this picture from time to time, as the environment changes. But really thinking in uncommon ways about where you and your team are heading will help you to foresee and construct problems and make effective decisions about a way forward.

Planning the route

It is at this third stage that our simple decision-making model lets us down. It provides no help in thinking about the most difficult task of all, which is *the means* of getting to B when you are starting out from A.

The process of getting from A to B expressed in its simplest terms would be 'Do X' but unfortunately in real life the question which immediately follows and which is the real crux of effective decision making (and incidentally, the beginning of creative problem solving) is 'How?' If the process of getting from A to B is clear-cut then it may be a question of deciding between a number of routes as suggested by the rational planning model. If the routes are not obvious then the question 'How?' is not easily resolved and what you are dealing with is a problem and not a simple decision.

Making a decision about which option to select from a number of possibilities is a clearly part of problem solving. Recognizing that there is no simple answer to the question 'How?' indicates that there is a problem to be 'resolved'. Defining what it is and then generating possible options takes you outside the scope of the simple decision-making model, and this is where the use of creative thinking techniques is essential. Our simple rational model now looks more like Figure 12.2.

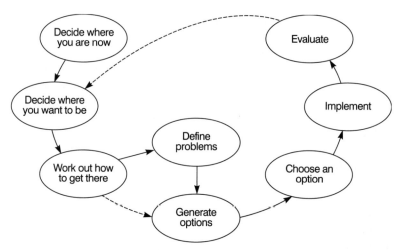

Figure 12.2   An extended decision-making model

Getting there

Having decided upon a course of action, planning and executing its implementation should be relatively straightforward. In rational terms any imagined plan for making progress from A to B would follow a simple linear programming approach, where one step forward leads on to the next, to the next and so on, inexorably towards the goal. Your management decision about which option to select for implementation will probably include the assumption that you will be able to progress by a series of interdependent steps.

In practice, of course, you may find that step 1 produces an unexpected problem or is more difficult to implement than anticipated. This delays the start of step 2, which depended upon step 1 having been completed. Steps 3 and 4 could probably go ahead even so, but the resource which had been allocated has been shifted elsewhere because of an unrelated problem. A number of people who had never previously expressed an interest in this particular issue decide that they have definite views about some of the steps you are trying to take because they might have an impact on them in the future. In the end you re-examine the possible options or perhaps decide that trying to reach B was an impossible objective and you settle instead for a route that will lead you to what C. Lindblom (1968) called this incremental approach 'the science of muddling through'. However it is only incrementalism if C as well as B is within your overall vision or strategy (see Figure 12.3).

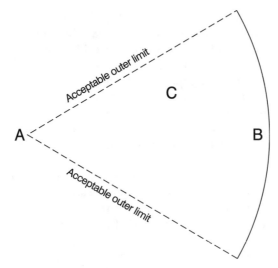

Figure 12.3   Incremental decision making

If this description of the implementation process at work seems realistic to you (and in practice we may find ourselves going through a number of iterations like this in progressing a plan or project), it is clear that to be effective you need to think beyond the rational. Neither of the two models we have looked at emphasize how crucial it is to monitor what is happening once implementation begins. However, the notion of building in some form of control or monitoring into your implementation programme, as described in Chapter 5, is in itself a rational approach.

Whether you are taking steps to resolve a problem or are managing a process of change, you need to be able to detect any changes in the environment which might cause you to alter your course. Having sensed an environmental shift you will then need to go back through the steps of whatever adapted model you were following in order to make adjustments. Even the most innovative ideas, born of creativity rather than an emergent strategy, must be monitored in this way.

Being realistic

Fortunately, one thing that most of us learn in our management lives is not to expect that things will turn out as planned and that we shall be able to achieve our entire objective. Our efforts to behave as a rational being are limited by the constraints imposed by the environment within which we work, largely those of time, finance, human and other resources. These factors, plus the fact that the human mind cannot comprehend the complexity of the real world, ensure that we have to 'satisfice', to settle for something that is a good enough option, to look for some means of getting part of the way there. It is still a rational process because it follows the steps set out in the rational planning model. You might argue that it is even more rational in one sense because it takes account of the fact that we do not operate in an ideal world and it means that we consciously apply limits to the goals that we have in mind.

In terms of the steps that we need to take towards our overall, and possibly limited, goals sometimes we may decide to take ones which will only result in marginal changes to the status quo, rather than more radical ones, again recognizing the constraints of operating within a complex and less than ideal world. I suspect many managers will empathize with Lindblom's description of how progress towards new goals is actually accomplished.

Being more than rational

We said earlier in the book that management is more like an art than a science, although, for many years it was discussed as if it were a science. Rationality, which has to do with systematic, logical analysis, seems much closer to a scientific approach, where facts can be established, assumptions can be proved or disproved and their validity tested. This does not mean that you should abandon all attempts to be rational, just that you need to apply rational models with caution.

However, management is perhaps more accurately described as a craft. Crafting is about using knowledge and acquired skills as well as special ways of thinking. There are certain things you can know or learn about, for example the kind of resources available to you, what their unique properties are, how to handle them, how extensive they are and so on. You can also understand the nature of the business you are in, and what your overall strategy should be. However, the skill lies in what you do with this understanding and knowledge in order to successfully 'craft' or create.

Crafting is not a haphazard, idiosyncratic pursuit. If you have watched someone making a piece of jewellery, for example, or an article made of wood, their actions are not random and illogical, but disciplined and sensible – rational in fact. A real craftsperson will also think creatively about the various materials they have, how they can be used in different ways to form new patterns or rework old designs. Their thinking may lead them to abandon some projects altogether.

In addition, crafting requires the ability to discover new potential in, as well as to recognize the limitations of, familiar materials. Successful craftwork also depends not just on being able to imagine a different pattern or arrangement, but also to make it a reality; to recognize when a project or a piece of work needs to be reassessed and it is time to 'go back to the drawing board'.

Crafting management requires an amalgam of rationality and the kind of uncommon thinking of which creativity is a part. The most effective crafting may mean that you have to work against the grain, sometimes out of choice, at others because it is the only way to create the effect that you want. It is this kind of balanced thinking which you need to bring to management. It is something more than rational.

Summary

This chapter has looked at rational models of decision making and the extent to which they are of value in practical management situations where the day-to-day business of managers includes making a number of non-routine, non-programmed decisions. From our understanding of how organizations behave, it is clear that even apparently 'lower-order' non-strategic decisions about the problems and situations which make up the day-to-day work of most managers can have profound effects on the organization.

Both rational decision-making models have their strengths and limitations. The planning model recognizes that in making decisions you need to explore possible options, and evaluate them in terms of their likely outcomes against your objective. On the other hand, it does not emphasize that your decision making should be grounded in a real understanding of where you are starting from. The three-stage model emphasizes both the need to be clear about the context in which you are working and to arrive at a vision of where you want to be, but it underplays the analytical skills needed to decide the best possible means of getting there.

Effective decision making is important not just because it is an essential aspect of those functions which traditionally define management but also because it is central to managing change and to the troubleshooting and problem-solving activities which are so much a part of the manager's role today. However, we cannot make decisions with comprehensive rationality, we can only aim to satisfice and muddle through.

If you cannot take a wholly rational approach to dealing with the problems, situations and decisions which are the day-to-day preoccupation of managers, and if relying on common sense is insufficient, what can you do? This book has argued that you can think smarter. You can challenge your assumptions and prejudices by recognizing that they are there. You can understand where people are 'coming from' by learning about their own perspective and motivation. Above all, you need to understand more about the context in which you work because the complexity of the environment in which you have to manage is a changing and ephemeral complexity which must be accounted for even if it cannot be comprehended. Rational models alone are not enough. The final chapter of this book re-emphasizes the importance of developing your own uncommon thinking.

Chapter 13
Making a habit of uncommon sense

You may have picked up this book originally because you have an unease about your own approach to management. You may have felt that, although you do a good enough job, you would like to manage more effectively. If this was the case then you were probably in the right frame of mind to take a critical look at some of the assumptions that you make about managing and to do some in-depth thinking about different approaches that you might adopt.

Lots of books on management offer advice on how to be more successful, but often these are in the form of lists of do's and don'ts, or prescriptions you can follow, as if management was another form of DIY. Other books offer you models which are aimed at helping you to reduce complexity by pretending that organizational life is comprehensible and that one way of understanding it is to put boundaries around it. There is plenty of advice about what to think and what to do, but very little about *how* to think and how to do things so that you avoid causing more problems than you already have.

We have tried to offer you a different way of thinking, one which means that you will never again want to depend upon the sort of common sense described at the start of this book. It is not a totally rational approach, because, as you have seen, perfect rationality is simply not possible. It is based upon an amalgam of rational and what we have called uncommon thinking. Uncommon thinking is more conscious, more active and more experimental than common sense. It encourages you to be tentative in making assumptions about the environment in which you work or the views and motivation of the people you work alongside. Uncommon thinking helps you begin to understand the relationships between the various elements in a situation and how these relate to the environment. It encourages you to challenge models and frameworks which you are offered, by thinking about them in terms of your own experience of management, so that you develop your understanding through reflection.

The managers who responded to the quiz in Chapter 3 found that it was their own experience which for the most part formed their approach to management. But supposing they never reflected upon their experience? What if the experience which they were relying upon was several years old? What if they consciously, or even unconsciously, rejected new experiences which cast doubts upon this common sense approach? Uncommon thinking uses techniques which can help you to break the constraints of your existing thinking habits. It will not mean that you discover that organizational life is any less complex, but it will help you to take this complexity and the range of different perspectives into account as you investigate problems, make decisions and manage change.

This chapter therefore aims to

- Bring together the different ideas and techniques covered earlier
- Show how they map onto the different stages of thinking
- Suggest some prompts that might help you to avoid slipping back into old-style common sense until the new way of thinking becomes a habit.

Stages in uncommon thinking

The starting point for looking at uncommon thinking is the rational model, because systematic, analytical thinking lies at the heart of effective management *whatever* you doing. But managers today need to develop other ways of thinking which take them 'beyond the box', and this includes the use of creative techniques to stimulate uncommon thought.

Uncommon thinking, therefore, is relevant whenever you have to think about a situation and make a decision, whether your goal is to resolve a problem, to turn a potential threat into an opportunity or to manage a process of change. You are familiar with the stages of the rational model for decision making and change from reading earlier chapters in this book. These are shown in Figure 13.1. You will notice that this doesn't exactly correspond to any of the diagrams which you have seen before. It includes the relationship between problems and opportunities and how thinking about these is part of a rational process. This is a good example of how you can use variations to diagrams to explain and extend your thinking.

The previous chapter examined the reasons why you cannot just simply follow the model as it stands. Uncommon thinking ensures that you *really* think about every stage as you work through them, frequently looping back to an earlier stage to check that the situation is still as it was, that you do not need to modify your objectives or generate new options. Whether it is your view of the situation that has changed, or the situation itself, you will need to rethink all subsequent stages.

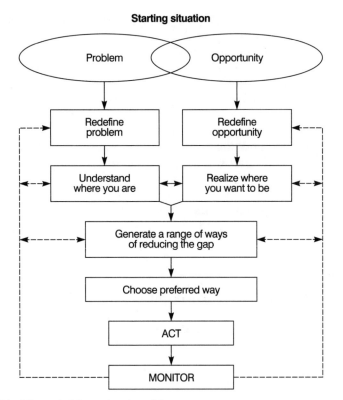

Figure 13.1   The underlying rational model

So although Figure 13.1 may look like a simple sequence, it is really a series of iterations. These are shown by the dotted lines. Depending upon the complexity of the situation, the time that you need to spend on each stage and the number of iterations will vary. Despite the iterations and revisions, you will find that you understand enough to able to move quite quickly to the final stage, because you will always have to satisfice – you aren't seeking perfection. We would not want to leave you with the idea that effective managers spend all their time going round in never-ending spirals!

We have taken each stage of the underlying rational model shown in Figure 13.1 and have suggested what you could usefully consider, techniques you might use and questions you might ask yourself to check that you have not slipped back to old habits of thought. Although we refer to the idea of 'constructing models', this does not mean that we expect you to spend huge amounts of time laboriously drawing version upon version of reality. As you become more used to uncommon thinking, these models will take shape very quickly in your head. And the sort of diagrams you use to clarify these stages should never be laborious – quick sketches are far more valuable than artistry!

The starting situation may have aspects of both opportunities and problems as discussed earlier in Chapter 9. As the environment changes the balance between problem and opportunity may change. What formerly seemed to consist largely of problems may now seem to contain opportunities as well.

You will also notice that we have shown two of the stages, 'Understanding where you are now' and 'Realizing where you want to be', in parallel. This is because where you start will depend upon the situation.

Ideas and techniques to use at each stage

Stage: Redefining the problem/opportunity

Use:

Diagrams
Creative techniques, such as goal orientation, five Ws and H

Stage: Understanding where you are now

Consider:

All stakeholders
  perspectives
  motivation
History of the situation
Organizational context
  sub-systems
  goals and hidden agendas
  culture, structure and power
  control loops
  other relationships
Wider environment
  SWOT
  STEP

Use:

Relationship diagrams
  systems maps
  multiple-cause diagrams
  metaphors
  team working
  creative techniques, picture imaging

Stage: Realize where you want to be

Consider:

Stakeholders especially any client
  plus their objectives for change
Organizational context
Wider environment
Measures of success

Use:

Ideas and techniques already listed
Creative techniques such as visioning, wishful thinking

Stage: Generate ideas for reducing the gap

Consider:

Non-obvious systems

Use:

Creative techniques such as wishful thinking; clichés, proverbs, maxims; brainstorming

Stage: Choose preferred way

Consider:

Results of earlier stages
Resources
Constraints

Use:

Simple evaluative techniques
Diagramming techniques for qualitative factors

Stage: Monitoring

Consider:

Control loops
Organizational context
Wider environment

This is only a selection of the most important ideas and techniques useful at each stage. Where it is fairly obvious that something used in an earlier stage will be needed again we have not repeated it.

Questions to ask yourself

In order to make sure that you are not slipping back into old habits you may find it helpful to ask yourself some at least of the following questions:

Stage: Redefining the problem/opportunity

Have you identified the *real* problem?
Have you looked for opportunities?

Stage: Understanding where you are

Have you involved a wide range of people with different perspectives?
Have you taken account of these perspectives?
Have you modelled different views of the situation and different aspects of the *problématique?*
Are at least some of your models diagrams?
Have you considered all the other parts of the organizations which are related to the situation?
Are you clear what values and assumptions you are starting with?
Has this made you think again about the roots of the problem?
Have you reconstructed your initial views to reflect a more in-depth understanding?

Stage: Realize where you want to be

Is it clear who 'owns' the situation and their objectives?
Is it clear how these relate to organizational and relevant sub-group objectives?
Do those affected, or whose cooperation is essential, agree on objectives (beware hidden agendas)?
Have you thought about how your success can be measured?
Have you remembered to include things that are important but hard to quantify?
Have you revised your initial view of the situation if necessary?

Stage: Generate ideas for reducing the gap

Have you used a range of idea generation techniques?
Has idea generation included all those with a stake in the situation?
Have you generated a really wide range of possibilities?
Do they address the real issue rather than superficial features?
Have you gone back to earlier stages to see if you need to modify them?

Stage: Choose preferred way

Has selection involved modelling as many aspects of each option as is realistic?
Have you used the measures of success agreed earlier?
Have you checked that the situation, and the desired future state have not changed since you started?
Did you remember the context in which any changes would be made?
Did your evaluation include qualitative as well as quantitative measures?
Have you taken constraints into consideration?

Stage: Monitoring

Did you plan your action carefully enough?

Stage: Learning from the experience (this is not a stage in the rational approach, but is an essential part of uncommon thinking, and deserving of some questions)

Have you reflected, preferably with team members, on techniques which helped and those which didn't and why?
Have you reflected upon models and theories which changed your approach to managing?
Have you noted areas where you could usefully find out more, either through study, training or effective networking?
Have you shared your learning with colleagues?

Going forward

From this point on you are on your own, or at least working with your colleagues to try to change the kinds of thinking which take place in your own organization. If you are using the ideas critically, and reading management articles and internal reports with a hard eye on what they offer for your own personal toolkit, your job should become more interesting and your increasing effectiveness should start to be noticed!

We should very much like to hear from you which of the ideas and techniques you found most helpful. Please contact us via the publishers if you have the time, to tell us which parts of the book you liked and whether there were any which seemed bizarre or downright unhelpful. Tell us of any things you would like to have been included or any examples of success you have had using the approaches described. If there is a next edition they can then be included!

References

Adair, J. (1983) *Effective Leadership,* Gower.

Belbin, R.M. (1981) *Management Teams,* Butterworth-Heinemann.

von Bertalanffy, L. (1947) 'Vom Sinn und der Einheit der Wissenschaften', *Der Student,* Wien, **2**, No.7/8.

von Bertalanffy, L. (1950) 'An outline of general system theory', *Brit. J. Philos. Sci.* **1**, 134–65.

Blake, R.R., and Mouton, J.S. (1964) *The Managerial Grid,* Gulf Publishing.

Burns, T., and Stalker, G.H. (1966) *The Management of Innovation,* Tavistock.

Daft, R.L. (1989) *Organization Theory and Design* (3rd edn), West Publishing.

Fayol, H. (1949) *General and Industrial Management,* Pitman, translated from the original *Administration Industrielle et Générale* (1916).

Handy, C. (1990) *The Age of Unreason,* Arrow.

Handy, C. (1993) *Understanding Organizations* (4th edn), Penguin.

Herzberg, F. (1968) 'One more time: how do you motivate employees?' *Harvard Business Review,* **46**, 53–62, January–February.

Isenberg, D.J. (1984) 'How senior managers think', *Harvard Business Review,* November–December, 81–90.

Jay, A. (1987) *Management and Machiavelli,* Hutchinson.

Johnson, G. (1988) 'Processes of managing strategic change', *Management Research News,* **11**, No. 4/5, 43–46.

Kirton, M.J. (1980) 'Adaptors and innovators: the way people approach problems', *Planned Innovation,* **3**, 51–54.

Kirton, M.J. (1984) 'Adaptors and innovators – why new initiatives get blocked', *Long Range Planning,* **17**, 2, 137–143.

Lawler, E.E., III and Porter, L. (1967) 'Antecedent attitudes of effective managerial performance', *Organizational Behavior and Human Performance,* **2**, 122–42.

Lindblom, C.E. (1968) *The Policy Making Process,* Prentice Hall.

Luthans, F.(1988) 'Successful versus effective real managers', *Academy of Management Executive,* **II**, No. 2.

Mangham, I. L. (1995) 'Scripts, talk and double talk', *Management Learning,* **26**, No. 4, 493–511.

Mayo, E. (1933) *The Human Problems of an Industrial Civilization,* Macmillan.

McGregor, D. (1960) *The Human Side of Enterprise,* McGraw-Hill.

Maslow, A.H. (1943) 'A theory of human motivation', *Psychological Review,* **50**, 370–96.

Mintzberg, H. (1973) *The Nature of Managerial Work,* Harper & Row.

Mintzberg, H. (1976) 'Planning on the left side and managing on the right', *Harvard Business Review,* **54**, July–August 49–58.

Mitroff, I.I. and Linstone, H.A. (1993) *The Unbounded Mind,* Oxford University Press.

Morgan, G. (1986) *Images of Organization,* Sage.

Morgan, G. (1988) *Riding the Waves of Change: Developing Management Competencies for a Turbulent World,* Jossey-Bass.

Morgan, G. (1993) *Imaginization,* Sage.

Rickards, T. (1974) *Problem-solving through Creative Analysis,* Gower.

Schnelle, E. *The Metaplan Method: Communication Tools for Planning and Learning Groups,* Metaplan Series No. 7, from Metaplan Gmbh, 2085, Quichborn, Goethestrasse 16, Germany.

Senge, P.M. (1990) *The Fifth Discipline,* Doubleday.

Simon, H. (1960) *Administrative Behaviour* (2nd edn), Macmillan.

Simon, H. (1960) *The New Science of Management Decision,* Harper & Row.

Taylor, F. W. (1903) *Shop Management,* republished in *Scientific Management* (1947), Harper and Row.

Taylor, F.W. (1911) *The Principles of Scientific Management,* Harper.

Tuckman, B.W. (1965) 'Development sequence in small groups', *Psychological Bulletin.*

Van Grundy, A.B. (1988) *Techniques of Structured Problem Solving.* (2nd edn), Van Nostrand Reinhold.

Vroom, V. (1964) *Work and Motivation,* Penguin.

Weber, M. (1971) *The Theory of Social and Economic Organizations,* Free Press.

Zuckerman, E. (1990) 'William Gates III', *People Weekly,* 20 August, 95–97.

Index